Pass CAPM in 21 Days –
the Ultimate Study Guide

Comprehensive Review Materials and Practice Questions Included

KAVITA SHARMA
ACP, AgileBA, CAPM, RMP, PRINCE2

Based on the new ECO
Released: Apr 2023, Version: 3

CHANGE LOG

Release Number	Date of release	Details of changes
Ver 2	Jan 2021	New version Based on PMBOK6
Ver 3	Jan 2023	New ECO as per 2023 updates by PMI

*I want to thank all my students for making this book possible and continue updating it.
Your feedback emails/WhatsApp keep me motivated.
Thanks to all of you. You made this book the way it is.*

कर्मण्येवाधिकारस्ते मा फलेषु कदाचन ।
मा कर्मफलहेतुर्भुर्मा ते संगोऽस्त्वकर्मणि ॥

It is the work that you control and not the outcome.

Table of Contents

A. FOREWORD

With India now at the crossroads towards implementation of National Education Policy 2020 (NEP 2020), the NEP 2020 challenge is to bridge the gap between academia and industry with a focus on developing skills such as critical thinking, problem-solving, creativity, communication, and collaboration making employability ready on the global perspective. Industries, on the one hand, are increasingly looking for employees who possess a diverse set of skills. And in addition to technical skills, employers are also looking for employees who have strong communication, problem-solving, and critical thinking skills and who have a global perspective and experience in a multicultural environment.

Project management is an essential skill that is highly valued in many industries. As companies strive to become more efficient and competitive within and on the global map, the demand for qualified project managers continues to grow. As a result, the future is for skilled, certified project managers. The Certified Associate in Project Management (CAPM) certification is globally recognized for project management professionals. In 2021, the Project Management Institute (PMI) announced a new pattern for the CAPM exam, which is designed to better align with the current industry standards and practices and as updated.

Pass CAPM in 21 Days - Study Guide, ONE BOOK TO REFER, is a resource guidebook with New ECO as per 2023 updates by PMI, and where the author provides a comprehensive overview of the CAPM certification exam and the principles of project management. The book is written in an easy-to-understand manner and is suitable for both novice and experienced project managers. The book starts by introducing the core concepts: project, operations and product, selection mechanism, organizational structure, organization types, PMO, and other fundamental concepts of Project management.

Followed by a detailed chapter on Business Analysis; Agile methodology with an introduction to agile thinking, teams, roles, and other concepts; Stakeholders; Predictive Processes; Execution, and monitoring and Control. Every chapter has been beautifully added with module end questions to solve and better understanding. The 21 Days Test Prep plan at the end of this resource guidebook is the icing on the cake added by the author, making one ready to be for a certification assessment and passing it with flying colors.

This guidebook is an invaluable resource for anyone who is interested in pursuing a career in project management or wants to enhance their existing project management skills. By mastering the principles of project management and obtaining the CAPM certification, readers will be well-positioned to excel in their careers and contribute to the success of their organizations.

I congratulate the author for this commendable work and highly recommend this guidebook to anyone considering pursuing the CAPM certification or wanting to enhance their project management knowledge and skills. The author's clear explanations and practical examples make this book indispensable for any aspiring project manager.

Wishing all a great success

Dr. Nitin Malik

Registrar | Dr. B R Ambedkar University Delhi

A.1 HI FROM KAVITA SHARMA

This book is the result of extensive research on CAPM courses and study materials. The CAPM exam is designed for new managers, and a lot is expected from them. However, since they are new to the field, it's essential to have a good understanding of the concepts, tools, and techniques to achieve results. Therefore, this book focuses on helping you understand the topics logically.

With the introduction of PMBOK6 and PMBOK7 confusion from 2023 and the eco

(CAPM exam content outline), it can be overwhelming to figure out what to study. This book aligns with the CAPM eco, and the mapping is provided in the annexures. You don't have to refer to multiple books to prepare for the CAPM exam. Follow this book, and you will pass. This book is a comprehensive reference to help you prepare for the CAPM exam. Its content aligns with the CAPM eco, providing a logical and straightforward approach to understanding the concepts.

Whether you're a new manager or just starting project management, this book will provide you with the knowledge and skills needed to pass the CAPM exam.

I wish you all the best!

A.2 DESIGN PRINCIPLES:

1. **One book to refer**
2. PMBOK and other standards as the source
    - Processes from PMBOK6
    - Agile from Agile Standard
    - Business analysis from BMBOK
3. Explain using videos
4. Use concise learning
    - Study Capsules
    - Let's Play
    - Keywords
5. Use examples where possible
6. Baseline tests and end test – full-length CAPM style

A.3 ABOUT THE BOOK

An adult mind can grasp concepts for 10-15 mins. More than that – it becomes too overwhelming.

Also, whatever you read goes into short-term memory; if you do not recall that, the mind fades the information. This book uses **scientific learning techniques** to help you understand the key concepts by giving you capsule size information and the Let's Play element as the study capsule. That way, one understands the concepts in a small entity and recalls and evaluates the knowledge. This affirms the mind, and you move forward to more complex concepts.

You may find the following terms for easy targeted learning:

KEYWORDS

If you see a definition – try and find the keyword for that. By default, the keywords are marked as BOLD for you. Try and pay attention when you see them. Keywords are a way to concise the learning and capture the essence of the concept. It will help you a lot in the CAPM exam.

LET'S PLAY

A chapter is divided into a logical set of study capsules. Once you learn a concept, the Let's Play is placed at the end of the concept. This helps with:

1. Help you evaluate your knowledge.
2. Boost confidence.
3. The studies feel easy.

MODULE END QUESTIONS

These are complex CAPM-style questions. Please complete them. It is important to complete and review the Module End questions to prepare for the CAPM exam.

MIND MAPS:

You will see mind maps to help you see the concepts in a picture. It helps (visual readers) to set the context and get all the information in graphics.

VIDEOS AT YOUTUBE

If you need help understanding the concept, you can search for the video with the keywords on my YouTube channel. Then, you **will find the video**. I'm working towards creating more videos as this book is published. You can also request a video through email or comment on my channel.

A.4 HOW TO READ THIS BOOK

Your prep for CAPM starts with this study guide. The first step is to understand the concepts.

Read the book chapter by chapter to understand concepts. Then, Let's Play quizzes will help you see if you understand the topic.

Module-end quizzes are more like CAPM tests. So do attempt them to assess your knowledge.

All answers are placed at the end of the chapters.

Once you finish the book, follow the 21 days plan. The plan requires you to have access to day wise tests and full-length tests.

You can enrol for the tests at https://kavitasharma.net

Use the coupon code: **CAPMBOOK** to avail discount.

1. CORE CONCEPTS

CAPM ECO TOPICS COVERED IN THIS CHAPTER

1.1	Demonstrate an understanding of the various project life cycles and processes.
1.1	Distinguish between a project, program, and a portfolio.
1.1	Distinguish between a project and operations.
1.1	Distinguish between predictive and adaptive approaches.
1.1	Explain how a project can be a vehicle for change.
1.3	Compare and contrast the roles and responsibilities of project managers and project sponsors.
1.3	Compare and contrast the roles and responsibilities of the project team and the project sponsor.
1.3	Explain the importance of the project manager's role (e.g., initiator, negotiator, listener, coach, working member, and facilitator).
1.3	Explain the differences between leadership and management.
2.1	Explain when it is appropriate to use a predictive, plan-based approach.
2.1	Identify the suitability of a predictive, plan-based approach for the organizational structure (e.g., virtual, colocation, matrix structure, hierarchical, etc.).
3.1	Compare the pros and cons of adaptive and predictive, plan-based projects.
3.1	Identify the suitability of adaptive approaches for the organizational structure (e.g., virtual, colocation, matrix structure, hierarchical, etc.).
3.1	Identify organizational process assets and environmental factors that facilitate the use of adaptive approaches.

The chapter is divided into sections as displayed:

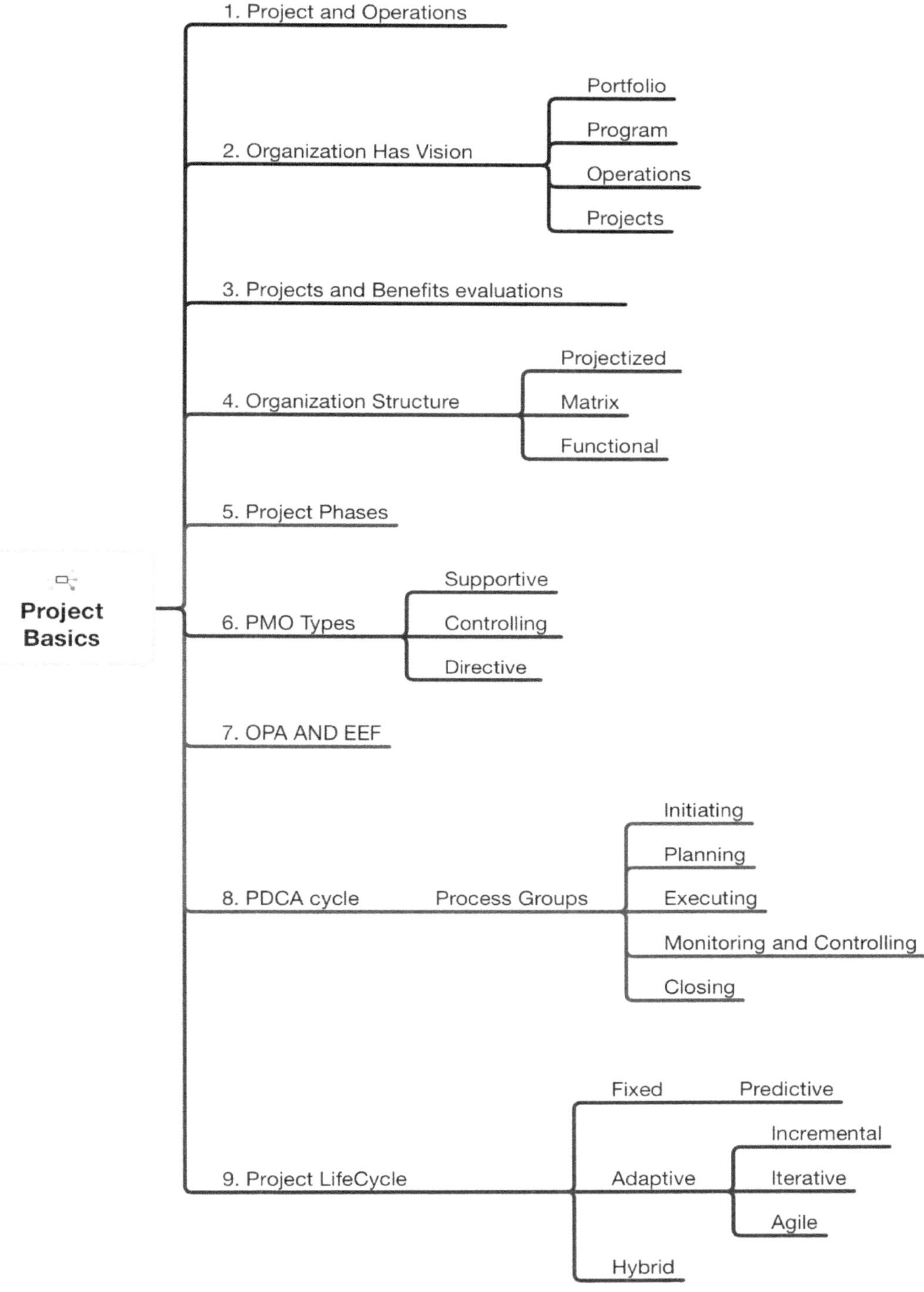

1.1 PROJECT, OPERATIONS, AND PRODUCT

We will be dealing with these terms throughout the book; hence, it's a good time to understand the difference between them.

A project is **temporary** (with a start date and end date) and creates something **unique**.
How about operations?
Operations are continuous and ongoing.
Think of your mom cooking for you(if she cooks regularly). She knows how to deal with anything going wrong with the dish, i.e., she knows the SOPs (Standard Operating Procedures) to create the deliverables. Whereas if you want to prepare an elaborate cake for her Birthday, then you may need to plan and think of all the risks, keep aside the recipe YouTube or book for the same. And things may go wrong – why? Since you are doing it for the first time, There are high chances of things going wrong—many risks.
In the above case, the deliverable is a cake. We plan and do the required work to get a perfect cake. This is called deliverable in this case.
A project is executed to get the required results. The results can be one or many deliverables. Here, in this case, it is just one deliverable.

Now think bigger. If you want to organize a party for your special ones' Birthday, that will have many deliverables:

- Cake
- Venue
- All invitees
- Gifts
- Food
- A party!!

This could be a project to throw a birthday party; the deliverables are as written above. Let's recap:

PROJECT

A project is temporary. It has a start date and an end date. It creates a unique offering. The offering could be a product or a service result.

OPERATIONS

An operation is repetitive in nature and is ongoing. Therefore, look for keywords like daily, monthly, and yearly - That is, operations.

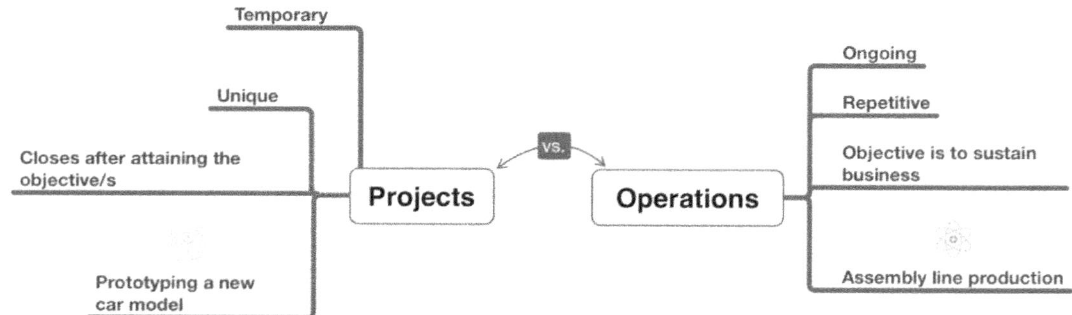

1.1.1 LET'S PLAY: PROJECT VS. OPERATIONS

Select if the scenario given represents a project or an operation.

1. **Construction of a new building at a new location.**

   A. Project

   B. Operations

2. **Baking a grand cake at home for a 50th Birthday celebration.**

   A. Project

   B. Operations

3. **Crossing the road every day while coming back home.**

   A. Project

   B. Operations

4. **A college student selecting the theme and venue for an upcoming fresher party. They are planning the party for the first time.**

   A. Project

   B. Operations

5. **Watching TV after work every day.**

   A. Project

   B. Operations

6. **The teacher prepares the quarterly tests for the class.**

   A. Project

   B. Operations

7. **A seasoned writer writing a new article for an old publication.**

   A. Project

   B. Operations

8. **Conducting disaster recovery drills every quarter by the operations head.**

   A. Project

   B. Operations

9. **Getting a dental checkup every year.**

   A. Project

   B. Operations

10. **Setting up a game station with the TV for the first time.**

    A. Project

    B. Operations

11. **The disaster recovery drills procedure to be implemented for the first time in a new building.**

    A. Project

    B. Operations

12. **The student needs to prepare for upcoming exams for the boards. It's a difficult task, as the student is taking it for the first time and wants to pass the exam with flying colors.**

    A. Project

    B. Operations

13. **The tuition center, ABC, is conducting coaching for all the students. This year there has been a 20% increase in students.**

    A. Project

    B. Operations

14. **A bakery chef is known for his wedding and birthday cakes. He gets an order to bake a cake for a 50th Birthday celebration.**

    A. Project

    B. Operations

15. **A new writer plans to write and publish a book on a technical subject. He is the SME (Subject Matter Expert) on the subject. This book will be his first.**

    A. Project

    B. Operations

1.2 PROJECT IS PART OF A PROGRAM OR A PORTFOLIO

An organization is created to achieve some results. The organization has a vision, the kind of work they do, and future aspirations. Organizations can be organized in specific ways and grouped in certain manners to do the work efficiently. If you are working in an organization, look around you. Are you part of a delivery unit, support unit, sales, or some other structure? Do you report to a supervisor? Off course you do. Is your supervisor managing a group (Business group) or a function or part of the middle management? When you look around yourself, you will find that you are working with other skilled people and are working towards achieving some goals. The supervisor you will have can be a program manager or portfolio manager. Now who are they, and the kind of authorities do they have?

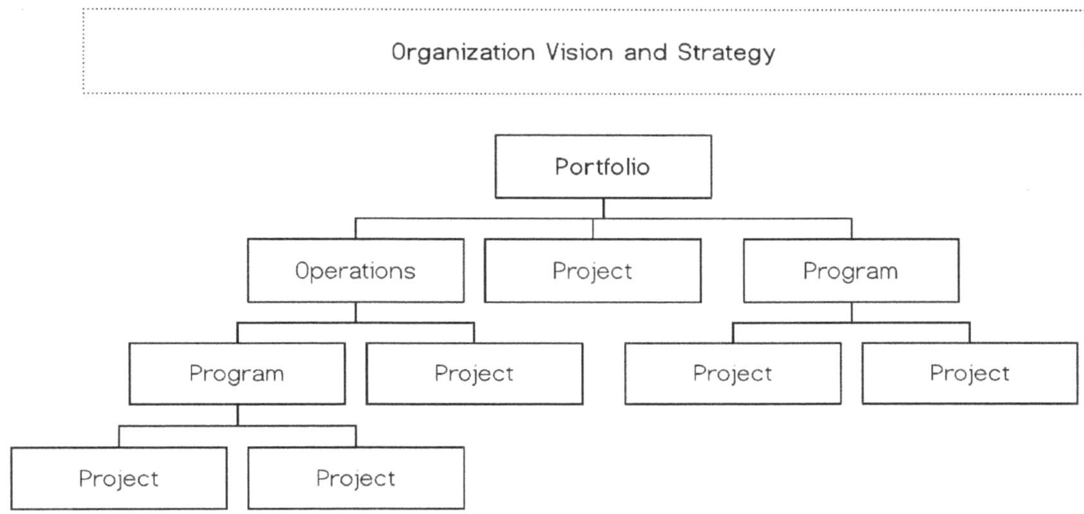

PROGRAM

A program is a collection of **related projects**.
Why do we combine related projects? So that we can get cumulative benefits by managing them under one umbrella. Think of one customer who may have outsourced a few projects and operations work to your organization. To manage the customer efficiently, you will have a Program/account manager for the customer and a few project and operations managers to cover the work by the customer organization.
Sometimes you may be part of specialized units example – robotics. Now each division of the organization may need your expertise, and your time may be divided where ever needed. The Program Manager ensures your allocation to the right project/initiative based on urgency.
A program manager may not be able to kill or initiate a new project. The main goal of Program Managers is to align/**optimize resources.**

PORTFOLIO

A portfolio manager is the decision-maker in the organization. Think of the CEO or people who can start new initiatives and close certain projects. Think of the sales head, who can request a new vertical based on customer demand.
The organization typically divides the work into portfolios to achieve the short- and long-term vision and goals. Think of the CEO of the Organization as the main portfolio manager. The portfolio manager can have a few delegations to smaller portfolio managers. Think of portfolios for a real estate firm as:
- Carting high-end Villas
- Creating managed services serviced apartments (Project and operations)
- Creating commercial spaces

Now based on the complexity of the portfolio or the expertise or the comfort, the portfolio groupings can be changed at any time. That's why you may have organizational structure changing all the time (at least in a few years). The people who manage the portfolios or those profit centers are portfolio managers. Let's summarize:

- A portfolio is aligned with the organization's **vision and strategy**.
- A portfolio may consist of projects, operations, and programs or sub-portfolios. These are called components in the portfolio.
- A portfolio manager **can kill** or can start new components for portfolio optimization.

1.2.1 LET'S PLAY: PROJECT, OPERATION, PROGRAM, PORTFOLIO

Find if you are managing a project, operation, program, or portfolio:

1. **You work with an airline help desk. Your job is to ensure that each passenger is given help when needed. You also issue tickets after verifying passenger details. The processes are described, and you follow them to ensure smooth work.**

    A. Project

    B. Operation

    C. Program

    D. Portfolio

2. **You are planning the initiative SMART per your organization's vision of being lean and green. This initiative must be taken across the entire organization and will affect all divisions. The success or failure of SMART will impact next year's profits and employee salaries.**

    A. Project

    B. Operation

    C. Program

    D. Portfolio

3. **You have a few team managers reporting to you. Each Manager complains of having difficulties in getting the right workforce. For example, team ALPHA forecasts 1 technical resource, team BETA wants 3 technical resources, and team GAMMA forecasts 5 resources by next month. When you analyzed this closely, you found that Team GAMMA has 2 underutilized resources from the last few weeks. They only need them in the coming month. So you get the resources reallocated to team ALPHA and BETA.**

    A. Project

    B. Operation

    C. Program

    D. Portfolio

4. **You are managing the project CLASSIC HOMES. This is the name given to the project to construct a residential township. Per the blueprint, it comprises 7 high-rise buildings and 30 low-rise studio apartments.**

    A. Project

    B. Operation

    C. Program

    D. Portfolio

1.3 Projects are Initiated to Achieve Results

PORTFOLIO MANAGEMENT AND PROJECTS:

Portfolio managers keep evaluating the market, risks, and other factors and decide to introduce a new component in the portfolio. The new component may introduce a few new initiatives, re-bundling old elements, and a few changes/upgrades to current components. Any of the changes lead to a project within the portfolio.
A project typically can be initiated by:
- → New technology
- → Competition
- → Material issues
- → Political changes
- → Market demand
- → Economic changes
- → Customer request/Stakeholder demand
- → Legal requirement
- → Business process improvement
- → Strategic opportunity
- → Social need
- → Environmental considerations

PROJECT SELECTION METHODS

Project selection methods are techniques used to evaluate and select the most appropriate project(s) to undertake based on various criteria. These methods help organizations prioritize their project portfolio and allocate resources effectively. Here are some common project selection methods:

BENEFIT-COST ANALYSIS
This method compares the expected benefits of a project with its costs. The project with the highest benefit-cost ratio is selected.

PAYBACK PERIOD
This method measures the time it takes for a project to generate enough cash flow to recover its initial investment. The project with the shortest payback period is selected.

NET PRESENT VALUE
This method calculates the present value of future cash flows expected from a project, considering the time value of money. Then, the project with the highest net present value is selected.

INTERNAL RATE OF RETURN
This method calculates the discount rate at which the present value of future cash flows equals the initial investment. The project with the highest internal rate of Return is selected.

SCORING MODEL
This method assigns project scores based on various criteria such as strategic fit, financial viability, technical feasibility, and risk. The project with the highest total score is selected.

PORTFOLIO ANALYSIS
This method involves analyzing the entire project portfolio to ensure that the mix of projects aligns with the organization's strategic objectives and risk tolerance.

EXPERT JUDGMENT
This method involves using the expertise of individuals or groups within the organization to evaluate and select projects based on their knowledge and experience.

These methods can be used alone or in Combination, depending on the organization's needs and priorities.

QUICK RECAP ON THE PROJECT SELECTION METHODS

Project Selection Method	Selection Criteria
Payback Period	Lowest
Benefit Cost Ratio	Highest
Net Present Value (NPV)	Highest
IRR	Highest
ROI	Highest

1.3.1 LET'S PLAY: PROJECT SELECTION MECHANISM

A local construction firm is evaluating retail projects to be undertaken to build. They researched the following information.

Projects	Payback Period (Years)	Benefits/Cost Ratio	NPV (Million)	IRR (%)	ROI
Project A	3	2.5	3	12	250
Project B	2	1.5	4	11.5	200
Project C	2.5	1.6	3.2	23.2	160
Project D	6	2	5.3	12.1	210

1. **Which project would you select if the selection criteria are the payback period?**

    A.   Project A

    B.   Project B

    C.   Project C

    D.   Project D

2. **Which project would you select if the selection criteria are IRR?**

    A.   Project A

    B.   Project B

    C.   Project C

    D.   Project D

3. **Which project would you select if the selection criteria are Return on investment?**

    A.   Project A

    B.   Project B

    C.   Project C

    D.   Project D

4. **Which project would you select if the selection criteria are Present Net Value?**

    A.   Project A

    B.   Project B

    C.   Project C

    D.   Project D

1.4 ORGANIZATION STRUCTURES

Does the structure of the organization influence the way projects are carried out?
Yes, for sure.
Organizations are structured to optimize the work which they perform. As a result, the work can either be unique or repetitive.
A car manufacturing company mostly works in the assembly line production of cars. Therefore, they want the people to be experts in their work. Therefore, functional structure is the best fit for this type of organization.
Some organization does projects for their clients, like advertising. The work is a unique burst of work to be finished within a timeline. A projectized structure is the best structure for them.
A virtual organization is required in covid like pandemic situations and can perform optimally even when the team is spread worldwide.
Senior management decides on the org structure. A Project Manager has no authority to define the structure. However, it is a good idea to know the org structure you work with so that you can perform the work better.

TYPES OF ORGANIZATIONS

Org. Type	Subtype	Work in	Allocations	Headed By	Keywords
Simple/ Organic		Flexible	Part-Time	Owner	No Formal Division Of Work
Functional	Centralized	Departments	Part-Time	Functional Head	Departments, One Boss
Functional	Decentralized	Departments	Part-Time	Functional Head	Departments, One Boss
Matrix	Weak	Departments	Part-Time	Functional Head, Project Manager	Departments, Two Or More Bosses
Matrix	Balanced	Departments	Part-Time	Many	Departments, Many Supervisors
Matrix	Strong	Departments	Part-Time - Full Time	Project Manager	Departments, Two Or More Bosses
Virtual	Matrix	Network, Assignment Based	Part-Time	Functional Head, Project Manager	Departments, Two Or More Bosses
Project-Based	By PM	Projects	Full Time	Project Manager	Project - One Boss
Project-Based	By PMO	Projects	Full Time	Project Manager	Project - One Boss
Hybrid		Mixed	Mixed	Mixed	Mixed

PROJECTIZED ORGANIZATION:

Senior management forms this type of organization when they expect **most work as projects**. In this structure, the team members report to the Project Manager. The teams are formed at the time of project initiation and adjourn when the project/phase terminates.

This structure gives **a lot of authority to the Project Manager** since the Project Manager controls all resources once they are allocated to the project, including the people reporting to the PM.

So, what happens when a project is closed?

You are aware that a project is temporary, which means that the project has a start date and an end date. Now, if the project ends, what would happen to people under the Project Manager hierarchy? But first, what happens to the Project Manager himself?

Typically, in this type of organization, a support function, which might be called RMG (Resource Management Group) or PMO (Project Management Office), is responsible for people not allocated to a project. If you have heard of a **bench** period in an organization, then you would know for sure that the organization type is Projectized.

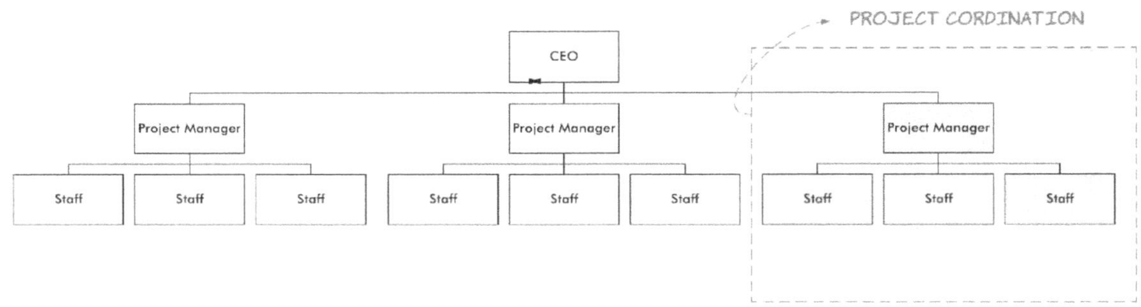

FUNCTIONAL ORGANIZATION:

These types of organizations are formed where the **expected work is repetitive**. In other words, this type of organization is formed around functions that are repetitive and form the overall operations. Now, we know from the definition of operations that these are ongoing; **work is ongoing.**

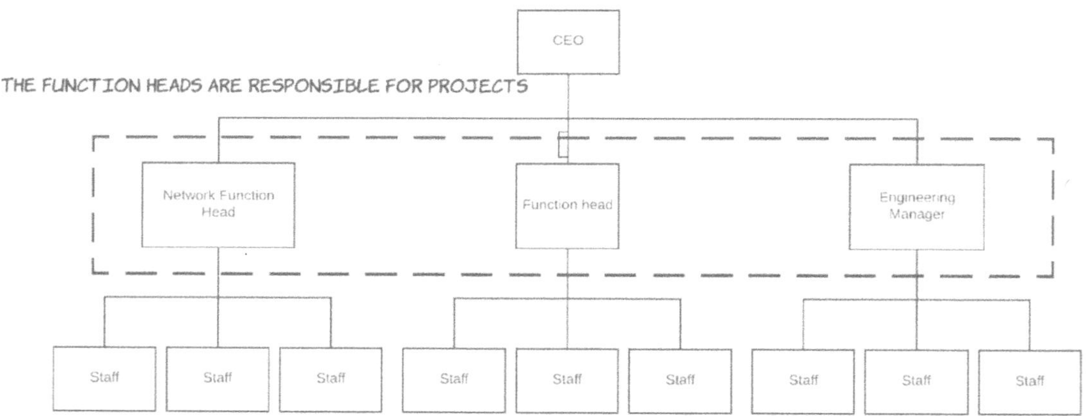

The teams are **structured around operations/functions**. Since this is repetitive work and is always going on, the hierarchy of the function is **permanent**. This means there is no bench period in a team member's life. Why? Because operations/functions are ongoing and typically never cease to exist, unlike projects.

Now, if this type of organization gets a project to work on, who would be carrying out the project? **Typically, the responsibility of completing projects will fall to the Functional**

Manager. They might choose someone from their team to help take notes, but the Functional Manager would be responsible for the project.

What will happen if any issue comes up in operations? What would be the priority for the Functional Manager? Would it be a new project or operation work?

If you thought about operations, then you are correct! A Functional Manager's core task is to keep the operations continuous. In such a scenario, the projects take a back seat.

…But, some organizations want to prioritize both the projects and operations, and they typically form a matrix structure.

MATRIX ORGANIZATIONS

These are the type of organizations that expect both project and operation work to happen. Typical features of matrix organization:

→ The team members report to more than one boss.

→ The team reports to both the Function Manager and the Project Manager (more than 1 supervisor)

→ Project coordination happens across departments.

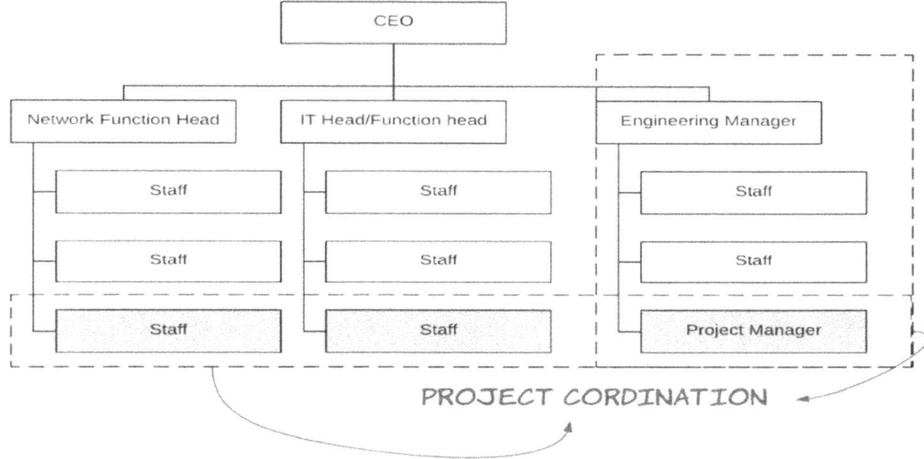

The detailing of weak and strong matrix organization is omitted because you won't see such questions in the new CAPM exam. Just remember the key features of the matrix organizations:

→ Two supervisors

→ The presence of a home, i.e., a functional head

→ The temporary allocation to a project and a PM

PROJECT MANAGER'S AUTHORITY GRAPH

The diagram below shows that the more you move toward a functional organization, the lower the PM's authority. Conversely, the more we move towards a Projectized organization, The more the PM gains authority. In the real world, most of us may work in a matrix organization where the authority is shared among the functional head and the PM.

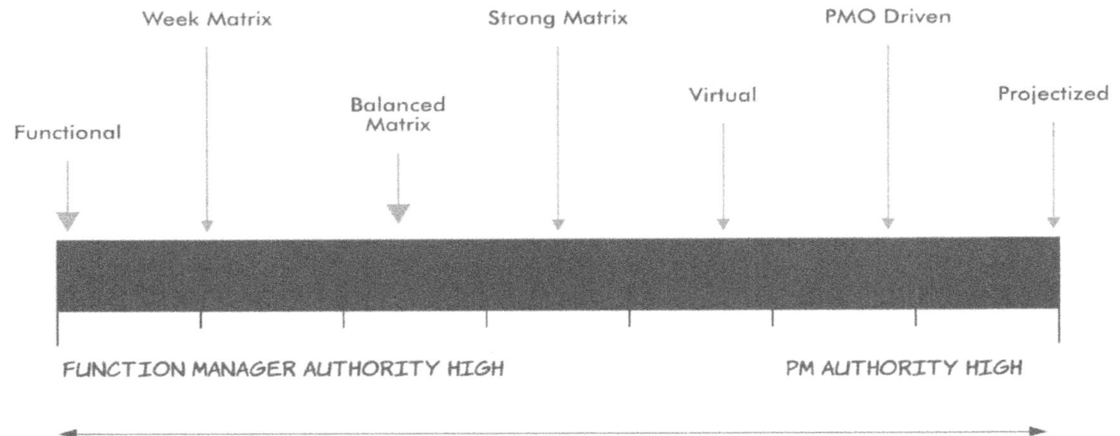
Functional
Week Matrix
Balanced Matrix
Strong Matrix
Virtual
PMO Driven
Projectized
FUNCTION MANAGER AUTHORITY HIGH
PM AUTHORITY HIGH

1.4.1 LET'S PLAY: ORGANIZATION TYPES

Can you find out the organization type, as represented by the interviewer?

1. **We are looking for an end-to-end program lead. You'd be responsible for working with the finance, sales, and marketing department. It would be best to work with specialists to ensure better architecture. Remember, these people will be working in their respective teams and should be busy with their work. The trick is to get your work done on time. Are you up to it?**

A.	Functional	B.	Matrix
C.	Projectized	D.	Simple

2. **We have a very difficult client who can behave abruptly. We need a Project Manager who can understand the business context and client requirements and deliver as per the organization's framework. We need people who can think and deliver. The team will report to you, and you will be responsible for the project outcome. It's a big responsibility, are you up to it?**

A.	Functional	B.	Matrix
C.	Projectized	D.	Simple

3. **Our stakeholders have been pressured to look at alternate energy sources. Everyone in the department is fully occupied with work, so we need someone who could help us accelerate work on this new initiative. I need you to take notes in the meetings. The functional head will make all the decisions, so talk to him in case of doubt.**

A.	Functional	B.	Matrix
C.	Projectized	D.	Simple

4. **I need someone dynamic who can multitask. We have had some great success with one home automation product named MAALEE. Currently, half of the team is busy with fulfillment and customer care. We are also developing low-cost variants of MAALEE, which may require your expertise. I need you to be part of as many initiatives as possible. Can you do it?**

A.	Functional	B.	Matrix
C.	Projectized	D.	Simple

1.5 PROJECTS ARE DIVIDED INTO PHASES

A project phase is a collection of related project activities that results in completing one or more deliverables. A variety of attributes can describe the phases in a life cycle. Attributes may be measurable and unique for a specific phase.

A phase is a logical division between project work.
Some Project Managers may want to divide the project work into types of work. For example:

- → Construction
- → Coding
- → Integration testing
- → Testing etc.

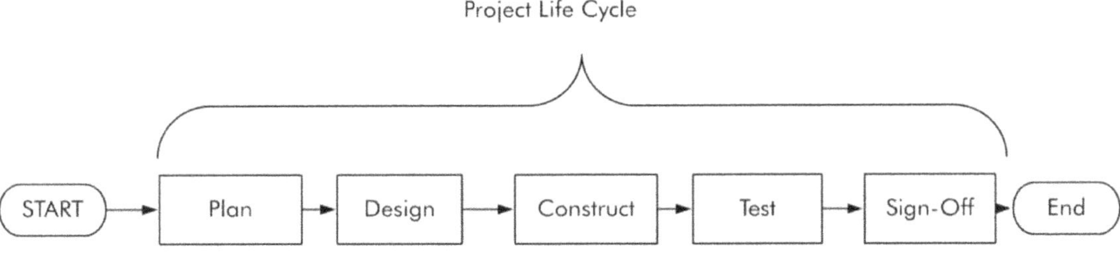

Some project managers may want to divide the work using deliverables/location or any other parameter which works. For example:

- → Phase 1 – Roll out in the USA
- → Phase 2 – Europe
- → Phase 3 – The rest of the world

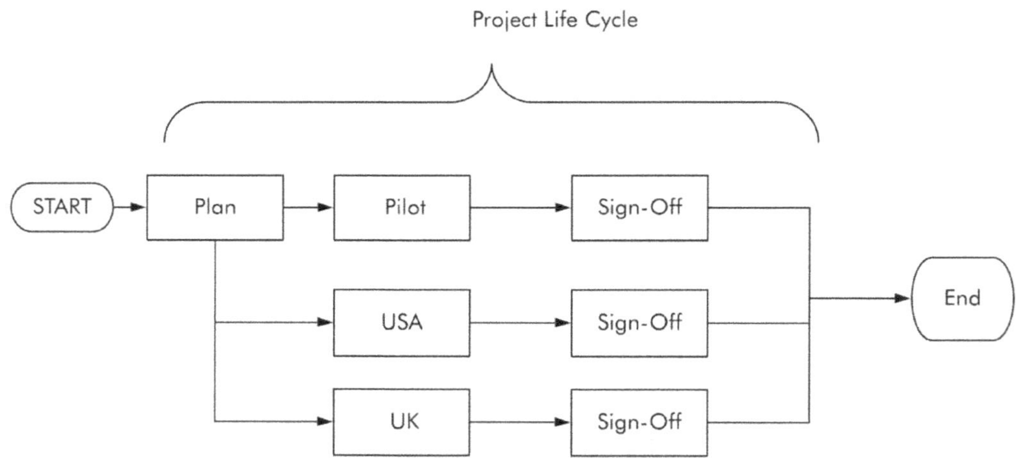

A few managers divide the work according to features. For example:
 Phase 1 – Site's basic features up and running
 Phase 2 – Extra features up and running
Combining all the phases is called a project life cycle.

PHASE-END REVIEWS:
A phase-end review by senior management is a point where the portfolio manager can evaluate the project's effectiveness and the environment. The decision to give the nod to continue the project or not is one of the key decisions taken by the portfolio managers in GO/NO-GO review meetings. Thus these meetings are also referred to as **kill points.**

1.6 PROJECT MANAGEMENT OFFICE

Have you heard of the following groups?
- PMO
- RMG (Resource Management Group)
- Quality
- Excellence

Combine all of them for your reference and call them PMO.

The PMO is responsible for helping projects so that project management practices can be standardized, measured, and improved.

In some organizations, the PMO supplies the templates, while in others, it is referred to as the quality department and audits the projects. Different level of authority is exerted by different PMOs.

SUPPORTIVE PMO

Supportive PMOs provide a consultative role to projects by providing templates, best practices, training, and access to information and lessons learned from other projects. In addition, this type of PMO serves as a project repository.
The degree of control provided by the PMO is low.

CONTROLLING PMO

Controlling PMOs provide support and require compliance through various means. For example, compliance may involve adopting project management frameworks or methodologies, using specific templates, forms, and tools, or conformance to governance.
The degree of control provided by the PMO is moderate.

DIRECTIVE PMO

Directive PMOs take control of the projects by directly managing them.
The degree of control provided by the PMO is high.

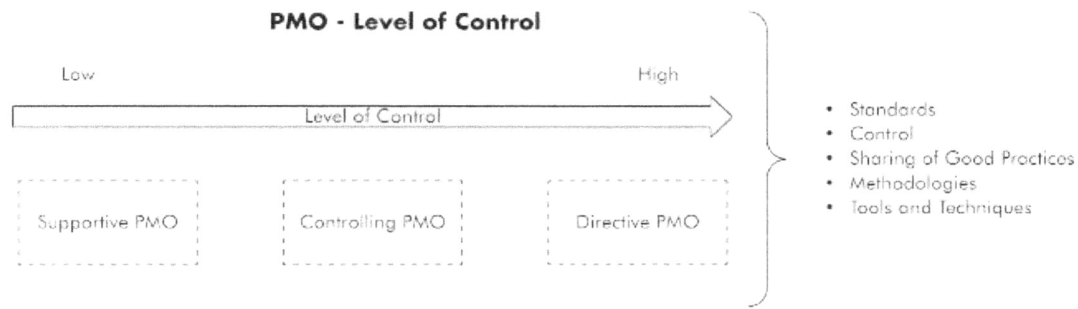

1.7 OPA AND EEF

ORGANIZATIONAL PROCESS ASSETS (OPA)

When an organization claims that they have specialized in telecom software integrators, what does that mean?
Does it mean that every employee in the organization understands telecom? Not necessarily.
Then what does it signify?
It means that the organization is learning and compiling the best practices for telecom software integration (SI) over time, so it can help them be more efficient in executing telecom-related projects. These assets may include:
> → Lessons learned
> → Plans
> → Templates
> → Best practices
> → Estimation guidelines
> → Execution guidelines
> → Risk information

Organizational Process Assets **help the organization and Project** Managers to be **more effective** in their work.
PMO is the custodian of Organizational Process Assets
OPAs are enablers.

ENTERPRISE ENVIRONMENTAL FACTORS (EEF)

Let's consider an example to understand EEF:

EXAMPLE 1:
You must staff your team and align the work hours with another country. To have maximum overlap hours, you decided to work from 12 noon till 9 pm. However, per your state's policy, you must ensure that any female employee is safely dropped back home. Your organization is a start-up and has yet to make any drop-off arrangements. Considering the drop-off costs, do you think twice before selecting female staff for the project?

EXAMPLE 2:
You have a team member who is always late. His attitude towards work could be better, and on top of that, he does not even attend the daily team meetings. You gave him feedback twice in the last month. This is getting out of control, and you are not happy with the situation. You can do better without this person on your team. What would you do?
> → Can you terminate the person's employment?
> → Would you go to HR and ask HR to put him on a PIP (Personal Improvement Plan)?
> → Would you ask the Functional Manager to replace him with another team member? Of course, your action depends on the company policy, right?

In the given examples, certain factors can influence your behavior/work in specific ways. These factors could be external (Example1) or internal (Example2).

Typically, an Enterprise Environmental Factor would constrain you. Enterprise Environmental Factors refer to conditions not under the project team's control that influence, constrain, or direct the project.

Enterprise Environmental Factors are CONSTRAINTS.

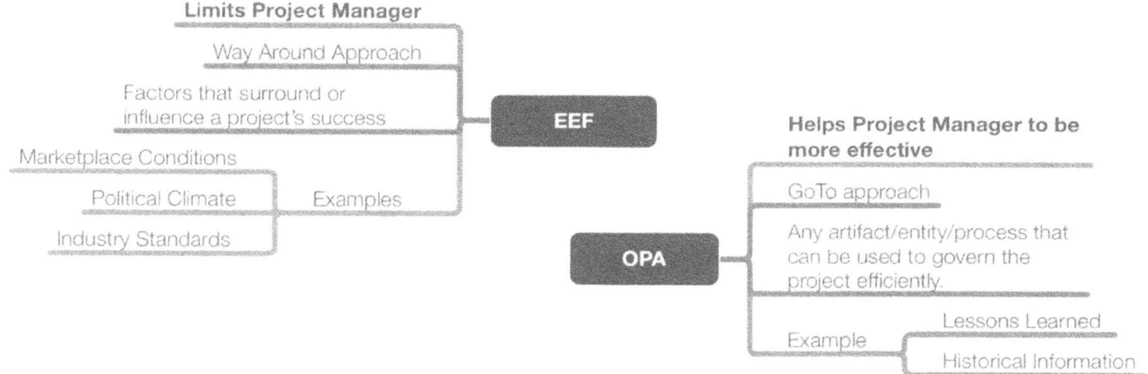

1.7.1 LET'S PLAY: OPA VS. EEF

Select if the scenario suggests OPA or EEF:

1. **A team member complains of a sexually oriented remark made by a colleague. You refer to the human resource policy on harassment to initiate appropriate action.**

    A.   Organizational Process Assets

    B.   Enterprise Environmental Factors

2. **To develop the Project Management Plan, you look for a predefined template.**

    A.   Organizational Process Assets

    B.   Enterprise Environmental Factors

3. **Since the office is in a remote place, you must arrange for pickup and drop-offs so that people can commute to the office safely.**

    A.   Organizational Process Assets

    B.   Enterprise Environmental Factors

4. **You change the project team timings from 11 am to 7 pm because no one seems to be at 11 am at the customer's office. This will help you overlap with customer times and give better project efficiency.**

    A.   Organizational Process Assets

    B.   Enterprise Environmental Factors

1.8 THE PDCA

INTRODUCTION: INDIAN WEDDING

Think of a Big Fat Indian Wedding. How do people plan it? Is there any planning for that? When I was a kid, we used to have a meeting with all the Chachas and Taus (Uncles), and responsibilities were assigned to people. I remember that keeping track of the money was one responsibility, and there were others, like:

→ Food menu
→ Beds
→ Getting the rooms cleaned
→ Flowers
→ The puja pandal

And you name it.

Was it a project? Yes, you bet!

Our elders have some re-defined ways of carrying out the project work.

Therefore, PMBOK has divided the project into SIMILAR types of work, called the KNOWLEDGE AREA. The examples of the knowledge areas are:

→ Cost
→ Quality
→ Scope
→ Etc.

Understand that a project goes through certain stages (initiation, planning, and execution). PMBOK refers to these as PROCESS GROUPS.

Process groups are not project phases.

Every project phase goes through all the process groups. What does it mean? Each phase will be initiated, planned, executed, and closed, along with monitoring and closing processes.

PROCESS GROUP INTERACTION

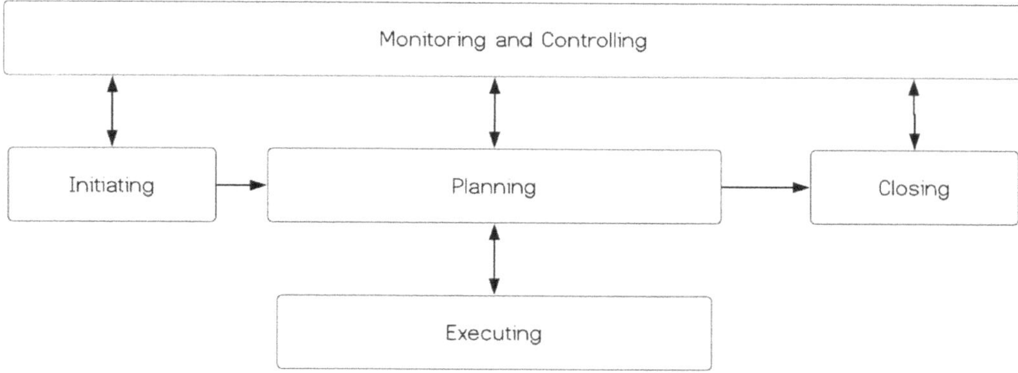

The process interaction shows that:

→ Initiating processes happen first.

→ Planning and execution are conducted simultaneously.

→ Monitoring and controlling processes are umbrella processes and are performed all the time, starting from project initiation until the closing of the project.

→ There is a trigger in monitoring and controlling, which would trigger the close of the project.

→ Closing processes are performed together.

PROCESS GROUPS

INITIATING

Each project is initiated. This means that the organization has committed to putting resources into the project and has allocated a Project Manager.

PLANNING

Once the project is initiated, the Project Manager plans the scope, time, and other success factors, including the quality necessary to meet the project objectives.

EXECUTING

The actual work happens here. Your team does the work and produces deliverables.

MONITORING AND CONTROLLING

The Project Manager creates dashboards every month/week to determine the project status.

In an Agile project, the monitoring and controlling happen DAILY. The team updates the burndown charts and takes control of the work.

CLOSING

These processes are performed to finalize all activities across all Process Groups and formally close the project or phase.

KNOWLEDGE AREAS

A Knowledge Area is a complete set of concepts/activities performed in an area of specialization.

The Knowledge Areas as per PMBOK 6th are:
1. Project Integration Management
2. Project Scope Management
3. Project Schedule Management
4. Project Cost Management
5. Project Quality Management
6. Project Resource Management
7. Project Communications Management
8. Project Risk Management
9. Project Procurement Management
10. Project Stakeholder Management

LET'S GO BACK TO THE WEDDING:

Imagine that you are managing the cash/payments, etc. You estimated the wedding. At the end of every day, you may have to look at how much money you are left with and ask yourself — Is it enough? These activities or areas of specialization can be combined under the Cost Management Knowledge Area.

Managing activities and completing them on time is a schedule management knowledge area. Similarly, the rest of the knowledge area follows.

Let's see what happens in each process group:

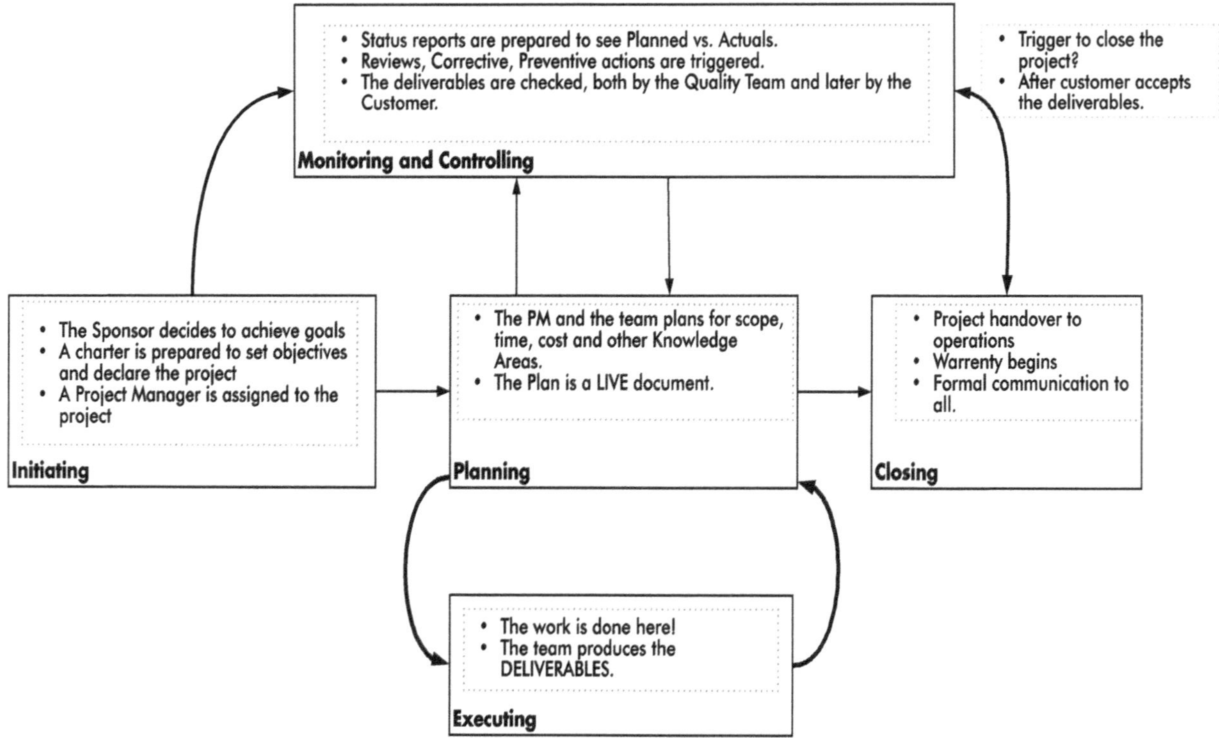

PMBOK6TH PROCESS MAP

	INITIATING	PLANNING	EXECUTING	MONITORING & CONTROLLING	CLOSING
INTEGRATION	Develop Project Charter	Develop Project Management Plan	Direct & Manage Project Work Manage Project Knowledge	Monitor & Control Project Work Perform Integrated Change Control	Close Project or Phase
SCOPE		Plan Scope Management Collect Requirements Define Scope Create WBS		Validate Scope Control Scope	
SCHEDULE		Plan Schedule Management Define Activities Sequence Activities Estimate Activity durations Develop Schedule		Control Schedule	
COST		Plan Cost Management Estimate Costs Determine Budget		Control Costs	
QUALITY		Plan Quality Management	Manage Quality	Control Quality	
RESOURCES		Plan Resource Management Estimate Activity Resources	Acquire Resources Develop Team Manage Team	Control Resources	
COMMUNICA-TIONS		Plan Communications Management	Manage Communications	Monitor Communications	
RISK		Plan Risk Management Identify Risks Perform Qualitative Risk Analysis Perform Quantitative Risk Analysis Plan Risk Responses	Implement Risk Responses	Monitor Risks	
PROCUREMENT		Plan Procurement Management	Conduct Procurements	Control Procurements	
STAKEHOLDER	Identify Stakeholders	Plan Stakeholder Management	Manage Stakeholder Engagement	Monitor Stakeholder Engagement	

1.8.1 LET'S PLAY: PMBOK PROCESS GROUPS

Refer to the PMBOK process chart and map the activities with the relevant process group:

Activity Description	Process Group
1. The team plans for the overall work and delivery approach.	Planning
2. The team does the work per the allocated task and updates the task information.	
3. Forecasts are created in the group.	
4. A status is compiled to check whether the project is within the schedule.	
5. Audit happens here	
6. Testing happens here	
7. A schedule is created in this process group.	
8. The work is divided into smaller, manageable units.	
9. Handover is performed	
10. Plans are created in this process group.	
11. The project goals are defined, and resources are committed to achieving goals.	
12. Daily stand-up meetings to understand progress and update the task progress	

1.9 PROJECT LIFE CYCLE

How would you define the project life cycle? What methodologies are available, and which methodology could be best for your project? That's a complicated question, so let's try to solve it.

EXAMPLE 1:

There are a few industries where the cost of change needs to be lowered. You want to **do it right the first time**. For example, the construction of a building of 25 floors. Would you finish the 25th floor first and then think the Design needs to be optimized? Let's rebuild the entire building. That's just not feasible.

So, in this case, you should ensure that you get the specifications right, do due diligence on the type of surface, soil, air, and water, and get adequate regulatory nods, then start the actual development/construction of the building. Here:

→ The cost of change is huge
→ Specifications are clear
→ The construction industry has mature regulations and processes

EXAMPLE 2:

Another example. A new technology (IT – software) has evolved, and many things can be achieved. You, as a customer, want some work to be done using new technology. However, you are not aware of the capabilities of the new technology. The relevant new feature can bring immense value to the business. You want to explore and build those features based on market feedback and available features. Here in this scenario:

→ The cost of change is low.
→ Specifications are changing
→ Industry is new

How would you go about developing the project for each scenario?

Before we ask this question, let us understand various ways to develop and deliver the product (Project Life Cycle - PLC).

PREDICTIVE LIFE CYCLES

This is also known as **fully plan-driven**. A predictive life cycle is an excellent methodology when customer requirements are **precise**, the industry is **mature**, and the cost of change **is high**. Think construction.

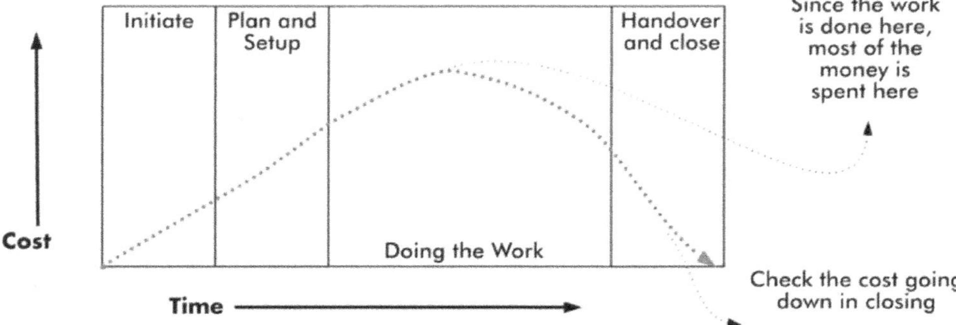

When we speak about predictive life cycles, things to keep in mind are:
- → Cost and staffing levels are low at the start, at their peak as the work is carried out, and drop as the project moves towards closing.
- → Risks in any project are greatest at the start and decrease during the later stages.
- → The ability to implement the changes in the product is lowest at the start.
- → Changes cost a lot as the project progresses toward completion.

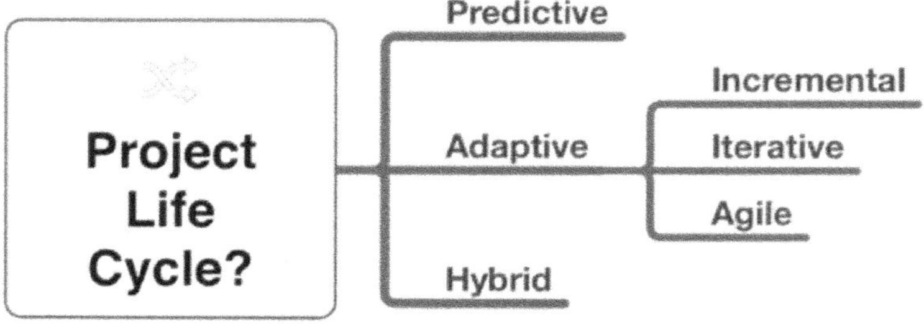

ADAPTIVE LIFE CYCLES

If the requirements are evolving, do you wait to get all of them uncovered before you start the project? That's not even possible in some scenarios where the next set of requirements will evolve only when the customer sees the response from the market of the product/project. In such cases, we can opt for an adaptive life cycle. We deliver some parts of the requirements and then build on them. The approaches to work on adaptive life cycles are:

INCREMENTAL LIFE CYCLES

Deliver in phases. We do it all the time. The requirements are mature. We finalize, develop, and deliver them in the first phase. We then work with the customer for the next requirements set and deliver them in the next phase. We deliver in phases.

ITERATIVE LIFE CYCLES

Think products! Windows and Mac's operating systems are the best examples that may come to mind. But, if you are a gamer, think of the different Wii or Play station versions.

A product team can think of releasing a major version as and when the industry demands or as per the team release cycle. Each version may focus on new additional features for the customer.

AGILE LIFE CYCLES

Agile projects follow the Agile Manifesto. The delivery approach combines the iterative and incremental lifestyle to deliver customer value. Many agile techniques exist, but remember that agile follows the Agile Manifesto. **Iterations are released in short burst cycles of a week or a month.** These small iterations are focused on new features or additional functionality. Then, the iterations are repeated until the whole product is released.

Small cycle iterations help the project team seek customer input in a shorter time frame. Any changes can then be incorporated into later iterations. This allows both the customer and the project team to work through details on the fly and can be very useful when the requirements need to be clarified.

Agile Manifesto

Individuals And Interactions	over	Processes And Tools
Working Software	over	Comprehensive Documentation
Customer Collaboration	over	Contract Negotiation
Responding To Change	over	Following a Plan

That is, while there is value in the items on the right, we value the items on the left more.

* Taken from: http://agilemanifesto.org/

PLC SUMMARY

	Requirements	Activities	Delivery	Goal
Predictive	Fixed	Performed once	Single delivery	Manage cost
Iterative	Dynamic	Repeated until correct	Single delivery	Correctness of solution
Incremental	Dynamic	Performed once for a given increment	Frequent small deliveries	Speed
Agile	Dynamic	Repeated until correct	Frequent small deliveries	Customer value via frequent deliveries and feedback

1.9.1 LET'S PLAY: PROJECT LIFE CYCLE

Suggest the life cycle suitable for the scenarios:

1. **The customer is new to mobile application development. Their requirements keep changing as the team learns new possibilities of features in mobile development/applications every day. They are very excited to start rolling out new features to their users. The key focus is to roll out valuable features, see the market feedback, and build on the feedback.**

   A. Agile
   B. Hybrid
   C. Incremental
   D. Iterative
   E. Predictive

2. **The customer wants to build a website for their upcoming new segment of clothing lines. The clothing lines are supposed to be rolled out in a specific sequence. There are few designers that the fashion brand employs, and they are expected to launch their collection soon (The dates keep changing). Once finished, each designer's work can be showcased on the new platform. However, the current emphasis is to roll out a campaign to showcase the upcoming new fashion lines and build excitement. The next set of rollouts would depend on the designers and their completion of the designs. The designers are yet to commit to the timelines.**

   A. Agile
   B. Hybrid
   C. Incremental
   D. Iterative
   E. Predictive

3. **You are managing a product called OPLAY. The product is a collaboration platform where people can find friends or communities and play games with them. You have a few games in mind to launch. Some of the games are Tetris (2-player game), UNO (2 and 4-player game), and Checkers (2-player game). You want to ensure that each game variant works perfectly on all mobile platforms. No errors can be tolerated, as this will harm your brand and application.**

   A. Agile
   B. Hybrid
   C. Incremental
   D. Iterative
   E. Predictive

4. You are tasked to make a bridge between two villages over a river. The bridge should be constructed to allow a seamless journey for vehicles and people from both villages. The government body issued a contract to your organization with the required specifications. The emphasis is that the bridge should be rolled out at a fixed cost soon.

   A. Agile
   B. Hybrid
   C. Incremental
   D. Iterative
   E. Predictive

5. You work as a manager with an automobile manufacturing unit. The company is facing a challenge now that the government has created new emission and safety laws. This would require redesigning the engine and interior, including safety gears, to pass the new tests mandated by the law. The engine design is complex and goes through lots of trials and errors. For the rest of the other phases of vehicle production, once the engine and safety norms are satisfied, they are easier to follow. They follow the standard development approach, like assembly, painting, and testing jobs.

   A. Agile
   B. Hybrid
   C. Incremental
   D. Iterative
   E. Predictive

1. MODULE END QUESTIONS

1. You are asked to coordinate a new initiative named CODE-B. This is a new and complex initiative requiring other departments' involvement. You are published as the coordinator for CODE-B. You are given the authority to call meetings. At any point, the team member is working on multiple initiatives. Your core responsibility as the project coordinator is to track progress and flag any issues so that action can be initiated at the management level. Which type of organization do you work with?

    A.   Projectized
    B.   Functional
    C.   Matrix
    D.   Organic

2. The research division head asks you to develop a prototype for facial recognition. He further tells you that you have the authority to get the resource allocation as needed, but the product needs to be ready within the next 6 months. The product needing to be ready within the next 6 months is an example of:

    A.   A requirement
    B.   Stakeholder expectation
    C.   An assumption
    D.   A constraint

3. Your organization is structured to do projects. Once a project is completed, the team member searches for another appropriate project matching his skill set and growth path. The PMO helps the team member with the next allocation per his skill match. Once the project is completed, to whom would the team member report?

    A.   Functional Head
    B.   Project Manager
    C.   Manager of Project Manager
    D.   Project Management Office

4. **The research division head asks you to develop a prototype for facial recognition. First, of course, the software should be accurate. However, a few features, like searching the federal database for prints and health records, can be added as features later. Which methodology can work for your project?**

   A.   Agile so that the customer gains confidence in the team

   B.   Incremental to keep on adding required functionality

   C.   Iterative so that features are accurate and function works well

   D.   Predictive as its straight forward project

5. **You are managing the project GHANA. The project is to develop services for telecom network operators. You are also part of the PMO (Project Management Office). Which type of organization do you work with?**

   A.   Projectized

   B.   PMO

   C.   Matrix

   D.   Organic

6. **You are working with a robotics firm. A new robot for a manufacturing client will be delivered in the next ten months. You seek advice and historical data from the PMO. They have all the information. The PMO is rather helpful and does not question your authority as the Project Manager. Which type of PMO is discussed in this scenario?**

   A.   Supportive

   B.   Controlling

   C.   Directive

   D.   Servant-leader

7. **Select the incorrect statement:**

   A.   A stakeholder can be a project resource

   B.   A stakeholder can be a group

   C.   A stakeholder can be an organization

   D.   A stakeholder can be a vendor human resource

8. **You joined an organization as a team member. You have one supervisor. Your role and growth path are clearly defined. Which type of organization did you join?**

   A.   Projectized

   B.   Weak Matrix

   C.   Strong Matrix

   D.   Functional

9. **The following scenario depicts a project EXCEPT:**

    A. Temporary endeavor by one person

    B. Temporary endeavor by team & Manager

    C. Implementing the changed standard operating procedures (SOPs)

    D. Adhering to the standard operating procedures (SOPs)

10. **To get started on the project, you spoke to the PMO and obtained the old project estimates and historical data. This will help you to plan and control the project. This is an example of the:**

    A. Controlling PMO

    B. Organizational Process Assets

    C. Enterprise Environmental Factors

    D. Directive PMO

11. **The customer wants an innovative, cutting-edge designed product. The customer can explain the functionality, and your technical team has developed the specifications. Design, on the other hand, has yet to be evolved. The challenge is that no one (including the customer) knows what they want. What time of project/phase life cycle would you choose for Design and why?**

    A. Design should be developed iteratively by redesigning till the team achieves what the customer likes.

    B. Design should be developed incrementally by developing features in phases.

    C. Design should be developed as a predictive life cycle using a prototype approach.

    D. Design should be developed as an agile life cycle with active customer inputs.

12. **Your firm makes bestseller vehicles for the rural market. The final product launched two years back was a major hit with the consumers, and your team won several awards. Now you are developing a new model, YANNA, which should comply with newly announced government regulations. The extent of the work is mostly known, but one of the components is tricky and needs lots of iterations to be perfect. This is the most crucial component of the project, which can make or break the product. What and how would you select the project life cycle for the new-age truck, YANNA?**

    A. Combination of predictive for known components plus agile development for unknown component

    B. Use predictive life cycle for the project

    C. Use an iterative life cycle for the project

    D. Use an agile life cycle for the project

13. **You have joined as a service lead with one of the leading organizations. You work on several leads at any time and form different teams from across departments to fulfill the services. The team members report to you part-time. It isn't easy to coordinate because the team is not even collocated. This is also good and works well because you save on project costs and get resources from across all the departments and geographies. This helps get a better global output. Which type of organization do you work with?**

    A. Projectized

    B. Virtual Matrix

    C. Co-located Matrix

    D. Functional

14. **Which project stage takes huge effort and expenditures?**

    A. Controlling stage

    B. Closing stage

    C. Planning stage

    D. Executing stage

15. **Select the TRUE statement when we think of predictive projects:**

    A. The cost of implementing a change is huge at the start and diminishes later

    B. It's OK to make changes at later stages

    C. The cost of change at the start is less

    D. A change management process can be created when the need arises

1. ALL ANSWERS

ANSWERS: 1.1.1 LET'S PLAY: PROJECT VS. OPERATIONS

Question No	Select the answer	Why?
1.	Project	Unique
2.	Project	Unique
3.	Operations	Daily
4.	Project	Unique
5.	Operations	Daily
6.	Operations	Quarterly
7.	Project	New article
8.	Operations	Quarterly
9.	Operations	Yearly
10.	Project	First time
11.	Project	First time
12.	Project	First time/Unique
13.	Operations	Every year
14.	Operations	Daily work
15.	Project	Now, the First book

ANSWERS: 1.2.1 LET'S PLAY: PROJECT, OPERATION, PROGRAM, PORTFOLIO

Question No	Answer	Why
1.	Operation	Processes are followed.
2.	Portfolio	Across Organization.
3.	Program	Resource optimization.
4.	Project	Clear goals, unique start and end date.

ANSWERS: 1.3.1 LET'S PLAY: PROJECT SELECTION MECHANISM

Question No.	Answer
1.	Project B has the lowest payback period.
2.	Project C has the highest IRR.
3.	Project A has the highest ROI.
4.	Project D has the highest NPV.

ANSWERS: 1.4.1 LET'S PLAY: ORGANIZATION TYPES

1. MATRIX - Check the allocation
2. PROJECTIZED - One Boss

3.   FUNCTIONAL - Check that the person has no authority
4.   MATRIX - Check the allocation

ANSWERS: 1.7.1 LET'S PLAY: OPA VS EEF

Question.	Answer	Why
1.	Enterprise Environmental Factors	You need to follow the policy even if your first choice is something else.
2.	Organizational Process Assets	It aids you in creating a plan in a shorter time frame.
3.	Enterprise Environmental Factors	Limiting factor.
4.	Enterprise Environmental Factors	It would be best to find a way to deal with a limitation.

ANSWERS: 1.8.1 LET'S PLAY: PMBOK PROCESS GROUPS

ACTIVITY DESCRIPTION	PROCESS GROUP
1. The team plans for the overall work and delivery approach	Planning
2. The team does the work per the allocated task and updates the task information.	Executing
3. Forecasts are created in the group	Monitoring and Controlling
4. A status is compiled to check if the project is within the schedule or not	Monitoring and Controlling
5. Audit happens here	Executing
6. Testing happens here	Monitoring and Controlling
7. A schedule is created in this process group	Planning
8. The work is divided into smaller, manageable units	Planning
9. Handover is performed	Closing
10. Plans are created in this process group	Planning
11. The project goals are defined, and resources are committed to achieving goals.	Initiating
12. Daily stand-up meetings to understand progress and update the task progress	Executing

ANSWERS: 1.9.1 LET'S PLAY: PROJECT LIFE CYCLE

Scenario	Life Cycle
1.	Agile Value, Market feedback – all points toward Agile PLC
2.	Incremental Changing dates and specifications, Few Requirements, at least the first phase is clear.
3.	Iterative

	Complete game, No errors.
4.	Predictive Clear requirements Fixed cost Physical outcome – rework is a lot of waste
5.	Hybrid One phase – new engine design can follow agile The rest of the phases can be Predictive

ANSWERS: 1 MODULE END QUIZ

Answer	Why of the Answer
1. C	You can call meetings, and people are reporting to more than one boss—a typical matrix organization. However, most of the decisions are made by the departmental head. This shows that it is a MATRIX organization.
2. D	Six months is a constraint to be accounted for while planning the project.
3. D	This is a great question. First, you need to find the type of organization in the given scenario. Then, it would be best if you found the reporting authority. The scenario showcases a Projectized organization. We know that in a Projectized organization, the team does not have a HOME/ Department. Once the project is over, the team, including the Project Manager, goes to the BENCH or waiting area. PMOs in Projectized organizations manage these bench/ unallocated resources.
4. C	The emphasis is on the accuracy of the features. An iterative approach will work best.
5. B	The controlling PMO gets involved in managing the project directly. The Project Manager is thus part of the PMO itself.
6. A	A supportive PMO manages the Organizational Process Assets and does not have the authority to control the project aspects
7. A	Using the TRUE/FALSE method: A. A stakeholder can be a project resource: This looks like an OK statement, but let's see if the rests of them are more TRUE or False B. A stakeholder can be a group: TRUE C. A stakeholder can be an organization: TRUE D. A stakeholder can be a project human resource: TRUE Now by looking at all the options, you know that options B, C, and D are TRUE, whereas option A contains the word resource. This could be a printer or an office meeting room. So, choice A is most correct.

8. D	One supervisor means that it is either Projectized or Functional. In this case, it is a functional organization. Notice the keywords, roles, and growth paths are defined.
9. D	Using the TRUE/FALSE technique to select the right option: A. Temporary endeavor by one person – TRUE B. Temporary endeavor by the team & Manager - TRUE C. Implementing the changed Standard operating process (SOPs) – TRUE. D. Adhering to SOPs (Temporary and unique) – FALSE – This is ongoing, and operations
10. B	This is an example of how well you read the question's intent. The question asks you about the historical data that can help you in your project. This is a clear example of the usage of Organizational Process Assets. If you get side-tracked into finding the PMO, then you may not be able to select the PMO type because only a little information on the role of PMO is described in the question.
11. D	In the case of new technology and where the specifications are evolving, the agile approach can be used to work and firm up the specifications.
12. A	See that some of the phases are known, and the customer performs them in earlier products. However, only one component is evolving. This can be the best example of a mixed (Hybrid) lifecycle. Predictive for the phases which are known and agile for the ones that need to be evolved.
13. B	The team is virtual (Not collocated) and reports to many bosses. Gets formed only for the project—all the keywords for Virtual teams.
14. D	Most of the efforts and costs are incurred when your team starts putting in efforts to develop the deliverables (i.e., carrying out the work/executing stage).
15. C	Do not necessarily go with the most verbose answer! Those could be wrong as well. The picture shows that the cost of change is low in the starting phases of the project and expends a huge amount of money and effort to incorporate the change towards the later stages of the project. Thus, a Project Manager's emphasis should be on getting the correct requirement from the customer so that changes due to incorrect requirements are eliminated.

2. BUSINESS ANALYSIS

CAPM ECO TOPICS COVERED IN THIS CHAPTER

1.5	Explain the purpose of focus groups, standup meetings, brainstorming, etc.
4.1	Demonstrate an understanding of business analysis (BA) roles and responsibilities.
4.3	Determine how to gather requirements.
4.3	Match tools to scenarios (e.g., user stories, use cases, etc.).
4.3	Identify the requirements gathering approach for a situation (e.g., conduct stakeholder interviews, surveys, workshops, lessons learned, etc.).
4.3	Explain a requirements traceability matrix/product backlog.
4.4	Demonstrate an understanding of product roadmaps.
4.4	Explain the application of a product roadmap.
4.4	Determine which components go to which releases.
4.5	Determine how project methodologies influence business analysis processes.
4.5	Determine the role of a business analyst in adaptive and/or predictive, plan-based approaches.
4.6	Validate requirements through product delivery.
4.6	Define acceptance criteria (the action of defining changes based on the situation).
4.6	Determine if a project/product is ready for delivery based on a requirements traceability matrix/product backlog.

Business analysis is a professional discipline of identifying business needs and determining solutions to business problems. Solutions often include a software-systems development component but may also consist of process improvements, organizational change, or strategic planning and policy development. – From Wikipedia

The steps to gather business needs are:

1. Gather business needs
2. Prioritize them.
3. Document them.
4. Establish Requirement traceability.

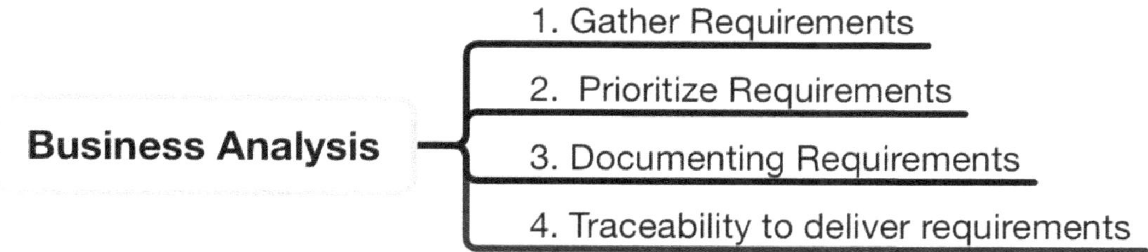

2.1 GATHERING REQUIREMENTS

We create a plan as how do we gather and deliver the asks by the stakeholders; we create a plan – which plan – Requirements management plan.

The Requirement Management Plan describes how requirements will be collected, analyzed, documented, and managed.

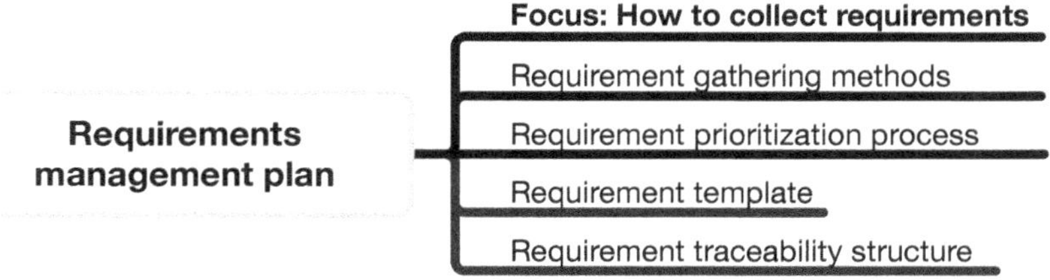

TECHNIQUES TO GATHER BUSINESS NEEDS

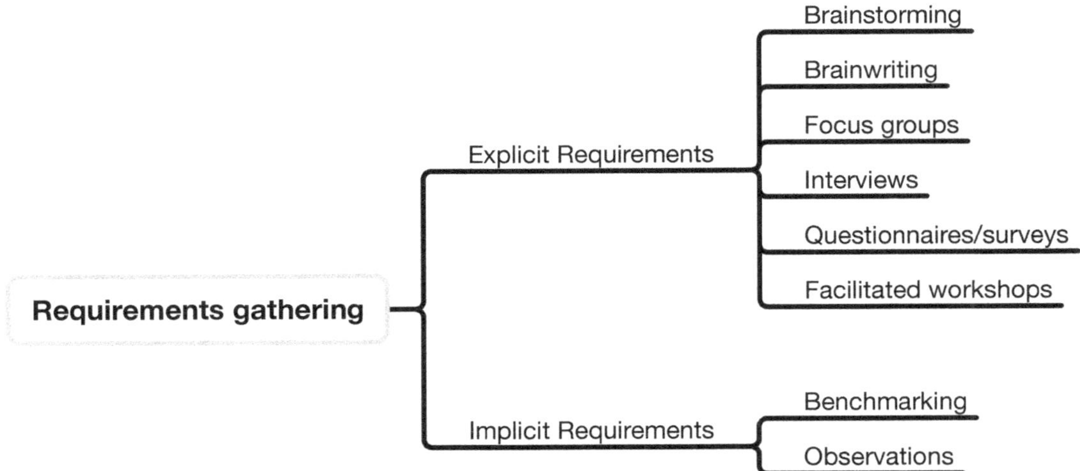

BRAINSTORMING

Think of working with your customers or team to generate various ideas on a few ways to develop the new housing blueprint or process flow.
Brainwriting is when you ask your team to prepare before the meeting and come up with ideas. The keyword is IDEAS.

BRAINWRITING

If you ask the stakeholders to think about the topic and write their thoughts before coming to the brainstorming session to optimize the meeting time – the technique is called Brain-writing.

INTERVIEWS

Predefined questions are asked to the stakeholders in an interview, and responses are collected. The mode of conducting an interview can be a one-to-one discussion or a meeting.
Interviews can be used to gather information on complex scenarios and from important stakeholders like senior management or SMEs (Subject Matter Experts). It requires your time and the other person's time and is a very expensive tool. You can use it to gather information from the KEY stakeholders

Effectiveness: High
Time Requirement: High
When to use:
- → For important stakeholders to gather information.
- → For complex requirements, which require two-way discussions.

QUESTIONNAIRES AND SURVEYS

Can be used when the target audience is vast and geographically dispersed. These are

termed passive information exchange to reach out to a broad respondent base in a short time. The technique comes in handy when the respondent base is geographically dispersed.

Effectiveness: Low
Time Requirement: Low
Geo Spread: High
When to use:

→ To reach out to larger participants.
→ For an easier set of requirements that can be expressed simply.

FOCUS GROUPS

A broad agenda is prepared to get people from **similar backgrounds** or similar domains to discuss requirements, views, and perceptions to get more information. In a focus group, people are asked about their perceptions, opinions, beliefs, and attitudes toward a product, service, concept, advertisement, idea, or packaging.
Focus groups are two-way, interactive, and effective in gathering thoughts around focused requirements or domains.

Effectiveness: High
Time Requirement: High
When to use:

→   To get multiple viewpoints.
→ For complex requirements, which require two-way discussions.

DOCUMENT ANALYSIS

To collect the requirement, a project team can refer to various documents like:

→ Agreements
→ Business case
→ Issue logs
→ Request for proposal
→ SOPs (Standard operating processes, etc.)

FACILITATION/FACILITATED WORKSHOP

Facilitated workshops are two-way, interactive, and a very effective technique to gather thoughts around cross-functional requirements or domains.
Since people from different backgrounds participate in the group discussion, a facilitator must control and modulate the discussion. Joint Application Development Sessions (JAD) and Quality Function Deployment (QFD) used in the manufacturing industry are examples of facilitated workshops.

What is the difference between a focus group and a facilitated workshop? The keyword is cross-domain participation. So people from various backgrounds may have different viewpoints, and you need facilitation techniques like a parking lot to get the meeting going.

NOMINAL GROUP TECHNIQUE

How many times have you brainstormed and then selected the top 3 ideas? Many times. The technique you used then is called the nominal group technique. See, you have been doing it all along. You just did not know the name. The nominal group technique enhances brainstorming with a voting process to rank the most useful ideas for further brainstorming or prioritization.

Keywords: Ranking/rating of ideas

DELPHI TECHNIQUE

Suppose you want unbiased opinions from experts/SMEs or user groups. Let's take an example. You created two book covers and want to know the feedback firsthand. But you also do not want your users to talk to each other and create biases (They are in the same room). So, you give them a yellow sticky and ask them to rate the covers on a scale of 1-5, 5 being the best liked. The participants don't have to write their names. This way, you can compile honest feedback on both covers and select the one with the better ratings. **Keywords: unbiased and anonymous.**

BENCHMARKING

Used to compare the planned products or features with comparable organizations to identify the best practices and generate improvement ideas. Benchmarking helps in getting the implicit requirements (Assumed or non-spoken).

Benchmarking is one of the BEST ways to ensure you do not miss out on implicit requirements.

OBSERVATIONS

Also known as work/job shadowing.
Observations can be used when the process is very complex, language exchange is difficult, or when there is a verbal or mental block to exchanging information. An observer observes the people performing their job or processes and collects the requirements.

PROJECT REQUIREMENTS CATEGORIES:

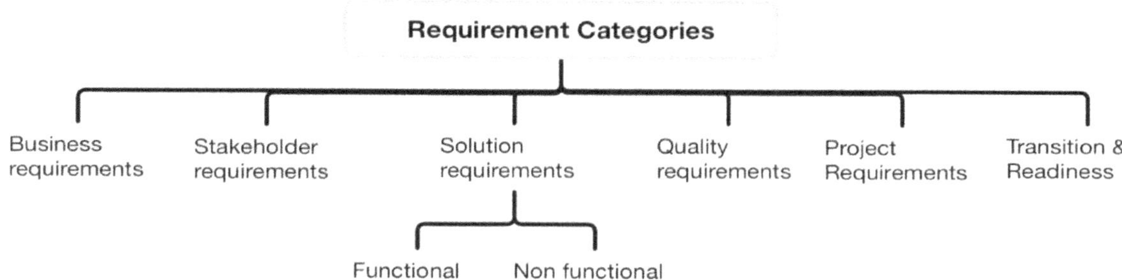

BUSINESS REQUIREMENTS:
The high-level organization needs come from portfolio management. Examples of business requirements are:
1. We need to train at least 50 engineers on Microsoft BI capability by the end of this year. Success Criteria: 50 People who have at least 5 months in setting up Microsoft BI capability so that we can win the BI projects.

STAKEHOLDER REQUIREMENTS:
Different groups of stakeholders may have different requirements. For example, if we are setting up the video conference room for the office, various requirements can be:
Stakeholder 1:
1. At least 10 people capability
2. Big screen
3. It Should feel like one on one call in front.
Stakeholder 2:
The reoccurring maintenance cost should be less than XYZ USD per year.

SOLUTION REQUIREMENTS:
The term is mostly used in software projects. The requirements of the requested solution can be further categorized as FUNCTIONAL (Interaction, data, workflow, etc.) And NON- FUNCTIONAL (reliability, security, safety, etc.) These are supplementary requirements. Examples are:
1. The website should be up 99% of the time
2. The website should be able to take up a concurrent user load of 100 at any time.

TRANSITION AND READINESS REQUIREMENTS:
The term is mostly used in business process outsourcing projects describing data conversion, as if, and future states.

PROJECT REQUIREMENTS:
The specific conditions or processes which the project needs to meet, e.g., constraints (milestones or costs), agreement specifications, etc.

QUALITY REQUIREMENTS

Processes to test the requirements, e.g., test cycles and process certifications like ISO or CMMI.

REQUIREMENT DOCUMENTATION

CONTEXT DIAGRAMS

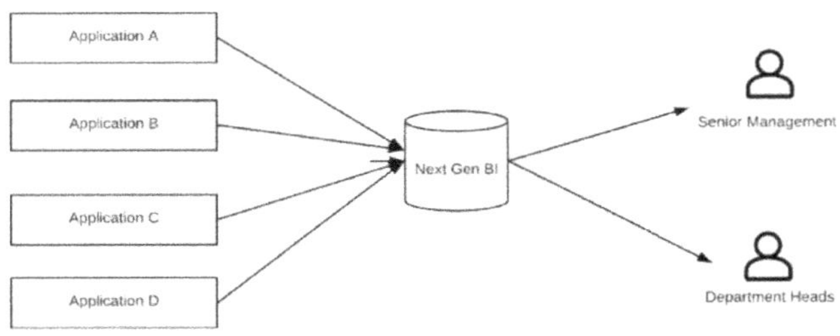

Visual representation to show at a broad level how other people or systems interact with the new upcoming product.
System Context Diagrams represent all external entities that may interact with the system in consideration.

A context diagram shows the system at the center, with no details of its interior structure, surrounded by all its interacting systems, environments, and activities.

The objective of the system context diagram is to focus attention on external factors and events that should be considered for the project under development.

IDEA/MIND MAPPING

You have seen mind maps in the book. Idea mapping, also called mind maps, uses free-flow danglers to showcase related ideas.

Keywords: Picture, Related Ideas

AFFINITY DIAGRAM

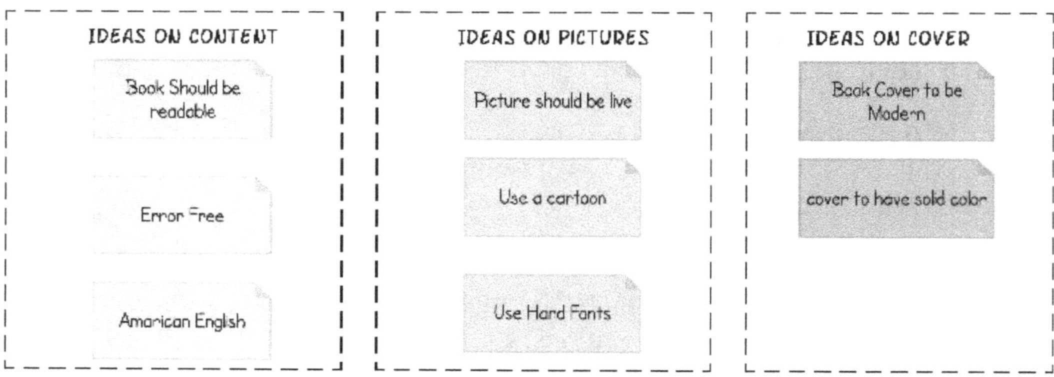

As the name suggests, similar ideas are clubbed together. You can use sticky notes to write the ideas and then rearrange them to form groups. Very useful to categorize the requirements in groups.
Keywords: Category, Bucket

PROTOTYPES

One of the MOST effective methods to get requirements verified at the start of the project.
A prototype will help the project group to get early confirmation of the requirements, thus, reducing the overall rework time.
Storyboarding is a type of prototype where various frames are shown with the overall action steps in visual design.
A prototype can be a small miniature model that can be reused or a throwaway. It is made to gather feedback on requirements from stakeholders. Examples of prototypes are wireframes in IT projects.
Storyboarding is a visual prototype for advertisement or visual industries
Keywords: Miniature/Model, Customer signoff

USER STORY-BASED REQUIREMENTS

A user story describes the type of user (persona) they want and why. A user story can help understand the specific requirement of typical users. A user story also will help you find the value it holds for the user and, thus, the business.
A user story has a format:

As a user, I would like to _____________(feature), So that _____________________ (Value)

USE CASE DIAGRAMS

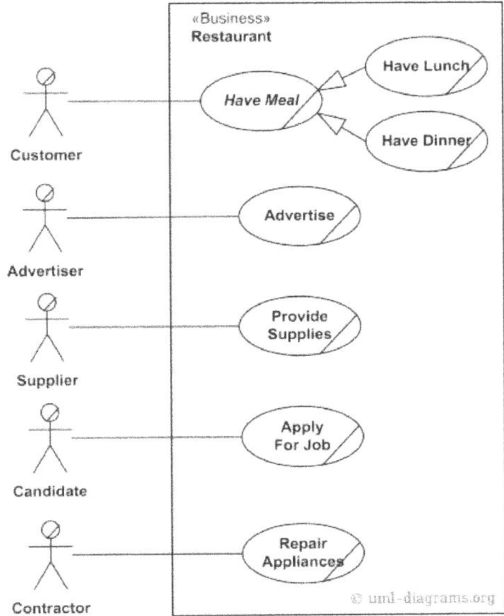

The purpose of a use case diagram in UML is to demonstrate how a user might interact with a system. The use case diagram uses the following components:
Actors
The users that interact with a system. An actor can be a person, an organization, or an external system that interacts with your application or system. They must be external objects that produce or consume data.
Use cases
Horizontally shaped ovals represent the different uses that a user might have.
Associations
A line between actors and use cases. Knowing which actors are associated with which use cases in complex diagrams is important.

PRODUCT ROADMAP

A product roadmap is a high-level visual summary that shows the vision and direction of a product's features over time.
The product roadmap can be used for the following:
- Describe the vision and strategy
- Get stakeholders in alignment
- Facilitate discussion of options and scenario planning
- Help communicate with stakeholders

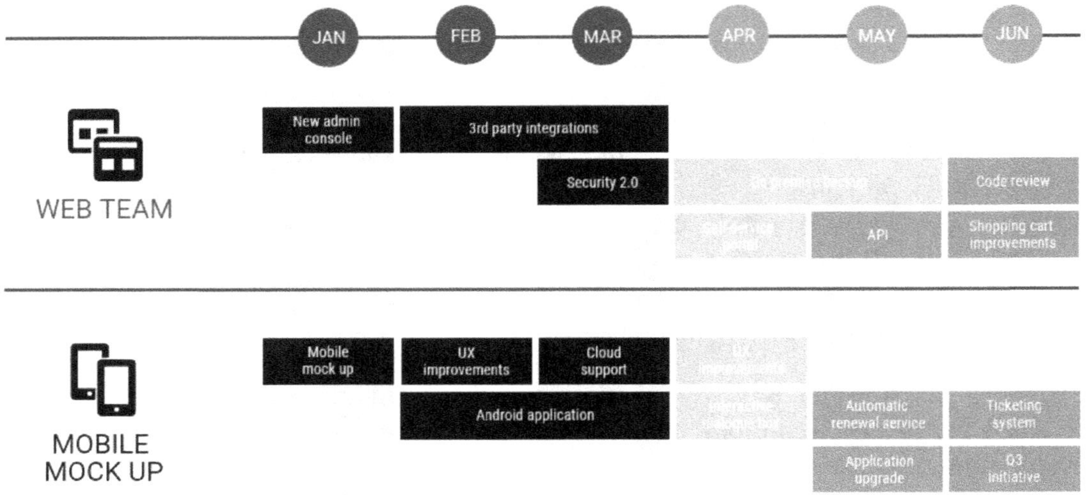

A product roadmap is a high-level visual representation of a product's strategy and direction over time. It provides a shared understanding of the product vision, the major initiatives, and the planned releases.

The product roadmap typically includes a timeline that outlines the major milestones and initiatives, along with the key features and capabilities planned for each release. It may also include information about the target market, the product's competitive landscape, and technical or operational considerations.

The product manager typically creates the product roadmap in collaboration with the cross-functional team, which may include engineering, design, marketing, and sales stakeholders. The product manager is responsible for prioritizing features, defining the product vision, and developing the product strategy. The team then works together to create the roadmap, considering the dependencies between initiatives, technical feasibility, and resource availability.

The product roadmap serves several important purposes, including:

Communicating the product vision: The roadmap helps to communicate the product's vision and strategy to stakeholders, including the development team, customers, and executives.
Aligning the team: The roadmap helps align the team around the product vision and strategy, ensuring everyone is working towards the same goals.

Prioritizing features: The roadmap helps to prioritize features based on their value, feasibility, and strategic importance, ensuring that the team is working on the most important initiatives.
Managing expectations: The roadmap helps to manage stakeholder expectations by providing a clear view of the product's direction and timeline.

Overall, the product roadmap is an important tool for product managers to plan and communicate the product's strategy and direction, align the team around a common vision, and prioritize features based on value and feasibility.

2.1.1 LET'S PLAY: REQUIREMENT GATHERING TECHNIQUES

Select the appropriate technique selected in the below scenarios:

1. **The marketing team met to generate ideas for a new product advertisement. The team leader grouped ideas into relevant categories.**

   A.   Facilitated workshop

   B.   Context diagram

   C.   Delphi technique

   D.   Affinity diagram

2. **The training manager sought responses from the participants on how the workshop went. For example, they used yellow sticky paper, and the participants were asked NOT to write their names. The training manager did this to get unbiased feedback.**

   A.   Facilitated workshop

   B.   Context diagram

   C.   Delphi technique

   D.   Affinity diagram

3. **The business analyst put together a diagram that showed the system interaction with all the users and old systems.**

   A.   Facilitated workshop

   B.   Context diagram

   C.   Delphi technique

   D.   Affinity diagram

4. **To start collecting a general idea of the new process and process gaps, the manager called a meeting with all the vendors, buyers, and the finance team. This could be chaotic, so a seasoned transition manager controlled the discussion.**

   A.   Facilitated workshop

   B.   Context diagram

   C.   Delphi technique

   D.   Affinity diagram

2.2 REQUIREMENT PRIORITIZATION METHODS

You can use them with customers or in the sprint planning meetings to decide on the correct (high-value) features for development for the iteration or a phase(in the case of the predictive approach).

KANO MODEL

Must-be Quality	One-dimensional Quality	Attractive Quality	Indifferent Quality	Reverse Quality
Must be included Think MVP	Satisfaction when fulfilled Dissatisfaction when not fulfilled.	Exciters Not expected attributes	No one cares Does not help the product	Can lead to dissatisfaction Not to be included

Must-be Quality	These requirements must be included and are the price of entry into a market. (Think MVP)
One-dimensional Quality	These result in satisfaction when fulfilled and dissatisfaction when not fulfilled.
Attractive Quality	These product features result in higher satisfaction when provided but do not cause dissatisfaction if not achieved. These are generally not expected attributes, such as a thermometer on a milk package showing the temperature of the milk.
Indifferent Quality	These attributes refer to neither good nor bad aspects and do not result in customer satisfaction or dissatisfaction.
Reverse Quality	These features may result in dissatisfaction since not all customers are alike—for example, loud music in a restaurant.

MOSCOW

This method uses four priority groups: MUST have, SHOULD have, COULD have, and WON'T have. With this technique, stakeholders can collaboratively prioritize requirements. The acronym represents the following:
- MUST (Mandatory)
- SHOULD (Of high priority)
- COULD (Preferred but not necessary)
- WON'T (Can be postponed and suggested for future execution)

PAIRED COMPARISONS

A User Story is picked up and compared with the other User Stories of the Product Backlog items to arrive at the relative value. This will ensure that the most valued user stories are shortlisted.

$$PBI-1,\ PBI-2,\ PBI-3,\ PBI-4$$

$$PBI\ 2,\ \left.\begin{array}{c}PBI\ 1\\ PBI\ 3\end{array}\right\},\ PBI\ 4\ =\ PBI\ 2,\ PBI\ 3,\ PBI\ 1,\ PBI\ 4$$

100 POINT METHOD

Each stakeholder is given 100 points. The person can then give any point to their preferred feature.

Thus, value and prioritization are determined by calculating the total points allocated to each feature/ User Story.

This is also an example of a decision analysis matrix.

Functionality	Marketing Representative	IT Manager	Business Head
Customer sign-up	30	25	35
Social Media Sharing	20	15	25
Customer Profile	25	25	20
Track Order	25	35	20
Total	100	100	100

DOT VOTING

Individuals use sticky dots to prioritize items/PBIs for development. Typically, a team member/decision-maker is given fewer dots than the decisions. The person selects the choices and puts the dot as per their priority.

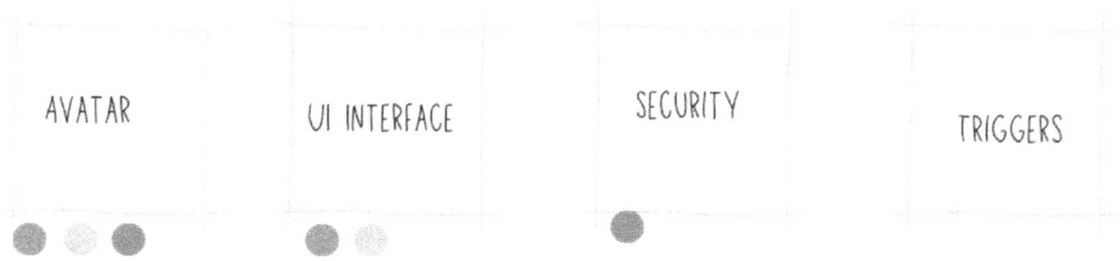

2.2.1 LET'S PLAY: REQUIREMENT PRIORITIZATION

1. **You are working with your team to select the essential product features. Your team has categorized the user stories in "Must be" and "Attractive" qualities. What other qualities should the team be aware of to get the maximum benefits of this prioritization method? (Select all that apply)**

   ☐ A.   One-dimensional Quality   ☐ B.   Indifferent Quality

   ☐ C.   Reverse Quality   ☐ D.   Nice to have Quality

2. **The Moscow prioritization scheme follows the following categorization techniques: (Select all that apply) Select one or more:**

   ☐. A.   Must have   ☐. B.   Should have

   ☐. C.   Could have   ☐. D.   Won't have

   ☐. E.   Exciters   ☐. F.   Delighters

   ☐. G.   Satisfiers   ☐. H.   Dissatisfiers

3. **Each Story is paired against all other stories for further prioritization. The Story, which comes first, is the only Story selected for execution in the Paired Comparisons technique. That way, the team is sure to have selected the winner feature.**

   A.   True
   B.   False

4. **You asked your team to select the top features of the product for the next iteration. To achieve the same, you asked your team to put their vote on the user story. The team member has only five votes. It is possible to give more than one vote to a feature/user story if they feel that the feature is essential. Which technique did you use?**

   A.   Dot voting
   B.   100-point method
   C.   Paired Comparison Analysis
   D.   Requirement Prioritization Meeting

2.3 REQUIREMENT TRACEABILITY MATRIX (RTM)

The requirement traceability matrix, as the name suggests, is a tool to trace the requirements from their origin and trace it to all the project stages until the requirement is finally delivered. A typical IT requirement traceability matrix is given below:

Requirement ID	Requirement Description	Business Need/Origin	Design Document	Code	Test Case	Acceptance Test Case
1.0 Use case no 1.0	Transformation of process1	XYZ	Design doc para 1.1	Page – abc.aspx Xyz.asp	TestCase1 Scenario 3.0	AT1 AT3 AT5
1.1 Use case 1.1	Transformation	The sponsor	DD para 1.4			
2.0	Requirement 3	ABZ	DD para 2.0			

Understand that an RTM is a live document. A live document is one that gets updated all the time in the project life cycle.

VALIDATING REQUIREMENTS THROUGH PRODUCT DELIVERY

Validating requirements through product delivery involves verifying that the delivered product meets the specified requirements and satisfies the customer's needs. The following are some steps to validate requirements through product delivery:

Create a test plan: The first step is to create a test plan that outlines the test cases and scenarios that will be used to validate the requirements. The test plan should include both functional and non-functional tests and should be based on the acceptance criteria.

Conduct testing: The next step is to conduct testing based on the test plan. This involves executing the test cases and scenarios to validate that the product meets the requirements. Again, testing can be done manually or using automated testing tools.

Document the results: Document the results of the testing and identify any defects or issues that were found. In addition, ensure that each requirement is validated and any changes made to the requirements during development are properly documented.

Conduct user acceptance testing (UAT): UAT involves testing the product with end-users to validate that it meets their needs and is easy to use. This step involves getting user feedback on the product's usability, functionality, and performance.

Address issues: Address any issues or defects identified during testing and UAT. Ensure that they are properly resolved and retested before the product is released.

Obtain signoff: Obtain signoff from the customer or stakeholders that the product meets the requirements and is ready for release.

By following these steps, you can validate requirements through product delivery and ensure that the delivered product meets the customer's needs and expectations.

THE DELIVERABLE JOURNEY

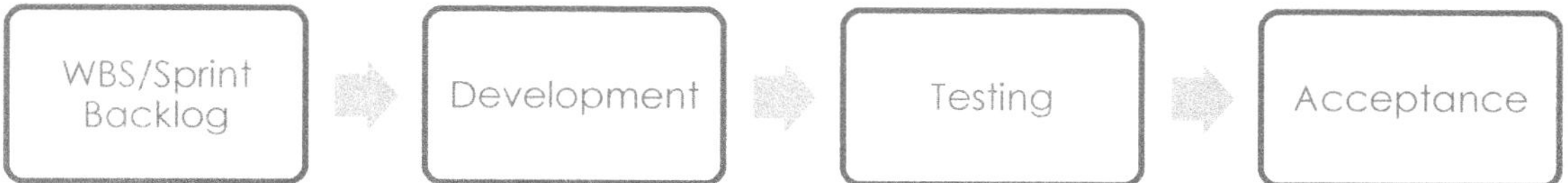

A deliverable is planned at the time of planning from the IN SCOPE items. The team works on it and develops it. Before we show this deliverable to the customer, It should be reviewed for errors (Who does it? QA/Testers)
(more details in chap 5)

2.4 ROLE OF BUSINESS ANALYST

A business analyst plays an important role in adaptive and predictive, plan-based approaches to project management.

In adaptive approaches like Agile, the business analyst is responsible for ensuring the product backlog is well-defined and prioritized. In addition, they work closely with the product owner to understand and clarify requirements and with the development team to ensure that the requirements are properly implemented. The business analyst also participates in sprint planning meetings, daily standups, and sprint reviews to ensure that the team stays on track and that any changes to the requirements are properly documented and communicated.

The business analyst is key in defining and documenting requirements in predictive, plan-based approaches, such as Waterfall. They work closely with stakeholders to gather and analyze requirements and create detailed specifications and use cases. The business analyst also works with the project manager to develop project plans and schedules and with the development team to ensure the requirements are properly implemented. In addition, the business analyst participates in testing and quality assurance activities to ensure that the final product meets the requirements and quality standards.

Overall, the business analyst's role in adaptive, predictive, plan-based approaches is bridging the gap between business needs and technical implementation. They are responsible for ensuring that requirements are properly defined, documented, and communicated and that the development team has a clear understanding of what needs to be built. By doing so, the business analyst helps to ensure that projects are completed on time, within budget, and to the satisfaction of all stakeholders.

2. MODULE END QUESTIONS

1. _______ method uses four priority groups: MUST have, SHOULD have, COULD have, and WON'T have. With this technique, stakeholders can collaboratively prioritize requirements.

    A.   Moscow
    B.   User Story
    C.   Dot Voting
    D.   KANO

2. The senior manager Noah was most concerned about customer acceptance for the project MOON. MOON is a huge construction project and has been going on for the last five years. Ana is managing the project MOON. While speaking with Ana, Noah asked her to ensure the complete delivery of the requirements at project closing. Which choices help Ana the most to ensure that all the needs have been met by the project team and get a hassle-free signoff from the client?

    A.   Project Plan
    B.   Scope Statement
    C.   Requirement Traceability Document
    D.   Scope Management Plan

3. There have been delays in the project due to changes in features requested by the customer. What's worse is that the changes are raised during customer acceptance. The customer is not able to firm up the features of the product. Which tool can help the project team to firm up the requirement in the early phases of the project?

    A.   Interviews
    B.   Surveys
    C.   Document Analysis
    D.   Prototype

4. "The user should be able to register on the website" – Is this a good user story?

    A.   TRUE
    B.   FALSE

5. The event management team kept a suggestion box at the reception to get unbiased and anonymous feedback or suggestions. The inputs will help the event management firm to plan the next bigger event in a better manner. Select the technique used by an event management firm.

    A. Survey
    B. Focus Group
    C. Interviews
    D. Facilitation

6. Sophie is one of the oldest and most experienced Project Managers the company, "Lion Airways," has ever had. The company has recently faced a few challenges in managing the lead-to-revenue process. First, there were revenue leakages due to major issues in the process. The CIO authorized Sophie to suggest process optimization changes to decrease revenue losses by 10% in the next six months. Sophie called a meeting with a few experts to get ideas on how to do this. The ideas were ranked, and she chose three of the most rated ideas to check for feasibility. Which technique did Sophie use?

    A. Brainstorming
    B. Nominal group technique
    C. Interviews
    D. Facilitation

7. You asked the team to write their ideas in a notebook before the team met in person. This will help you save time in the stakeholder meeting. Which technique did you use?

    A. Brainstorming
    B. Brainwriting
    C. Brainstorming with brainwriting
    D. Data analysis

8. Ethan is working on the redesign of the collaboration platform for the firm FXA. His team works with all the stakeholders to get company-specific policies and information around all business units. Today, he is meeting with team members from the marketing department to shortlist the collaboration feature list from the marketing group. Which information-gathering technique applies to the given scenario?

    A. Brainwriting
    B. Focus Group
    C. Interviews
    D. Facilitation

9. Ana is the most charismatic person you will ever meet. She is dynamic and gets the work done. Ana called for a meeting to get input on a recent project issue. The issue would cause major havoc if not contained early. The meeting included the project team members, user groups, and senior managers. Ana facilitated the meeting, where she used the drawing board to write the idea in a picture format and brainstormed on related ideas. At the end of the meeting, she could get a picture where all the related ideas were captured in a picture format. Which technique is used in the scenario?

   A.   Brainstorming
   B.   Nominal group technique
   C.   Affinity diagram
   D.   Idea/mind mapping

10. In the case of the MOSCOW requirement prioritization technique, the W stands for
    __________.

   A.   Would have
   B.   Won't have
   C.   Wise to have
   D.   Will have

11. Jack was given a project to develop the CIO dashboard. The CIO dashboard will be refreshed every day at 11 am to showcase governance, performance, and efficiency Key Performance Indicators. Your team created the dashboard after a few weeks of development. Unfortunately, the CIO rejected the dashboard and emphasized getting better drill-downs next time. What would you have done to avoid this?

   A.   You should have used screenplays
   B.   You should have used storyboards
   C.   You should have used a prototype before development
   D.   You should have used brainstorming

12. You are working on a creative project to design a new product. You had several mock-ups and wanted to get opinions from the team. Based on the voting, your team voted and shortlisted a few ideas to be explored further. Which tool is used in the scenario?

   A.   Nominal group technique
   B.   Focus group
   C.   Facilitated workshop
   D.   Brainstorming

13. **You are developing a cost-effective mechanism for bullet practice for the defense department. The team has put in much effort, and now the software is ready. However, the client is not happy with your simulation's features. What could you have done to avoid this gap in requirement understanding?**

    A.   You should have held more workshops

    B.   You should have created a requirement traceability matrix

    C.   You should have created a prototype to get your customer onboard

    D.   This is normal and is part of any project acceptance phase

14. **Joe, a marketing manager at a bike manufacturing company, is working on launching new super-fast blue bikes, set to release on the eve of Christmas. This means they must be ready for market by October for the annual trade fair, where dealers and consumers interact. Joe is in the process of ensuring that the bike meets federal safety standards, which it does. Still, the product has problems with additional non-federal safety issues that are only now being uncovered. Identify the assumption, constraint, and product description:**

    A.   Product Description: Federal safety regulations are sufficient for the bike. Constraint: The product must be market-ready by October. Assumption: The vehicle is a bike.

    B.   Assumption: The product must be market-ready by October. Constraint: The product should be fast. Product Description: The vehicle is a motorcycle. Risk: Federal safety regulations are sufficient for the bike. Issue: The product is facing non-federal-related issues.

    C.   Product Description: The vehicle is a fast bike with a blue theme. Constraint: The bike should be ready by October. Assumption: Federal safety standards are sufficient to launch the bike.

    D.   Product Description: The vehicle is a super-fast bike with a blue theme. Assumption: The product must be market-ready by October. Constraint: The product must be fast.

15. **You are in a requirement gathering workshop with Jack and Emma. James asked for better color combinations and has a strong opinion on the system's user interface. At the same time, Emma had some other requirement that was much more urgent than this. And these are only two people so far. Your team needs to meet with 5 more stakeholders to gather further requirements. A time constraint is already mentioned in the contract. What should you do?**

    A.   Implement all the requirements

    B.   Use requirement traceability matrix

    C.   Develop a requirement priority matrix

D.   Just ignore a few requirements to meet the timelines

16. The customer wanted a website that could handle a load of 99 concurrent users. This requirement can be categorized as follows:

A. Functional requirements

B. Non-functional requirements

C. Alternative requirement

D. Rolling Wave Planning

17. The customer has few requirements on the functions, but many of his requirements are on extensibility and error-free usage of the product. Where would you categorize these requirements?

A.   Functional requirements

B.   Non-functional requirements

C.   Transition requirements

D.   Business requirements

18. The formal acceptance of the deliverables should be taken from?

A.   The senior manager of the performing organization

B.   The PMO

C.   The head of sales of the customer organization

D.   The sponsor

19. The requirements may change at any point as the customer learns what is achievable. What should be the Project Manager's approach toward frequent requirement changes?

A.   Reject them

B.   Analyze the requirements and select the predictive life cycle

C.   Accept them

D.   Analyze the requirements and select the right project life cycle

20. You are working with an international client. The client's native language is not English. While discussing the requirements, you are unsure if the customer understands them fully. Which requirement-gathering tool could help the most?

A.   Interviews

B.   Focus Group

C.   Facilitated Workshop

D.   Observation

2. ALL ANSWERS

ANSWERS: 2.1.1 LET'S PLAY: REQUIREMENT GATHERING TECHNIQUES

Question	Correct Answer	Why?
1. The marketing team met to generate ideas for a new product advertisement. The team leader grouped ideas into relevant categories.	Affinity Diagram	Grouping of ideas
2. The training manager sought responses from the participants on how the workshop went. They used yellow sticky paper, and participants were not asked NOT to write their names. The training manager did this to get unbiased feedback.	Delphi technique	Unbiased feedback
3. The business analyst put together a diagram that showed the system interaction with all the users and old systems.	Context Diagram	System interaction
4. To start collecting a general idea of the new process and process gaps, the manager called a meeting with all vendors, buyers, and the finance team. This could be chaotic, so a seasoned transition manager controlled the discussion.	Facilitated workshop	Controlling discussions

ANSWERS: 2.2.1 LET'S PLAY: PRIORITIZATION

Sno	Answer	Why
1.	A, B, C	(KANO Model)
2.	A, B, C, D	(Moscow model)
3.	FALSE	In this technique, a list of all the User Stories in the Prioritized Product Backlog is prepared. Next, each User Story is taken individually and compared with the other User Stories in the list, one at a time. Each time two User Stories are compared, a decision is made regarding which of the two is more important. Through this process, a prioritized list of User Stories can be generated. Not one (many)
4.	A	You know, Dot Voting.

ANSWERS: 2. MODULE END QUESTIONS

1. A	[MoScoW] This method uses four priority groups: MUST have, SHOULD have, COULD have, and WON'T have. With this technique, stakeholders can collaboratively prioritize requirements.

2. C	The requirements traceability matrix links product requirements from their origin to the deliverables. Implementing a requirements traceability matrix helps ensure that each requirement adds business value by linking it to the business and project objectives. In addition, it provides a means to track requirements throughout the project life cycle, helping to ensure that requirements approved in the requirements documentation are delivered at the end of the project.
3. D	Prototyping is a method of obtaining early feedback on requirements by providing a working model of the expected product before actually building it. This can be used when the requirements are a little fuzzy, or the customer is not an expert in the domain.
4. FALSE	A user story has a format: *As a user, I would like to ______________(feature), So that ______________________ (Value)* The statement is just a requirement statement.
5. A	The unbiased and anonymous survey technique helps reduce bias in the data and keeps any one person from having undue influence on the inputs.
6. A	The unbiased and anonymous survey technique helps reduce bias in the data and keeps any one person from having undue influence on the inputs.
7. B	Brainwriting is asking the stakeholders to write their thoughts before the brainstorming meeting. This can be used to shorten the thinking time.
8. B	Check the keyword "same department." Focus groups bring together pre-qualified stakeholders and subject matter experts from similar domains to learn about their expectations and attitudes about a proposed product, service, or result.
9. D	Check the keywords PICTURE and IDEAS, and RELATIONSHIP. Idea/mind mapping is the technique in which ideas created through individual brainstorming sessions are consolidated into a single map to reflect commonality and differences in understanding and generate new ideas.
10. B	Won't have is the correct answer
11. C	A prototype helps in clarifying the requirement in the early requirement cycle. One of the best tools to use to avoid requirement validation.
12. A	The nominal group technique is where the ideas are ranked by voting.
13. C	A prototype helps in getting the requirement verification in the early phases of the project and helps in arriving at final requirements.
14. C	We keep looking until we get the best answer: Option A seems good, but let's see if we get a better fit. Option B, the assumption is wrong. Option C, by far, is a better answer than option A. Selecting it and checking if D is a better choice. Option D, Assumption is wrong. It's a constraint. Option C is the best answer.
15. C	A requirement priority matrix will help the project team prioritize the requirements to achieve a defined timeline.
16. B	Non-functional requirements, not related to the system functionality, define how the system should perform. Some examples are:

	• The website pages should load in 3 seconds with the total number of simultaneous users <5 thousand. • The system should be able to handle 20 million users without performance deterioration.
17. C	All the ilities are normally called non-functional requirements. E.g., extensibility, usability, etc.
18. D	The project's sponsor would be the ultimate authority to formally initiate a go-ahead to the handover process.
19. D	If requirements change too frequently and you struggle, maybe you selected the wrong project life cycle. Work with experts and customers, check the process maturity of the project domain, and then select the right project life cycle to stay ahead of the curve. A few changes are OK, but a lot of changes, if a predictive life cycle is selected, maybe the wrong option. Maybe agile works better in your project. Analyze and select the right methodology to execute and deliver the project work.
20. D	Observations as a requirement-gathering tool could be helpful in case of language issues or mental biases.

3. AGILE METHODOLOGY

CAPM ECO TOPICS COVERED IN THIS CHAPTER

3.1   Explain when it is appropriate to use an adaptive approach.
3.2   Determine how to plan project iterations.
3.2   Distinguish the logical units of iterations.
3.2   Interpret the pros and cons of the iteration.
3.2   Translate this WBS to an adaptive iteration.
        Explain the importance of adaptive project tracking versus predictive, plan-based
3.2   tracking.
        Determine how to document project controls for an adaptive project. · Identify
3.3   artifacts that are used in adaptive projects.
3.4   Explain the components of an adaptive plan.
        Distinguish between the components of different adaptive methodologies (e.g.,
        Scrum, Extreme Programming (XP), Scaled Adaptive Framework (SAFe®),
3.4   Kanban, etc.).
3.5   Interpret success criteria of an adaptive project management task.
3.5   Prioritize tasks in adaptive project management.

3.1 INTRODUCTION TO AGILE THINKING

The agile approach fits well when the requirements are changing, and the project team wants to deliver value to the customer in small increments.

In the earlier days (e.g., construction/ auto manufacturing), the project required good emphasis on requirement stability because if requirements change, then it would hugely impact the cost. Think of constructing a multistorey building.

However, code change is easier with software development, i.e., control Z.

So few developers came together and created an agile manifesto emphasizing customer collaboration more than firming up contracts/requirements.

AGILE MANIFESTO

Individuals And Interactions	over	Processes And Tools
Working Software	over	Comprehensive Documentation
Customer Collaboration	over	Contract Negotiation
Responding To Change	over	Following a Plan

That is, while there is value in the items on the right, we value the items on the left more.

Also, since software developers are highly skilled, they asked for a change in the managerial attitude, and new terms like servant leadership emerged. The SCRUM methodology (one of the most adopted agile methodologies recommends using the SCRUM Master role rather than calling it a project Manager)
It was also emphasized that the Development Team should have all the desired skillsets (multi-skilled or T-shaped) to deliver the working software using a smaller manageable team/group (7 plus or minus 2).

One of the key things agreed upon was that the agile teams should show something working in a required time frame, e.g., some teams agreed that a good time to show progress by showcasing the completed features in 2 weeks, and some said 4 weeks. However, it was later established as the best practice to have a rollout period of 1 - 4 weeks (No/little documentation -right) to show that the team is progressing in the right direction.
The concept of TIMEBOX emerged – It means that the agile teams would produce something of value within the selected period (1-4 weeks).
It changed everything. How?
In the standard (predictive) way of project management – the Project Manager and the team used to agree on the scope with the customer and then use it to estimate time and

cost and prepare the plan and milestones to get started. These plans were agreed upon by the customer and sign-off (baselined), and the team would start working to deliver the products – a building, a ship, or a road – you get the idea.

Since the agile team said that we would be producing something of value within some predefined time limit – it would mean that – The TIME IS FIXED, the team would now select the features to be developed within that period. So the estimation techniques are evolved to estimate scope. Since the Time was FIXED, and the Agile team members are fixed – The cost more or less is typically fixed (remains the same), so an emphasis on the cost tracking is gone.

We will revise the above concepts in each chapter and see how the agile way of working impacts when we think of cost or schedule.

But for now – Let's start with a new project – Using AGILE.

3.2 PROJECT WOOFED

You are a dog lover. You are faced with a problem. You had two dogs, and they gave birth to 6 puppies. You want the puppies to be adopted by good families. You are a software engineer, and you think it's a problem on a bigger scale. So you envision a solution (website/app) for the collaboration of people. Users can list their dogs for adoption. Interested people (Dog lovers) can browse the available dogs and adopt.

Can you think of other features for this offering?

Let me give you another one: Dog lovers should have some way to reach out to animal shelters or NGOs to report any problems.

3.2.1 LET'S PLAY: PRODUCT THINKING

Think to list the features of the proposed solution. List few features

1.

2.

3.

4.

Based on the kind of vision you have, you may have added features like:
1. Payment for the dogs (Dog Listing - prices)
2. Pictures or short clips of dogs
3. Details and care of various dogs (Breeds)
4. Healthcare/Animal shelters contacts (location-aware)
5. Most important – Registration for different users. (Dog owners, Lovers, Hospitals, NGOs, etc.)

A structured way to develop the product specifications is using Persona.

3.3 AGILE PERSONAS

A persona is a specific type of user who would interact with the system. It can be based on real users.

Let's try Persona with an example:

PERSONA - JERRY

Jerry owns a dog, works in a multinational firm, and lives alone. He has a girlfriend, but she lives in another town. Jerry travels often and needs someone to care for the dog in his absence.

PERSONA - KATIE

Katie loves dogs. She is an old lady and stays home most of the time. She walks regularly and calls the helpline to get the required help whenever she spots a pet in need. Due to her age, she cannot wait long on the streets.

Now you got the idea. Let us think and write a few more personas:

3.3.1 LET'S PLAY – PERSONA

Describe a few types of people who can interact with your WOOFED:

1.

2.

3

Each Persona would have some specific needs for the solution/product. Let's give this product a name - how about WOOFED? Or you can name it as you want.

3.4 USER STORY USING PERSONA

A user story describes the type of user (Persona) that they want and why. A user story can help understand the specific requirement of typical users. A user story also will help you find the value it holds for the user and, thus, the business.
A user story has a format:

As a user, I would like to _______________(feature), So that _______________________ (Value)

WRITING THE USER STORY FOR JERRY:

- As an executive, since I travel a lot, I would like WOOFED to provide pet care services so that I can travel without any guilt, knowing my dog is taken care of.

Let's write another one:

- As a person who cares for the pet, I would like to know the helpline numbers of nearby hospitals or NGOs so that I can inform them of any dog that needs care.
- As Katie, I would like to rate the hospitals/NGOs – based on the response and care so that other people know about the NGO/Hospital attitude and interactions.

Now you get the idea...

3.4.1 LET'S PLAY – USER STORIES

Let's write 2 user stories for each Persona which you created:

Persona 1: _______________

1.

2.

Persona 2: ________________

1.

2.

Persona 3: ________________

1.

2.

Great work so far. Let's dig deeper.

3.5 AGILE TEAM AND ROLES

Since we are talking about a timeboxed release and the requirements that keep evolving, a role that knows and owns the product vision and who can work with the team to clarify and feature or collaborate to build a vision for the product becomes very important. A customer can play that role. However, if you look around yourself, you will see that you are dealing with products everywhere. Think of the Zoom Product team, Think of your team for WOOFED, and so on. This person who owns the vision of the product and works with the Development Team would be called the Product Owner.

PRODUCT OWNER

The Product Owner owns the Product Backlog. They own the entire product portfolio and decide on the feature's priority or value. A Product Owner is responsible for grooming the Product Backlog (prioritizing it) and providing a sense of direction and vision of the product to the Development Team. Who can be this person? Normally a role within the performing organization (the organization where the project is getting developed).

TEAM

The agile team consists of T-shaped skillsets - enthusiastic individuals. Agile teams should be cross-functional. What does it mean? The Team members have a specialization in one skill plus a breadth of multiple skills.
These are also called **T Skill people**.
Think of it as a DBA (database administrator having testing and coding skills as well).
How are I shaped, skilled people? The people who have a single specialization.
Since Agile teams are small, the rule is plus or minus 7, i.e., 5 - 9 people in Agile development. Less than five is too few, and more than 9 is too big (SCRUM rule may only apply to some agile methodologies. But there is a general consensus that agile teams should be small. The agile team member should be:

COLLOCATED
Better coordination and trust lead to better productivity. What about geographically distributed teams? Can't they be agile? Yes, but then the recommendation is to create a **FISHBOWL WINDOW** (People can see each other while working) using a pre-configured daily video conferencing window.

FULLY COMMITTED
100% Allocated on the project (When a person multitasks between two projects, that person is not 50% on each project. Instead, due to the cost of task switching, the person is somewhere between 20% and 40% on each project * Agile Practice Standard)

PAIRED PROGRAMMING

One person does the actual work, and the other observes. This improves the code quality and adds another set of eyes to ensure quality. This practice also creates a backup resource just in case of any issue. It can be used in virtual teams by using the remote pairing concept, where the pairing is observed using a video conferencing link to have the overlap between the team pairs.

AGILE TEAM SPACE

Collaborative work environments, where the agile teams can share progress and update the progress for everyone to see.

SCRUM MASTER/ PROJECT MANAGER

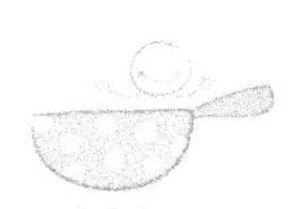

The project manager role is not recommended in the Agile teams. Why? Because Agile teams are supposed to be self-organizing, No manager is required to plan and control.

SCRUM Master is the new role that replaces the Project Manager in SCRUM methodology (One of the most adopted agile methodologies). However, Project Manager is still used in many agile teams like Disciplined Agile and XP. A manager is expected to serve as a coach rather than control and manage the development. They should show the traits of servant leadership, coach the team, and help and coordinate with the stakeholders. They are also responsible for ensuring that the Development Team focuses on the key deliverables. In case there is any issue/impediment they face, the PM/Coach pitch into work with the issues. So that the team does the work they are good at, ie. Programming. What are the traits of a servant leader?

- Educate stakeholders about why and how to be agile
- Support the team through mentoring and encouragement. Advocate for team members' training and career development. The quote "We lead teams by standing behind them."
- Help the team with technical project management activities like quantitative risk analysis.
- Celebrate team successes and support and bridge-building activities with external groups.

3.5.1 LET'S PLAY – AGILE ROLES

Identify the roles played in each scenario:

1. **Harry is responsible for working within a timeline. He attends daily team meetings to work with his peers. He is expected to call for help in case of issues beyond his control.**

A. Product Owner	B. Team Member
C. SCRUM Master	D. Stakeholder

2. **Ria is coaching the team on how to adopt Agile. She attends the daily meetings but does not lead them. She ensures that if the team is facing some blockers, she works with management to handle them.**

A. Product Owner	B. Team Member
C. SCRUM Master	D. Stakeholder

3. **Blu is working with the business to understand the requirements. He also works with the testing team to get the defects on the current product. The team comes to him for any clarity on the work under development. He does not attend the daily meetings.**

A. Product Owner	B. Team Member
C. SCRUM Master	D. Stakeholder

4. **Ray is emotional to the core and is very devoted to product success. He checks the competitor products and works on the feature list to outrun the competition. He maintains the features list and works with the Development Team to see the outcome.**

A. Product Owner	B. Team Member
C. SCRUM Master	D. Stakeholder

3.6 TIMEBOX

Timebox is an **agreed-upon time** to finish development and release the working software. The Development Team decides the duration of the timebox using considerations like customer preference /software complexity and organization guidelines. The iteration duration is one of the few things to establish when the team chooses to go agile. Also, note that **The team cannot continue the work beyond the timebox.**

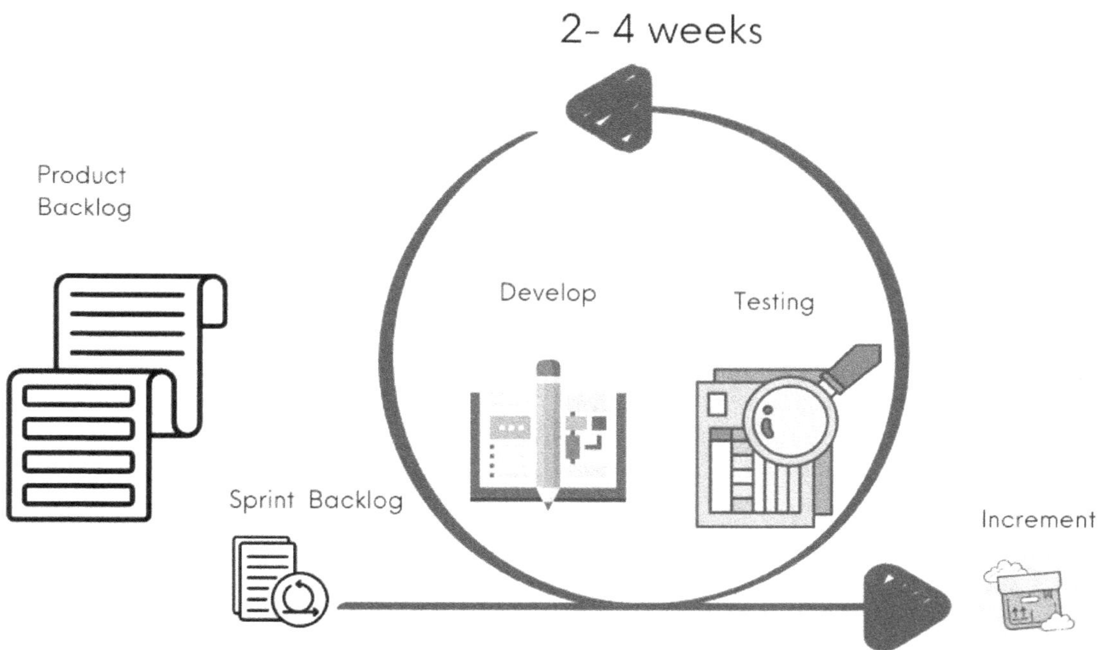

So what happens in the timebox?

The development team selects the features which are of high value as per the Product Owner (he has an ultimate say). The stories are estimated, and the team agrees to deliver them in the upcoming planned iteration of 2/4 week. There are different prioritization techniques that can be applied while selecting the Items for the upcoming sprint/iteration. The selected items for the Sprint are called SPRINT BACKLOG. *A Sprint Backlog is a SUBSET of a Product Backlog.*

The team works and shares status every day using daily standup meetings. And delivers the working product, also referred to as INCREMENT, at the end of the sprint/iteration.

If you are from predictive life cycle background, think that all the planning, execution, testing, and acceptance testing is done within the timebox. The duration of the phase is FIXED, i.e., Timeboxed.

In the case of traditional (Predictive models), the scope is fixed, and the team plans for schedule and cost.

However, in the case of Agile, the TIME of the phase/Iteration is fixed, and the team estimates which PBI Items can be developed in the iteration. i.e. The time is fixed, and the scope is estimated.

3.7 PRODUCT BACKLOG

A Product Backlog is a list of new features, changes to existing features, bug fixes, infrastructure changes, or other activities that a team may deliver to achieve a specific outcome. The Product Backlog is the authoritative source for things a team works on. (Definition from agile alliance). So who owns the Product Backlog? The Product Owner.
The Product Owner keeps the list of features or user stories in prioritized order. The variable which derives the prioritization is business value. The Product Owner gets feedback from the market, user polls, defect lists, and competitor analysis. With all that help, the Product Owner creates and adds items to the Product Backlog and puts the business value to each item in the Product Backlog.

PRODUCT BACKLOG ITEMS (PBIS)

The features which are yet to be developed. The bugs that are yet to be closed and other required items like regulations that must be adhered to. The Product Owner does many things like competitor analysis, regulations applicability, and defect reports and adds the required changes to the Product Backlog. So understand the PBIS are features to be developed but also defects and regulations requirements. But which should be developed first?

3.8 PRODUCT BACKLOG GROOMING

The Product Owner works with the Development Team to clarify the features. The meeting when the Development Team and Product Owner meet and discuss Product Backlog Items (PBI), which may result in the change of PBIs priority, is called the Product Grooming Session, and the activity is called Product Backlog Grooming. This is an ongoing exercise in general.

3.9 DEFINITION OF READY (DOR)

Each PBI should follow the DOR so that Development Team can clearly estimate the PBI's development for the upcoming iteration. If the PBI is unclear and broad, then the Development Team cannot complete the feature in the iteration. To ensure that requirements are good and ready to be developed, the team may establish a checklist for the Product Owner. This checklist could be like this:
- Is the PBI small enough to be developed in 2 weeks?
- Is the PBI clear?
- Can one team member develop the PBI?
- Is the PBI testable?

Having a DOR would make the Sprint planning meetings more productive. What is the Sprint planning meeting? We will discuss them next. The DOR may follow INVEST criteria, i.e., Individual, Negotiable, Valuable, Estimable, Small, and Testable for the Product Backlog Items.

I	(Independent).
	The PBI should be self-contained and it should be possible to bring it into progress without a dependency upon another PBI or an external resource.
N	(Negotiable).
	A good PBI should leave room for discussion regarding its optimal implementation.
V	(Valuable).
	The value a PBI delivers to stakeholders should be clear.
E	(Estimable).
	A PBI must have a size relative to other PBIs.
S	(Small).
	PBIs should be small enough to estimate with reasonable accuracy and to plan into a time-box such as a Sprint.
T	(Testable).
	Each PBI should have clear acceptance criteria which allow its satisfaction to be tested.

SPRINT PLANNING MEETINGS

At the start of the iteration, the Development Team and the Product Owner choose the PBIs, resulting in a valuable product for the business. This requires discussion on the PBIs to understand the feature in detail and estimates to select the total PBIs for the iteration development.

SPRINT BACKLOG

The selected list of user stories is called Sprint Backlog. The sprint backlog is a subset of the Product Backlog.

The team may use several methods to select the features/PBIs/user stories for development. For example, for the WOOFED product, I may have several features on the Product Backlog, and I may want all of them to be developed:

- Registration for the dog owner
- Registration for dog lovers
- Dog listings
- Breed caring videos
- Nearby pet care
- Discussion boards
- Meetups for dog owners
- Food services

The team has only 7 members and 2 weeks to develop the iteration. They need clarity on all the features to estimate and develop them. It is essential that the PBI items follow the INVEST criteria or DOR. What is DOR? Go back and read, pl.

3.10 SIZING THE STORY/FUNCTIONALITY

How do we estimate the work for the iteration? Which features should be selected in the upcoming sprint/iteration?
Thoughts?
This brings us to how we estimate if the stories/PBI items can fit in the iteration.
The Development Team can estimate using the following methods:
To stay away from absolute hours or days sizing, the Agile team works on some abstraction, and that makes the sizing very interesting.

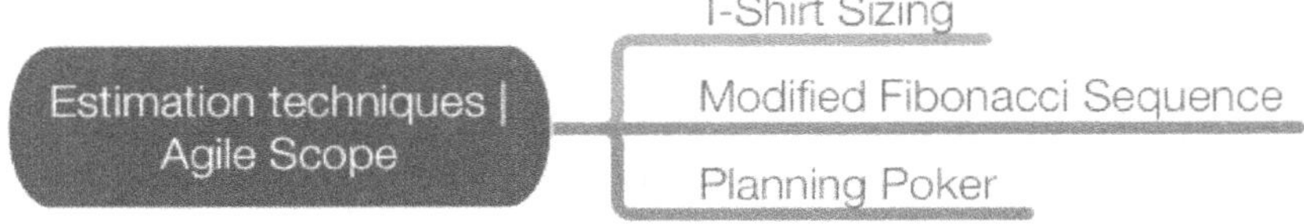

STORY POINT

Story point is an estimation technique where the team rates each user story to arrive at a general consensus on the effort to develop the feature/story.
A story point can be 5 hours of work for one team and 10 hours for another. So the team estimates each PBI item using RELATIVE sizing, i.e., using story points.

What is a story point? Think of a developer creating the smallest web page. The simple page is one story point for him. Now when he checks the requirement for a new web page, he can compare it with the simplest page and estimate if the new one is twice the size or more than that instead of thinking of how much time he would need to create entire page. This simplifies things.
Another example can be a carpenter. For him, let's say a simple item is to create a drawer. Now if he needs to make a table with 2 drawers, he can simply relatively say that this is 4X the amount of effort.

A few of the ways to size the PBI using story point is:

T-SHIRT SIZING

One of the simplest methods is to size a story or feature. The features are categorized as T-shirts starting from Extra small, medium, large, and extra-large. This will help the team establish a consensus on the feature under discussion. The team, in turn, may associate the sizes with story points or working hours. For example, the XS size of the PBI may mean that it can be finished in 1 day. Small may take 2 days. Medium - 4 days, Large may take 6 days, and XL may take 10 days to prepare.

MODIFIED FIBONACCI SEQUENCE

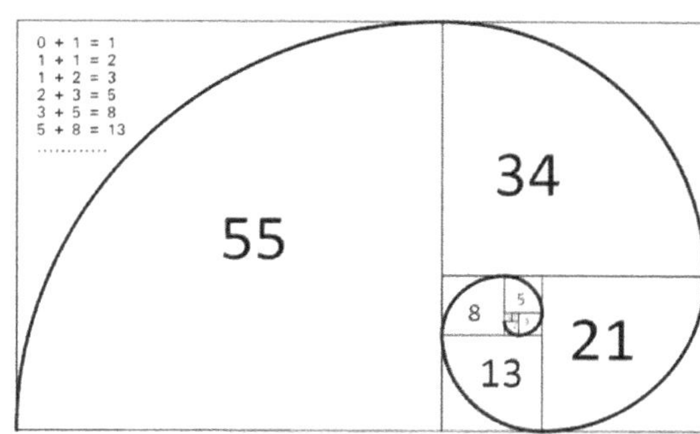

WHAT IS FIBONACCI SEQUENCE?
We start with numbers 0 and 1, add them with the last number, and get the sequence.
The formula gives us the series: 1, 1, 2, 3, 5, 8, 13, 21,...
The modified series is to calculate the size of the story as 1, 2, 3, 5, 8, 13,20,40,100
The numbers are referred to as story points. A story point can be 5 hours of work in one team and 10 hours in another. The team can then use the above numbers to establish the complexity and effort of the feature. 100 may mean that the story is too big to be built and needs to be divided into further sub-features.

PLANNING POKER GAME

In the Sprint Planning meeting, each team member is given a card to represent the effort on the user story/feature. Then, each feature is discussed, and all members pick their cards to show the efforts needed to develop the feature in the discussion. If there is slight variation - that's good - discussion would bring clarity and, finally, a consensus on the effort of the story.
If the team picks up cards that vary in the estimate, e.g., one developer feels that the story is small and another feels that the story is XL, then a discussion may be required to clarify the estimate. The team gets into discussion and arrives at the final size.
Planning poker can use any estimation technique (T-shirt size or Fibonacci series) to estimate each PBI.

3.10.1 LET'S PLAY | ESTIMATION AGILE

Select the correct estimation method.

1. **This estimation technique uses a format: 0, 0.5, 1, 2, 3, 5, 8, 13, 20, 40, and 100. It may sound counter-intuitive, but that abstraction is helpful because it pushes the team to make tougher decisions around the difficulty of work.**

A.	T-shirt sizing	B.	Story point
C.	Fibonacci series	D.	Planning poker

2. **The team will take an item from the backlog, discuss it briefly, and each member will mentally formulate an estimate. Then everyone holds up a card with the number that reflects their estimate. If everyone agrees, great! If not, take some time (but not too much time–just a couple of minutes) to understand the rationale behind various estimates.**

A.	T-shirt sizing	B.	Story point
C.	Fibonacci series	D.	Planning poker

3. **This is one of the story points sizing techniques to estimate user stories usually used in agile projects. It's a relative Estimation Technique. Rather than using several planning pokers, items are classified into XS, S, M, L, and XL.**

A.	T-shirt sizing	B.	Story point
C.	Fibonacci series	D.	Planning poker

4. **The team takes an item from the backlog, discusses it briefly, and each member will mentally formulate an estimate. Then everyone holds up a card that shows XL, L, M, and S that reflect their estimate. If everyone agrees, great! If not, take some time to understand the rationale behind various estimates. (Select two)**

A.	T-shirt sizing	B.	Story point
C.	Fibonacci series	D.	Planning poker

3.11 SCRUM EVENTS

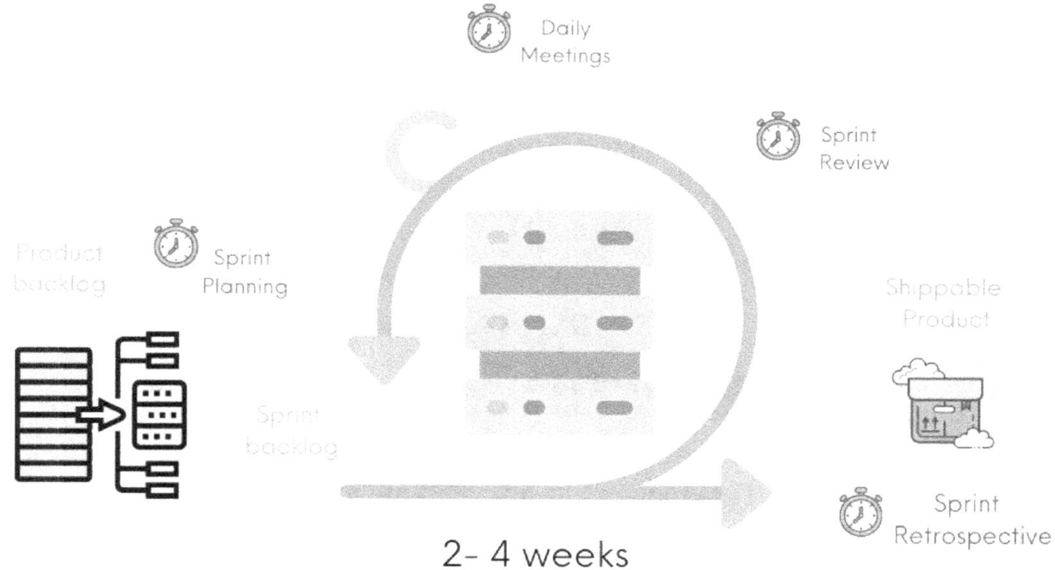

SPRINT PLANNING MEETING

The team meets before the start of the scrum/iteration and selects the PBI for the upcoming iteration. Then, they use various prioritization methods to arrive at the selected feature. The selected PBI items are called Sprint Backlog.

DAILY STANDUPS

The team meets daily to understand the progress and discuss any issues. This is a short meeting where the team discusses the progress and issues. The Agile Development Team is all that is required to be present in the meetings. For the Project Manager, also referred to here as the SCRUM Master, presence in the daily meetings is to coach and help - remember servant leadership.
The Development Team can use various tools like burndown, burnup charts, or Kanban to show and track the iteration progress.

SPRINT REVIEW MEETING

The team produces the deliverables by the end of the timebox. What if the timebox ends and the team has not completed the deliverables? It should not have happened if the team tracks the progress daily :)
So after the timebox, the team is ready with the deliverables. They invite a broad set of stakeholders to review the outcome. It could be the design or functionality concept or a prototype (per the Sprint backlog). Who should be the MUST person/role to attend the meeting?
The Product Owner

Why? Because the Product Owner was the one who worked on the product specifications and should be the one to review the outcome. The sprint review meeting will give inputs to the upcoming iterations (bugs/requirements)

SPRINT RETROSPECTIVE

After the Sprint Review meeting, the Development Team and the SCRUM Master meet to reflect on the iteration. The idea is to learn from mistakes in the Sprint and enhance team productivity. The team members discuss the failures, how they could have been avoided or handled, and the good things they liked. The Product Owner is optional to be part of the meeting but can be invited.

3.12 RECAP: SCRUM EVENTS, AGENDA, AND ROLES

SCRUM Event	Timebox	Roles to attend	The intent of the meeting
Sprint Planning Meeting	8 Hours	Product Owner Development Team SCRUM Master	Timeboxed event. This is done at the start of the iteration to select the Sprint Backlog Items. The team can use prioritization methods to select the user stories for Sprint.
Daily Standups	15 Mins	Development Team	The Development Team meets daily to discuss progress and any blockers/issues and update the progress in the burndown chart.
Sprint Review Meeting	4 Hours	Product Owner Development Team SCRUM Master Other Stakeholders	The SCRUM Team invites stakeholders to discuss and show the Sprint deliverables. The Product Owner can release any completed functionality if they feel so.
Sprint Retrospective	3 Hours	Development Team SCRUM Master Product Owner (Optional)	During a Sprint retrospective, the team discusses the top 3 questions: 1. What went well 2. What could have been better 3. Any better way of doing things

3.12.1 LET'S PLAY: MIX AND MATCH: SCRUM EVENTS

Match with the right event:

No	Situation	Event
1	Timeboxed event. This is done at the start of the iteration to select the Sprint Backlog Items. The team can use prioritization methods to select the user stories for Sprint.	Daily Scrum
2	The Development Team meets daily to discuss progress and any blockers/issues and update the progress in the burndown chart.	Sprint Review
3	The SCRUM Team invites stakeholders to discuss and show the Sprint deliverables. The Product Owner can release any completed functionality if they feel so.	Sprint Retrospective
4	During a Sprint retrospective, the team discusses the top 3 questions: 1. What went well 2. What could have been better 3. Any better way of doing things	Sprint Planning

3.13 TEAM VELOCITY

Velocity is the number of story points the team completes in the iteration/sprint. The Team velocity is calculated at the end of the iteration by adding all the completed User Stories.

If the team has completed many iterations, the team velocity is calculated using an average of all completed iterations.

Let's use an example to understand this: A team finished 3 iterations as below:

Q1: The story points completed by the team were 20 in Iteration One. They completed 22 story points in Iteration 2 and 24 in Iteration 3. What is the team velocity?

(20+22+24)/3 = 22
The team velocity is 22.

3.14 AGILE ARTIFACTS

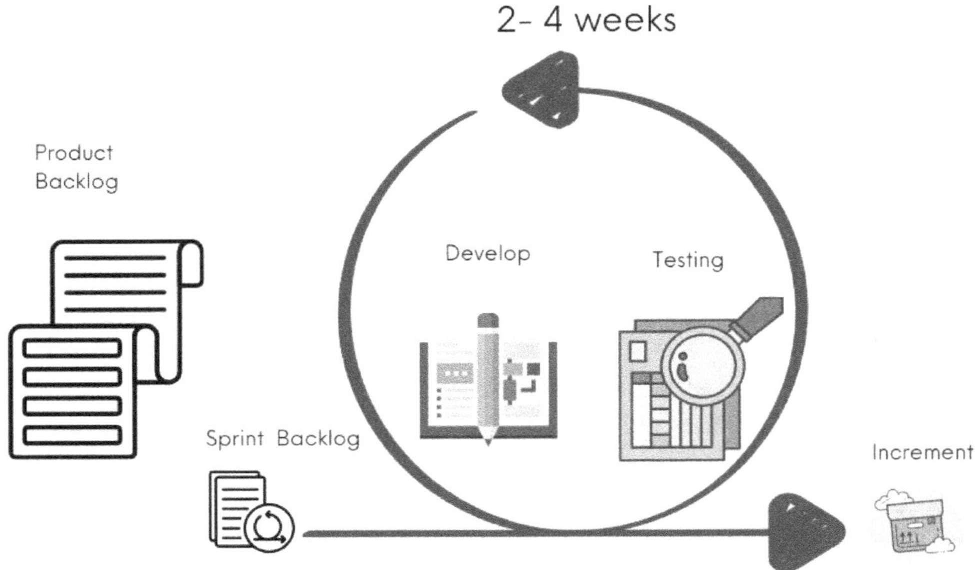

Product Backlog	The Product Backlog contains required features, errors, or improvements. The Product Owner can compile this list from competitor analysis, user feedback, and market demands.
Sprint backlog	The sprint backlog is the subset of the Product Backlog. The sprint backlog is the features selected for the current Sprint.
Product increment	The product increment is the outcome prepared by the team in a sprint. It is called increment because it contains the older features produced by the team.

3.15 DEFINITION OF DONE (DOD):

Each individual is different, especially the development members. They have their own definition of done. Typically when I ask if the work is done? The developer may say yes, but his done means that the code is working and documentation is left. But for the team, the done means:

- ☐ Code is completed
- ☐ Unit tests are written
- ☐ Unit test results are logged
- ☐ Integration tests are successful
- ☐ Updated Manuals, if applicable
- ☐ The code is labeled and checked in
- ☐ Anything else?

A checklist is a great tool to establish a definition of done (DOD).

3.16 TESTING MINDSET FOR AGILE PRODUCT/INCREMENT

Automated tests are preferred over manual testing in agile teams.

UNIT TESTS

The developer tests the code against the features.

INTEGRATION TESTS

The different features, when integrated together, should be able to perform the functionality as a whole. For example, the Security module should be able to work with buying books. A relevant person is shown only his/her history.

SYSTEM TESTING

The whole system should work as intended. Typically, system tests are performed before the functionality rollout.

REGRESSION TESTS

When one feature changes, the whole system should be tested again to see if that (new update) impacts the overall functionality. For example, if you change the website's logo, the checkout page should behave normally. Doing random checks to ensure that the system works fine is called regression testing.

ACCEPTANCE TEST-DRIVEN DEVELOPMENT (ATDD)

The tests are written first, and only then the development of the features begins. For example, in the WOOFED product, we write that the user should be able to create an account on the app. (That's the test). The code is developed later. Similarly, in construction, in a high seismic zone, the test criteria of the building should be able to sustain an earthquake of x intensity. The tests are written first, and then the development begins. Writing (automated) tests before developing the product helps design and mistake-proof the product.

Hardware and mechanical projects often use simulations for interim tests of their designs.

TEST-DRIVEN DEVELOPMENT (TDD)

Test-driven development applies at the developer level. The developer writes the test cases before writing the code.

SPIKES (TIMEBOXED RESEARCH/EXPERIMENTS)

A concept from Extreme Programming (XP). Spikes can be used to learn/prototype when we have uncertainty around various things, e.g. -
- We don't know how technology would work
- How the feature would look
- How to arrive at the final estimate (new team)

An iteration can be used to establish the prototype or that risky item. This iteration, where the developers work towards concept clarity, is called Spike.

3.17 DIFFERENT AGILE METHODOLOGIES

Adaptive methodologies are iterative and incremental approaches to software development that prioritize flexibility and responsiveness to change. While different adaptive methodologies share some common characteristics, each has distinct components and practices. Here are some of the key components of some popular adaptive methodologies:

SCRUM:

SCRUM is an agile framework for managing and completing complex projects. The key components of SCRUM include:
SCRUM roles: SCRUM has three roles - the Product Owner, SCRUM Master, and Development Team - each with specific responsibilities.
SCRUM events: SCRUM has several events, including Sprint Planning, Daily Scrum, Sprint Review, and Sprint Retrospective.
SCRUM artifacts: SCRUM has three artifacts - the Product Backlog, Sprint Backlog, and Increment - used to manage the work.

EXTREME PROGRAMMING (XP):

XP is an agile software development framework that emphasizes coding practices and customer involvement. The key components of XP include:
XP practices: XP includes practices such as Test-Driven Development (TDD), Pair Programming, and Continuous Integration (CI).
XP values: XP is based on five core values - Communication, Simplicity, Feedback, Courage, and Respect - that guide the team's behavior.
XP roles: XP has two roles - the Developer and Customer - each with specific responsibilities.

SCALED AGILE FRAMEWORK (SAFe®):

SAFe® is a framework for scaling agile to larger organizations. The key components of SAFe® include:

SAFe® values: SAFe® is based on four core values - Alignment, Built-in Quality, Transparency, and Program Execution - that guide the team's behavior.

SAFe® practices: SAFe® includes a range of practices, such as Agile Release Trains (ARTs), Portfolio Kanban, and Lean-Agile Leadership.

SAFe® roles: SAFe® has several roles, including the Product Manager, Release Train Engineer, and SCRUM Master, each with specific responsibilities.

KANBAN:

Kanban is a framework for managing and improving workflow. The key components of Kanban include:

Kanban board: A visual representation of the workflow, with cards representing work items.

Work-In-Progress (WIP) limits, the amount of work that can be in progress at any given time.

Kanban cadences: Regular meetings or checkpoints to review progress and identify improvements.

Overall, while different adaptive methodologies share some common characteristics, they also have their own distinct components and practices. Understanding these differences can help teams select the most appropriate methodology for their needs and effectively implement it.

3.18 AGILE PRINCIPLES

No	Principle	Implementation
1.	Our highest priority is to satisfy the customer through the early and continuous delivery of valuable software.	Product Backlog and Product Backlog grooming (valuable items at the top)
2.	Welcome changing requirements, even late in development. Agile processes harness change for the customer's competitive advantage.	Change-based methodology – no question on changes – shorter iterations. The Product Backlog is continuously updated.
3.	Deliver working software frequently, from a couple of weeks to a couple of months, with a preference for a shorter timescale.	Timebox
4.	Business people and developers must work together daily throughout the project.	Sprint Planning and Sprint Review
5.	Build projects around motivated individuals. Give them the environment and support they need, and trust them to get the job done.	T shaped Development Team. Servant leadership

6.	The most efficient and effective method of conveying information to and within a Development Team is face-to-face conversation.	Use of war rooms, Sliding window for virtual teams Collaboration tools
7.	Working software is the primary measure of progress.	Timebox and working increment
8.	Agile processes promote sustainable development. The sponsors, developers, and users should be able to maintain a constant pace indefinitely.	Team Velocity
9.	Continuous attention to technical excellence and good design enhances agility.	Dfx – Design for X is a concept you will learn in quality management
10.	Simplicity—the art of maximizing the amount of work not done—is essential.	4 events and 3 artifacts 3 roles Simple to follow
11.	The best architectures, requirements, and designs emerge from self-organizing teams.	Emphasis on Self-organizing teams with good skillsets and mindset
12.	At regular intervals, the team reflects on how to become more effective, then tunes and adjusts its behavior accordingly.	Retrospective Meetings

3. MODULE END QUESTIONS

1. What should be the sequence of the following activities? Put them in order.

- A.   Sprint Retrospective
- B.   Sprint Planning
- C.   Sprint Review
- D.   Team Formation

2. When multiple teams work together, each team should maintain a separate Product Backlog.

- A.   True
- B.   False

3. Match with the correct definition

1. A team's checklist of all the criteria must be met so that a deliverable can be considered ready for customer use.	Definition of Ready
2. A team's checklist for a user-centric requirement that has all the information the team needs to be able to begin working on it.	Acceptance Criteria
3. A set of conditions that are required to be met before deliverables are accepted.	Definition of Done
4. At or near the conclusion of a timeboxed iteration, the project team shares and demonstrates all the work produced during the iteration with the business and other stakeholders.	Variance Analysis
5. A technique for determining the cause and degree of difference between the baseline and actual performance.	Iteration Reviews

4. ______ method uses four priority groups: **MUST have, SHOULD have, COULD have, and WON'T have. With this technique, stakeholders can collaboratively prioritize requirements.**

    A.   Moscow

    B.   User Story

    C.   Dot Voting

    D.   Kano

5. **A project is in execution, and a member is delayed on his task. What should be the next step for the team?**

    A.   Discuss in the daily meeting and formulate a plan to complete the feature in the timebox

    B.   Escalate it to the SCRUM Master

    C.   Escalate it to the Product Owner

    D.   Do Nothing

6. **Which statement best describes the Sprint Review?**

    A.   It is a review of the team's activities during the Sprint.

    B.   It is when the SCRUM Team and stakeholders inspect the outcome of the Sprint and figure out what to do in the upcoming Sprint.

    C.   It is a demo at the end of the Sprint for everyone in the organization to provide feedback on the work done.

    D.   It is used to congratulate the Development Team if it did what it committed to doing or to punish the Development Team if it failed to meet its commitments.

7. **What does it mean to say that an event has a time box?**

    A.   The event must happen at a set time.

    B.   The event must happen by a given time.

    C.   The event must take at least a minimum amount of time.

    D.   The event can take no more than a maximum amount of time.

8. **The Product Backlog is ordered by:**

    A.   Small items at the top to large items at the bottom.

    B.   Safer items at the top to riskier items at the bottom.

    C.   Most valuable items at the top and least valuable at the bottom.

    D.   Least valuable items at the top to most valuable at the bottom.

9. **When using agile development methodology, who is primarily responsible for making scope versus schedule trade-off decisions?**

    A.   The SCRUM Master

    B.   The Team

    C.   The Product Owner/Sponsor

    D.   The Project Manager

10. **How does the Agile Manifesto address planning?**

    A.   Planning is not required in an agile project, as the project is focused on the current status

    B.   Responding to change is more important than following a plan

    C.   Sign-off on the detail of Product Backlog items is mandatory before any item can be planned into an iteration.

    D.   Upfront planning and design is an integral stage before development can begin.

11. **What is the relationship between Product Backlog and Sprint Backlog?**

    A.   A Sprint Backlog is a subset of a Product Backlog

    B.   A Product Backlog is a subset of Sprint Backlog

12. **Which tools can facilitate team collaboration in a virtual environment? (Select 2)**

    ☐ A.   Your laptop

    ☐ B.   Facebook

    ☐ C.   Task Boards

    ☐ D.   Kanban Board

13. **Your team is using planning poker, and you are given some cards. What are the most likely values in the cards?**

    A.   Random numbers as per your team's suggestions

    B.   T-shirt sizes S, M, L, XL, XXL, etc.

    C.   Fibonacci series like 1, 2, 3, 5, 8, 13, 21, 34, etc

    D.   Odd numbers 1, 3, 5, 7, 9, 11, etc.

14. **What are typical items discussed in the daily standup? (Select 3)**

    ☐ A.   What is the plan for today

    ☐ B.   Any issues hampering the progress

    ☐ C.   What did I do yesterday

    ☐ D.   Conflicts with other members, if any

    ☐ E.   How is my morale today

15. The Product Owner asked the developers to add a very important item to a Sprint that is in progress. What should be your response to it as a SCRUM Master/Project Manager?

A. Let's add this item to the Product Backlog and revisit it in the next iteration planning meeting.

B. Let's do this. Adapting to change is the reason we selected the agile methodology.

16. What is the recommended size of agile teams as per SCRUM methodology?

A. 5 to 10 members

B. 5 to 9 members

C. 4 to 11 members

D. 6 to 9 members

17. Which of the following is the best Agile team?

A. An Agile team that collaborates and self-organizes continuously.

B. An Agile team that has no one to blame if things go wrong.

C. An Agile team that avoids conflicts.

D. An Agile team with specialists.

18. You are part of an agile team working as a SCRUM Master. Which SCRUM events are mandatory for you to attend? (Select 3)

☐ A. Sprint Retrospective

☐ B. Sprint Planning

☐ C. Kick-off Meeting

☐ D. Daily Scrum

☐ E. Sprint Review

19. At the end of the iteration, the team observes that they have completed only 50% of the initially estimated stories of 12 story points. How many story points from these stories would count toward the team's velocity?

A. Zero story point

B. 50 story points

C. 6 story points

D. 12 story points

20. **Since the project required a faster outcome and more work, your agile coach made three teams of 8, 9, and 6 people to perform the work in parallel using an agile methodology. Which can tool/practice helps integrate the outcome? (Select 2)**

    ☐ A.   All Team Meet

    ☐ B.   SCRUM Practices

    ☐ C.   SCRUM of SCRUM

    ☐ D.   Scaled Agile Practices

21. **In the case of agile methodology, when does an iteration consider complete?**

    A.   When the timebox is completed

    B.   When the team finishes with all Sprint backlog items

    C.   When the Product Owner decides

    D.   When the customer acceptance is over

22. **Which of the following are SCRUM artifacts (select 4)**

    ☐. A.   Burndown Chart

    ☐. B.   Product Backlog

    ☐. C.   Communication Plan

    ☐. D.   Gantt Chart

    ☐. E.   Sprint Backlog

    ☐. F.   Project Backlog

    ☐. G.   Sprint Backlog

23. **Team Alfa has a velocity of 25 story points, and Team Beta has a velocity of 50 story points over a 2-week iteration. What does this mean?**

    A.   Velocity of two teams cannot be compared

    B.   Team Beta is more mature

    C.   Team Beta has more capacity

    D.   Team Beta is more efficient

24. **In the case of agile development methodology, who should know the most about the progress toward a business objective or a release and be able to explain the alternatives?**

    A.   SCRUM Master

    B.   Product Owner

    C.   Project Manager

    D.   Customer

25. Who should be responsible for Product Backlog grooming

A.   Product Backlog grooming is the sole responsibility of the Product Owner.

B.   Product Backlog grooming is a joint responsibility of the Product Owner and Development Team.

3. ALL ANSWERS

ANSWERS: 3.2.1 LET'S PLAY: PRODUCT THINKING

Based on the kind of vision you have, you may have added features like:
- Payment for the dogs (Dog Listing - prices)
- Pictures of short clips of dogs
- Details and care of various dogs (Breeds)
- Healthcare/Animal shelters contacts (location-aware)
- Most important – Registration for different users. (Dog owners, Lovers, Hospitals, NGOs, etc.)

ANSWERS: 3.3.1 LET'S PLAY – PERSONA

1. Admin, who is also the Product Owner, interested to see the results.
2. Rita, single, a working professional, stays away from their parents and has a dog.
3. Sam is a single sportsperson looking for pets that can help him burn calories.

ANSWERS: 3.4.1 LET'S PLAY – USER STORIES

ADMIN/PRODUCT OWNER
1. As an admin, I would like to see a list of users who enrolled today so that I can see how the app is performing.
2. As a Product Owner, I would like to see how many dogs have been adopted so that I can see the acceptance of the app.
3. As a Product Owner, I would like to see the comments and interactions of people to see the value the app brings to users.

RITA
1. I would like to be reminded of my dog's vaccinations so that I do not forget them.
2. I would like to meet other single dog owners to form a community
3. I would like to know the pet-care centers near me so that I can take my dog to the nearest one when needed

SAM
1. I would like to search for dogs so that I can shortlist them
2. I would be able to shortlist the required dog so that I optimize my time finding the correct species for me
3. I would like to interact with dog owners to understand the dog breed and the behaviors and care required so that I'm committed and prepared.

ANSWERS: 3.5.1 LET'S PLAY – AGILE ROLES

1. B (Harry is a team member)

Harry is responsible for working within a timeline. He attends daily team meetings to work with his peers. He is expected to call for help in case of issues beyond his control.

2. C (Ria is a SCRUM Master)

She is showing the traits of servant leadership.

Ria is coaching the team on how to adopt Agile. She attends the daily meetings but does not lead them. She ensures that if the team is facing some blockers, she works with management to handle them.

3.   A (Blu is a Product Owner)

Blu is working with the business to understand the requirements. He also works with the testing team to get the defects on the current product. The team comes to him for any clarity on the work under development. He does not attend the daily meetings.

4.   A (Ray is the Product Owner)

Ray is emotional to the core and is very devoted to the product's success. He checks out competitor products and works on the feature list to outrun the competition. He maintains the features list and works with the Development Team to see the outcome.

ANSWERS: 3.7.1 LET'S PLAY: PRIORITIZATION.

1. A,B,C (KANO Model)
2. A, B, C, D (Moscow model)
3. FALSE
In this technique, a list of all the User Stories in the Prioritized Product Backlog is prepared. Next, each User Story is taken individually and compared with the other User Stories in the list, one at a time. Each time two User Stories are compared, a decision is made regarding which of the two is more important. Through this process, a prioritized list of User Stories can be generated. Not one (many)
4. A You know, Dot Voting.

ANSWERS: 3.10.1 LET'S PLAY | ESTIMATION AGILE

1. **This estimation technique uses a format: 0, 0.5, 1, 2, 3, 5, 8, 13, 20, 40, and 100. It may sound counter-intuitive, but that abstraction is helpful because it pushes the team to make tougher decisions around the difficulty of work.**

   C. Fibonacci series

2. **The team will take an item from the backlog, discuss it briefly, and each member will mentally formulate an estimate. Then everyone holds up a card with the number that reflects their estimate. If everyone agrees, great! If not, take some time (but not too much time–just a couple of minutes) to understand the rationale behind various estimates.**

   D. Planning poker

3. **This is one of the story points sizing techniques to estimate user stories usually used in agile projects. It's a relative Estimation Technique. Rather than using several planning pokers, items are classified into XS, S, M, L, and XL.**

   A. T-shirt sizing

4. The team takes an item from the backlog, discusses it briefly, and each member will mentally formulate an estimate. Then everyone holds up a card that shows XL, L, M, and S that reflect their estimate. If everyone agrees, great! If not, take some time to understand the rationale behind various estimates. (Select two)

A. T-shirt sizing

D. Planning poker

ANSWERS: 3.12.1 LET'S PLAY: MIX AND MATCH: SCRUM EVENTS

Sprint Planning	Timeboxed event. This is done at the start of the iteration to select the Sprint Backlog Items. The team can use prioritization methods to select the user stories for Sprint.
Daily Scrum	The Development Team meets daily to discuss progress and any blockers/issues and updates the progress in the burndown chart.
Sprint Review	The SCRUM Team invites stakeholders to discuss and shows the Sprint deliverables. The Product Owner can release any of the completed functionality if they feel so.
Sprint Retrospective	During a Sprint retrospective, the team discusses the top 3 questions: 1. What went well 2. What could have been better 3. Any better way of doing things

ANSWERS: 3. MODULE END ANSWERS

1.	**Team Formation >> Sprint Planning >> Sprint Review >> Sprint Retrospective**
2. TRUE	To avoid confusion- there is only one Product Backlog and only one owner for the Product Backlog - what's that role?

3.		
	1. A team's checklist of all the criteria must be met so that a deliverable can be considered ready for customer use.	Definition of Done
	2. A team's checklist for a user-centric requirement has all the information that the team needs to be able to begin working on it.	Definition of Ready
	3. A set of conditions that are required to be met before deliverables are accepted.	Acceptance Criteria
	4. At or near the conclusion of a timeboxed iteration, the project team shares and demonstrates all the work produced during the	Iteration Reviews

	iteration with the business and other stakeholders.
	5. A technique for determining the cause and degree of difference between the baseline and actual performance. Variance Analysis
4. A	[MoScoW] This method uses four priority groups: MUST have, SHOULD have, COULD have, and WON'T have. With this technique, stakeholders can collaboratively prioritize requirements.
5. A	This is normal and should be handled at the team level. A daily meeting is the best place to discuss and take the next steps to solve the issue.
6. C	Sprint Review is a demo at the end of the Sprint for everyone in the organization to provide feedback on the work done.
7. D	A timebox is a previously agreed period of time during which a person or a team works steadily towards completing some goal. Rather than allowing work to continue until the goal is reached and evaluating the time taken, the timebox approach consists of stopping work when the time limit is reached and evaluating what was accomplished.
8. C	The Product Backlog lists any required deliverables. Its contents are ordered by business value. Backlog Item priority might change, and requirements can be added and removed - thus, the Product Backlog is a continuously maintained plan towards a growing business value.
9. C	The final decision lies with the Product Owner.
10. B	Individuals and interactions over processes and tools Working software over comprehensive documentation Responding to change over following a plan Customer collaboration over contract negotiation
11. A	A Sprint Backlog is a subset of the Product Backlog. Iteration backlog is a subset of Product Backlog. The development chooses the most valuable items for Sprint along with the Product Owner. The list of items selected for execution in the Sprint is called Sprint or Iteration backlog.
12. C, D	Using technology can work to bring the team closer. Working together using a shared taskboard to check progress and collaboration would be a great addon. (Laptop is a piece of equipment)
13. C	Planning poker is based on a list of features to be delivered, several copies of a deck of cards, and, optionally, an egg timer that can be used to limit the time spent in discussion of each item. The feature list, often a list of user stories, describes some software that needs to be developed. The cards in the deck have numbers on them. A typical deck has cards showing the Fibonacci sequence, including a zero: 0, 1, 2, 3, 5, 8, 13, 21, 34, 55, 89; other decks use similar progressions with a fixed ratio between each value, such as 1, 2, 4, 8, etc.
14. A, B, C	A. What is the plan for today B. Any issues hampering the progress C. What did I do yesterday The above questions are discussed in the daily standup.

15. A	Let's add this item to the Product Backlog and revisit it in the next iteration planning meeting. The iterations are short and should not be disturbed.
16. B	Most Agile and SCRUM training courses refer to a 7 +/- 2 rule. That is, agile or SCRUM teams should be of 5 to 9 members.
17. A	An Agile team is all about communication (usually daily), teamwork, problem-solving, technical development skills, and striving to improve the team's velocity with each iteration. ... Agile teams are composed of self-organized, cross-functional, highly effective groups of people
18. A, B, E	The SCRUM Master helps the SCRUM Team perform at their highest level. They also protect the team from both internal and external distractions. Scoutmaster holds the SCRUM Team accountable to their working agreements, SCRUM values, and the SCRUM framework itself. The daily meeting can be held without SCRUM Master
19. C	50% of 12 is 6 story point
20. C, D	SCRUM of SCRUM and scaled agile framework can be used in the case of more significant agile projects.
21. A	A sprint/iteration in agile projects is time-boxed. i.e., the iteration is over when the time finishes. Usually, the timebox can be anywhere from 1 - 4 weeks.
22. **A, B, E, G**	Burndown Chart - Agile Artifact Product Backlog - Agile Artifact Communication Plan - NA Gantt Chart- NA Sprint Backlog - Agile Artifact Project Backlog - NA Sprint Backlog - Agile Artifact
23. A	Team story point measures can be different, and hence the team velocity of any two teams cannot be compared.
24. B	The Product Owner is accountable for maximizing the value of the product resulting from the SCRUM Team's work. How this is done may vary widely across organizations, SCRUM Teams, and individuals. The Product Owner is also accountable for effective Product Backlog management, which includes: → Developing and explicitly communicating the Product Goal → Creating and clearly communicating Product Backlog items → Ensuring that the Product Backlog is transparent, visible, and understood. → Ordering Product Backlog items The Product Owner may do the above work or may delegate the responsibility to others. Regardless, the Product Owner remains accountable.
25. B	Product Backlog grooming is a joint responsibility of the Product Owner and Development Team. The Product Owner owns the Product Backlog, but the PBI grooming should be a team task, and joint team sessions are conducted to classify the PBI value.

4. STAKEHOLDERS

CAPM ECO TOPICS COVERED IN THIS CHAPTER

1.2	Use a stakeholder register in a given situation.
1.3	Demonstrate an understanding of project roles and responsibilities.
1.3	Explain emotional intelligence (EQ) and its impact on project management.
4.1	Outline the need for roles and responsibilities (Why do you need to identify stakeholders in the first place?).
4.1	Differentiate between internal and external roles.
4.2	Determine how to conduct stakeholder communication.
4.2	Recommend the most appropriate communication channel/tool (e.g., reporting, presentation, etc.).
4.2	Demonstrate why communication is important for a business analyst between various teams (features, requirements, etc.).

Stakeholders → Communications → Team.

INTRODUCTION: PROJECT VOLTA

An organization, BIGB, decided to transform the shared services operations. They called this project VOLTA. BIGB had around 15 offices across the globe. Each location had support services like marketing, human resources, payroll, benefits, and finance teams, making up 30% - 40% of the overall task force. Moving most of the shared services to a global shared service hub made a huge difference in the overall margins. It was decided that most of the roles could be transferred to India. The processes were to be streamlined along with SLAs (Service Level Agreements) so business goes on as usual.

Now, who will be impacted by this change?

- Everyone within the organization.
- Everyone within the organization is a stakeholder of Project VOLTA.
- Would there be people who oppose the change?
- Would there be people who accept the change?

The Project Manager of VOLTA had a huge task ahead of him to categorize each stakeholder and engage with them to be successful.

STAKEHOLDER MANAGEMENT OVERVIEW

Objective: Stakeholder management focuses on identifying stakeholders, understanding their expectations, and effectively engaging them through project execution.

Communication and stakeholder engagement go hand in hand, and both drive the way in which you would manage and engage people as you move toward successful project completion.

4.1 IDENTIFYING STAKEHOLDERS

The first thing to start with a project is to identify entities that **may affect or get affected by the activities or outcome of a project**. Then, as the project team, we gather information regarding **their interests, influence, and impact** to engage the stakeholders in the project—an engaged stakeholder results in project success.

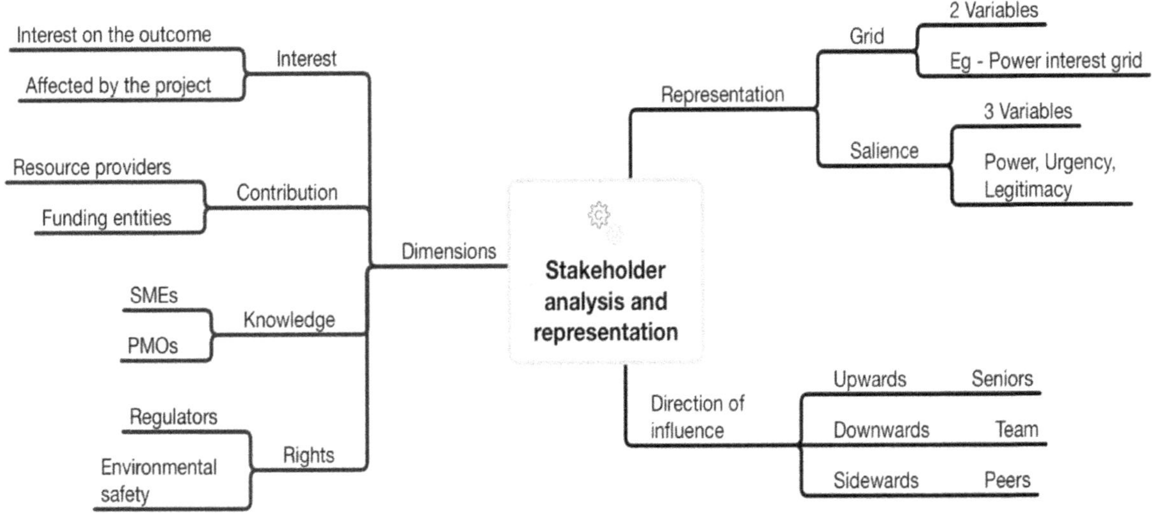

A stakeholder is an entity that gets impacted by the project outcome.

An entity/person who can influence your project toward success or failure is also considered a stakeholder.

Try to obtain a **list of all influencers and those impacted by the project outcome**. Do not leave anyone out. The rule of thumb is to write down everyone you can think of and add them to the project stakeholder register.

STAKEHOLDER ANALYSIS

You either start meeting the stakeholders, conducting workshops, or sending a survey to assess their interest in your project. Once you have the data, you can analyze the stakeholders in context.

Here is a sample stakeholder register. Check the column: Interest and Authority.

No	Type	Name	Contact Details	Email	Interest	Authority
1	Internal	ZZZ			High	High
2	Customer	VVV			Low	High
3	Seller	VVV			High	Low

POWER AND INTEREST GRID

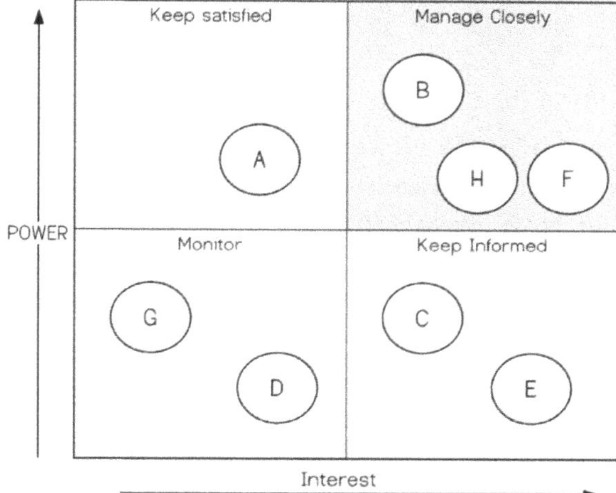

One of the categorizations which most people work with is the Power Interest grid, as shown in the picture Power Interest Grid.

A, B, C, etc., All are the identified stakeholders in a project. They have been plotted on the grid according to their interest and authority.

PERSON A:
This person is high in power and has a low interest.
How do you manage people like these? Send them correct and adequate information as and when they want it.

Not before, not after, not too much, and not too little. Keep them satisfied with the information they need.

These are the people whom you should not be CCing. If they are CCed, you may receive a shouting email – take me out of this communication thread. Never a good thing.

PERSON G AND D:
These people fall under low power and have low interest.
They cannot help in the project activities or affect you in a negative way. Also, they are not interested in knowing about the project.
How should you deal with them?
Do not do any extra work. For example, do not produce reports to send them as they are not interested in following the project's progress or any other information. However, keep track of them and see if they get promoted or if their interest level changes. If that happens, you need to change their mapping and manage them accordingly.

PERSON C AND E:
These people are low in power and have high interests.
These people are quite interested in the project but have low authority. Examples of these stakeholders can be sellers or team members.
Keep them informed on relevant project information. They are interested.

PERSON B, H, AND F:
These people are high in power and have high interests.
They can help the project when needed as they are powerful. Keep them engaged with the project.
But how?
Develop trust, engage in conversations, and keep them posted on project successes and setbacks.

SALIENCE MODEL

The salience model is used to describe the stakeholders using three dimensions which are given below:

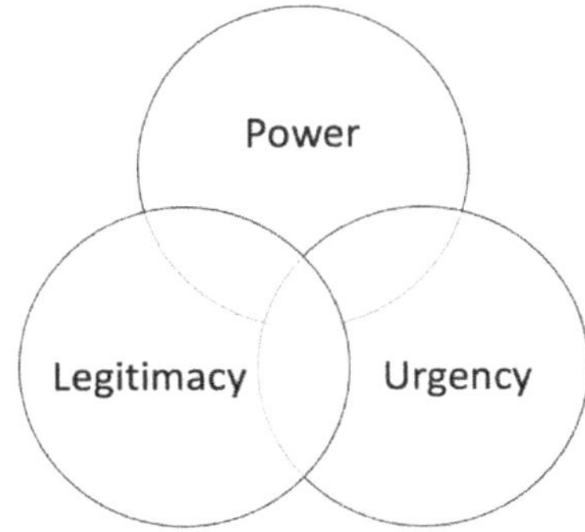

Power: Level of authority or influence.
Urgency: Need attention on a critical basis.
Legitimacy: Is the involvement reasonable?

How would you identify all the stakeholders? Start with the charter. Meet the person who signed the charter and get to know their expectations from the project. A good question to ask in this meeting would be:
How interested would you be in the project updates?
Daily, Weekly, or Monthly. This question would help you assess their interest level in the project.
Another assessment that you can do is find out their authority level. How do you assess the authority? Network, ask people, check organization chart, etc.
The sponsor may direct you to two or more people under him and say – these are your day-to-day contacts. That's good news. Meet with them and try understanding their authority and interest level by assessing, networking, and asking the right questions.

4.1.1 LET'S PLAY: STAKEHOLDER ANALYSIS

Match how you would plan to handle a given type of stakeholder:

Power	Interest	Strategy
1. High	High	A. No Extra Work-Monitor
2. High	Low	B. Manage Closely
3. Low	High	C. Keep Satisfied
4. Low	Low	D. Keep Informed

4.2 PLANNING STAKEHOLDER ENGAGEMENT

Once we understand the stakeholder's communication needs and interest in the project, we plan for better engagements.
For a project to be successful, a good stakeholder engagement plan will lead to better stakeholder management.

MAPPING STAKEHOLDER ATTITUDE TOWARD PROJECT

You can create the current engagement level and plan for future engagements and actions so that the stakeholders are involved. This requires one to understand the current engagement level. Stakeholder's attitude toward the project can be classified as follows:

Stakeholder Type	Color	Description
Supportive	Green	Aware of the project and potential impact and supportive of changes.
Leading	Dark Green	Aware of the project and potential impact and actively engaged in ensuring the project is a success.
Resistant	Red	Aware of the project and potential impact and resistance to change.
Unaware	No color	Unaware of the project and potential impact.
Neutral	White	Aware of the project yet neither supportive nor resistant.

Let's think of project VOLTA. Stakeholders will have various attitudes towards project VOLTA based on their roles.

- A few people, like senior management, will be pro-project – it will help them save money.
- Some will be losing jobs because of the change brought by VOLTA. These people will oppose the project.
- Some may not care.

The Project Manager of VOLTA needs to consider the current state and desired future state of all the stakeholders.

How can you influence stakeholders to change their attitude toward the project? Activities that can enhance engagement with stakeholders should be planned. These are:

- Building trust by communicating
- Showcasing the value/benefit of the project
- Develop Interpersonal relationships
- Show what's in it for them
- Find acceptable solutions

STAKEHOLDER ENGAGEMENT ASSESSMENT MATRIX

SAMPLE STAKEHOLDER REGISTER

No	Type	Name	Contact	Email	Interest	Authority	Current State	Desired State
1	Internal	ZZZ			High	High	White	Green
2	Customer	VVV			Low	High	Red	Green
3	Seller	VVV			High	Low	White	Green

4.2.1 LET'S PLAY: STAKEHOLDER ENGAGEMENT GRID

Match how you would plan to handle the type of stakeholders:

ENGAGEMENT LEVEL	DESCRIPTION
1. Unaware	Aware of the project and potential impacts and supportive of changes.
2. Resistant	Aware of the project and potential impacts and actively engaged in ensuring the project is a success.
3. Neutral	Aware of the project and potential impacts and resistance to change.
4. Supportive	Unaware of the project and potential impacts.
5. Leading	Aware of the project yet neither supportive nor resistant.

4.3 MANAGING COMMUNICATION WITH STAKEHOLDERS

Objective: Communication management focuses on developing and communicating artifacts that meet the information needs of stakeholders.

A gap in communication, no matter how small, impacts the project in an adverse way.
A Project Manager who is good at communication management is much more successful in managing the stakeholders.

Communication involves access to the **right information and distributing project information to achieve successful project results**.

COMMUNICATION DIMENSIONS

Communication takes place all the time, even while you are not communicating actively (voluntary versus involuntary)
There are various forms of communication, ranging from gestures, also called nonverbal communication, or tone of voice, known as para-lingual communication.

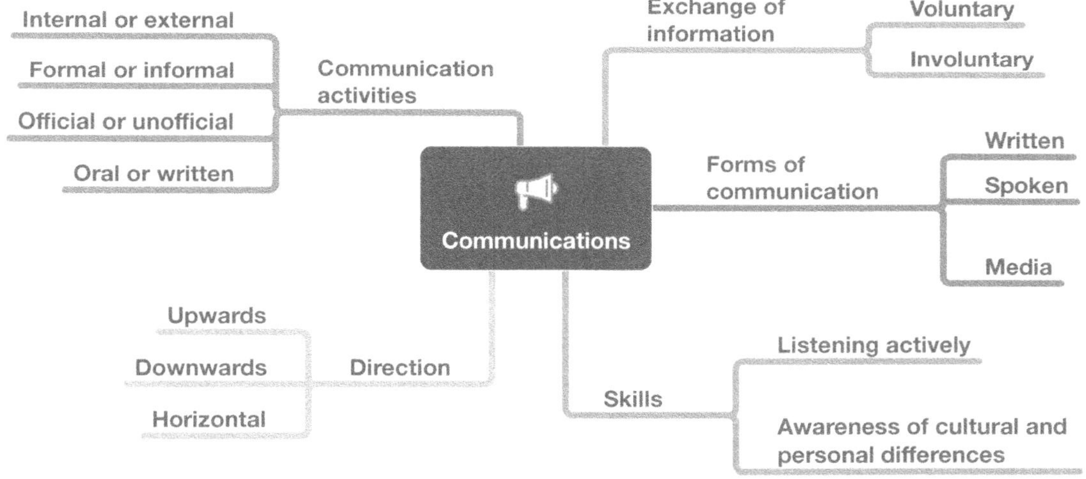

A Project Manager must also listen actively and manage stakeholders' expectations while understanding personal or cultural differences.
Efficient communication is the need of the hour to work with virtual teams comprising various cultures and beliefs.

4.3.1 LET'S PLAY: COMMUNICATION DIMENSIONS

Match the following

S.no.	Communication Characteristics	Category
1	Correct grammar, concise expression, clear purpose, coherent, logical flow, controlling the flow	With peers
2	Gestures	Internal, upwards
3	Horizontal communication	Communication skills
4	Sending an internal note to the supervisor	5Cs of communication
5	Listening actively	Nonverbal communication

4.4 PLANNING COMMUNICATIONS

To engage stakeholders, we need to communicate. Developing strategies to use various communication methods effectively and mentoring and adjusting the strategies results in better communication.

A communication plan typically has the following:

1. Reporting mechanism
2. Storage and artifact retrieval systems
3. Meetings
4. Escalation planning

Think of daily meetings, steering team meetings, Change Control Board (CCB) meetings, client calls, and the escalation matrix. All of this should be planned in the communication plan.

If I had to plan whom to communicate information to and when to communicate that information, how would I begin? First, I would check stakeholder attitude (interest in the project) and the project environment to start planning for any communication in my project.

COMMUNICATIONS REQUIREMENT ANALYSIS

Do you need to set up a complex system to communicate, or do you need to wave your hands and talk? All of this depends on many things. One very important aspect is finding and managing the number of communication channels.

COMMUNICATION CHANNELS

If there are only 2 members on a team, how many ways can information reach each of them - only one? If there are 5 team members, how many communication channels could there be?

It quickly becomes a web of communications, as shown.

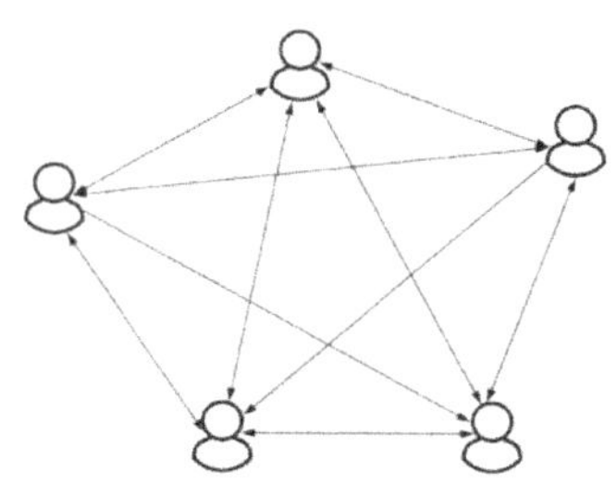

So how do you calculate the total no of communication channels?

Communication channels = n(n − 1)/2,

Where n represents the number of stakeholders.

For example, a project with 10 stakeholders has 10(10 − 1)/2 = 45 potential communication channels.

Why do we calculate the total number of communication channels? One reason is that there will be questions in the CAPM exam on this topic. :)

The customer and you, as Project Manager, are also involved in communication and should be considered an entity while calculating the communication channels.

How does knowing the number of communication channels help?

I suggest restricting the communication channels if there are too many. The way to achieve that is by ensuring that there is an official mapping of people for communication. It can be top-down communication or horizontal communication. What's that about?

HOW DO WE COMMUNICATE? (COMMUNICATION MODEL)

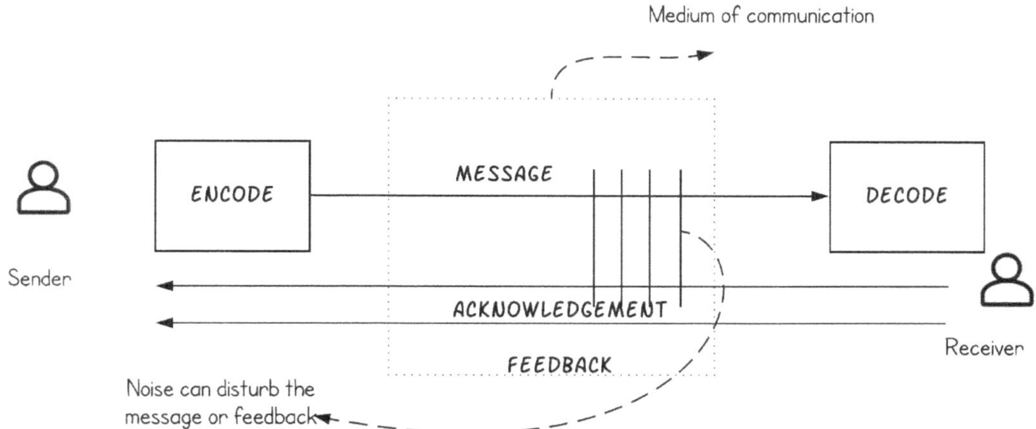

In any communication, there is a sender and a receiver. The sender has the responsibility to encode the message in such a way that the receiver understands the message. The receiver, on the other hand, has the responsibility to decode the message and provide feedback to the sender, explaining if he has understood the message or not.

Noise can be internal (things like views or perceptions about a person) or external (a car horn) and can alter the message.

Term	Meaning
Sender	The entity which initiates the message
Receiver	The entity the message is intended for
Medium	The mechanism by which a message is transmitted
Feedback	A response to the message
Noise	Can interfere with the message
Encode	Encryption/modification so that the message can be sent and is clear to all recipients
Decode	Decryption/modification ensures that the message is understood by all receivers.

4.4.1 LET'S PLAY: COMMUNICATION MODEL

Match the following

Element	Description
1. Sender	Used for transmitting the message
2. Receiver	The entity for which the message is intended
3. Medium	This can change the message
4. Feedback	Done at receiving end
5. Noise	Confirming the receipt of the message
6. Encoding	Done at the sender's end
7. Decoding	The entity that initiates the communication
8. Acknowledgment	Response to message

4.5 COMMUNICATION METHODS

When you plan for project communication, consider the environment, the urgency of the information, and what type of communication will work the best.
There are three types of communication methods, Interactive (two-way), Push (one-way from sender), and pull (receiver pulls communication in). Various situations demand different methods. A good project communication plan consists of all three methods.

INTERACTIVE COMMUNICATION.

A Multi-directional exchange of information. It is the **most efficient** way to ensure a common understanding.
Used when quick decisions are required or a complex discussion is needed. Examples are meetings, phone calls, video conferencing, etc.

PUSH COMMUNICATION

Push communication is initiated by the sender, and the receiver has no control over when they receive the information. Think SMS, emails, and notice boards. The push method does not certify that the message reached the recipient or was understood. Examples are letters, memos, reports, emails, faxes, voicemails, press releases, etc.

PULL COMMUNICATION.

Pull communication is a very good way to handle a large volume of data or information archives. Things like minutes, plans, and reports can be stored in a shared repository where the project team can look for information without disturbing others. Yes, you need to implement configuration management (who can access what), but that will make your life as a PM easier. In pull communications, recipients can access information when they need to.
Examples are Intranet sites, e-learning, knowledge repositories, etc.

FEW MORE THINGS TO REMEMBER

NONVERBAL COMMUNICATION

These are gestures, facial expressions, and physical appearance when communicating your message.

PARA LINGUAL COMMUNICATION

Is the tone and pitch of your voice when you are telling people what is going on with your project

4.5.1 LET'S PLAY: COMMUNICATION TYPES

Mia and Jay were selecting the candidates for replacing Alex. Choose the kind of communication used in the scenarios given:

1. **One applicant came in 30 minutes late and was dressed unprofessionally. Mia and Jay knew he would not be a good fit for the position.**

    A. Paralingual

    B. Nonverbal

    C. Feedback

    D. Communication competence

2. **Jay asked an applicant, Rachel, about her background. Her tone of voice was sarcastic, and Jay got the impression that she didn't take the job seriously. So Jay and Mia decided to pass on her, too.**

    A. Paralingual

    B. Nonverbal

    C. Feedback

    D. Communication competence

3. **Jay asked the next applicant, Ron, if he knew what the process requirements were. Ron inquired, "Can you please repeat the question?"**

    A. Paralingual

    B. Nonverbal

    C. Feedback

    D. Communication competence

4. **Ron told Jay and Mia about his background. As he spoke, he made eye contact with them and made sure to confirm agreement with them.**

    A. Paralingual

    B. Nonverbal

    C. Feedback

    D. Communication competence

4.6 PLANNING THE PROJECT TEAM

Resource planning includes identifying and documenting project roles & responsibilities, required skill sets, reporting relationships, and creating a staffing and resource management plan.

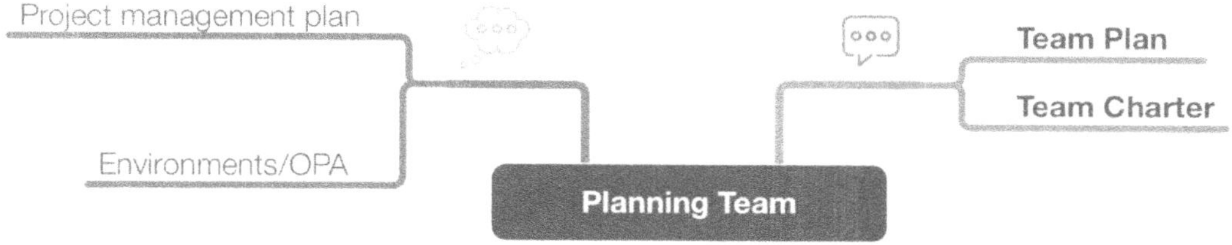

TEAM GOVERNANCE

- You can use hierarchical charts to show who reports to whom.
- A text format can be used to describe roles and responsibilities.
- RAM stands for Responsibility Assignment Matrix. A RAM chart can be used to clearly assign responsibilities of the work to your team.

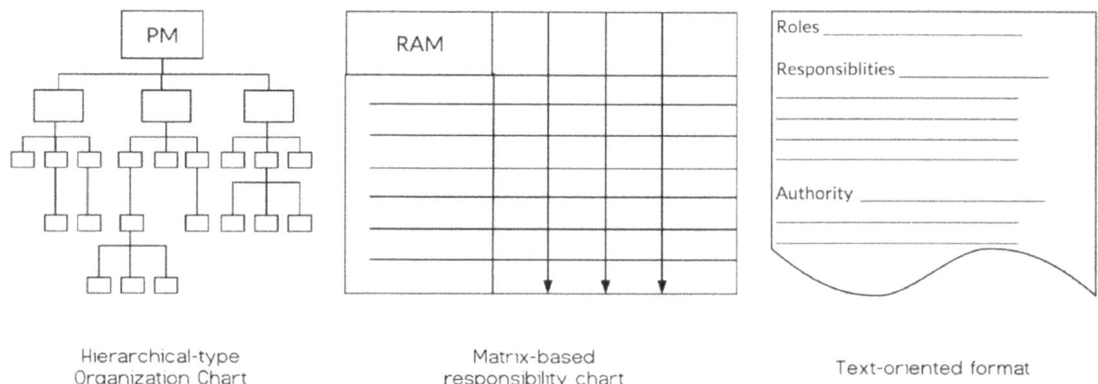

A good example of RAM is a RACI (Responsible, Accountable, Consult, Informed) chart. A RACI chart can be helpful in a matrix organization where the resources report to many supervisors. In such cases, a clear direction and accountability will help the team to function effectively.

Activity	Team Member				
	Emma	Ana	Mia	Ben	Ethan
Testing	A	R	I	I	C
Module 2 Plan	C	A	I	I	I
Module 4	I	C	A	R	I
Module 2	R	I	I	A	C

R = Responsible   A = Accountable   C = Consult   I = Inform

Follow the rule of clear accountability, so have only one A. You can have many R's.

A good example is creating the Project Plan. Project Manager(A) is accountable for making the project plan, but the module leads (R) can work and collaborate to fill in the module details.

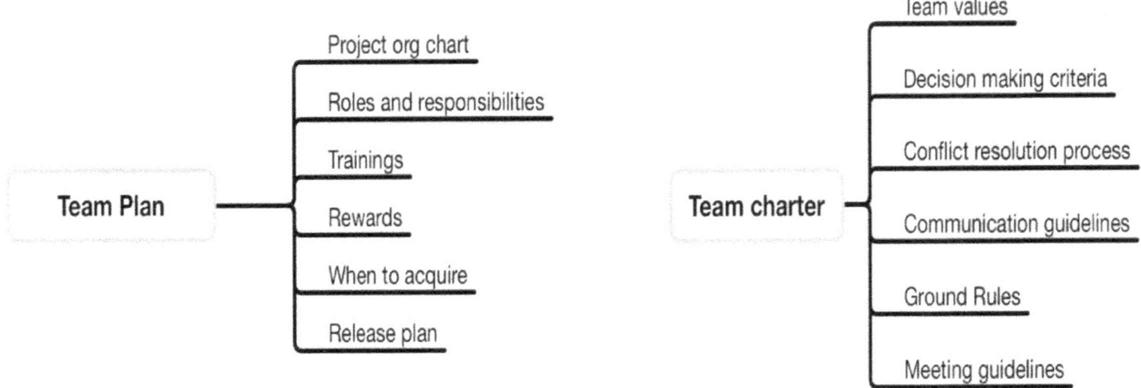

TEAM CHARTER

The team charter defines the group norms. This helps align the thought process, a vision of the group, and expected ways to behave.
Team Values like openness and respect will help the team come together and discuss conflicts when they arise.
Team culture can be built on the ways to communicate, e.g., open-door policy or WhatsApp any-time culture. You decide how formal your team could be.

GROUND RULES

Ground rules detail the code of conduct for a group, explaining the behavior that's expected of all members. Ideally, ground rules are created and agreed to by all on the team. A few ground rules as an example are:

→ Meetings on time
→ No interruptions while one speaks
→ Put your name as owner of a task only if you can make the target date

A fine can be imposed if you miss the target date or a ground rule. This will help the team come together and help to understand the acceptable behavior and non-acceptable behavior in the group.
A good idea is to publish the ground rules in a visible place for the team to view.

ACQUIRE AND DEVELOP TEAM

Get the team on board as per the project plan. The selection of the team members plays a tremendous role in getting the right people on board.

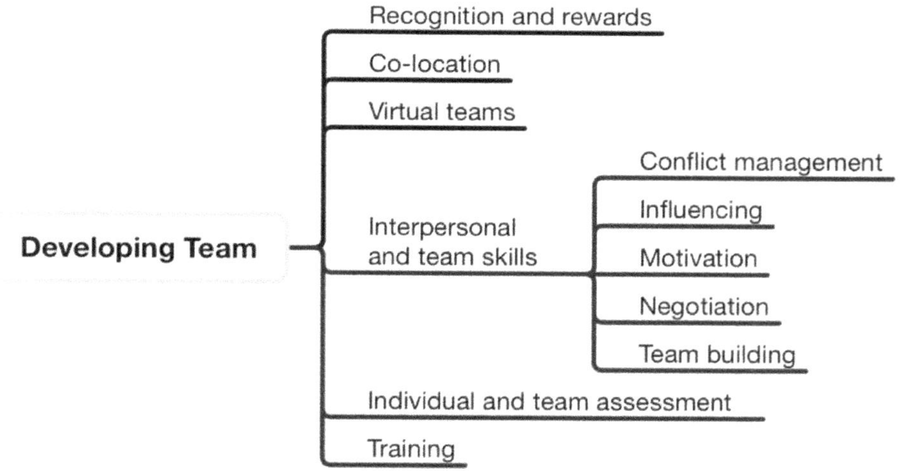

If you do not get people with the right skills in one place, you may opt for a virtual team and build the team.

A few of the methods to manage and develop teams are:

CO-LOCATION

Co-location, also referred to as Tight Matrix, involves placing many or all of the most active project team members in the same physical location to enhance their ability to perform as a team.

Tacit information is information in the air. That is the reason why a person located in headquarters knows the undercurrents. However, a person based in Canada and working from home might have little knowledge about the urgency in the air at the head office.

If you want your team to be aggressively working on a few critical milestones, the best thing to do is to co-locate your team. This way, you avoid all the miscommunication, or worse, lack of communication.

Co-location strategies can include a team meeting room (sometimes called a "war room"), places to post schedules, and other conveniences that enhance communication and a sense of alliance.

VIRTUAL TEAMS

Virtual teams are groups of people with a shared objective who fulfill their roles with little or zero time spent meeting face-to-face. There can be disadvantages related to virtual teams. For example, the possibility of misinterpretations, feeling of loneliness, and one head to catch. Communication planning becomes increasingly important in a virtual team environment.

Tools that can be used by virtual teams to work effectively:

COMMUNICATING EFFECTIVELY
→ Schedule some time for teams to get together using the group conferencing tools. A daily meeting with all group members will help. Find a common time.
→ Chat windows – let your team have a way to leave messages using WhatsApp group or any official tool like Zoom chat

→ Shared storage space like Dropbox or SharePoint site can help the team to refer to the right documents without wasting time.
→ Use pair programming with the virtual conferencing tool. You don't have to talk. It is just on so that it feels like you are working together, also referred to as sliding windows.
→ Use collaboration tools to share the tasks and progress.

TASK ALLOCATION AND TRACKING
A clear understanding of tasks and tracking the progress using tools like ZIRA or common workspace tools can help the team understand the tasks and update the progress without dependencies.

BUILD TRUST
Using a virtual game hub or chit-chat space will help the team to feel together. There are games like Guess the Movie or Let's Make a Dish. Find out some time for your team to spend some chill time together.

SCHEDULING MENTORSHIP CALLS
A great leader should know the team, and the best way is to spend some time in a one-on-one meeting. This is a time to understand any challenges faced by your team members at an individual level and coach/mentor them.

Here we focus on improving competencies and team member interactions to improve overall team productivity.

INTERPERSONAL SKILLS

You build your team by spending time with them, bonding with them, and using your interpersonal skills.
I know a manager who remembers most of the things about his team, like location preference, the way of working, and even personal issues if someone is facing distracting challenges. The result? Teams love him and are willing to do whatever he asks for.

RECOGNITION AND REWARDS

Part of the team development process involves recognizing and rewarding desirable behavior.
People are motivated if they feel they are valued in the organization, and this value is demonstrated by the rewards given to them.
Money is viewed as a tangible aspect of any reward system, but intangible rewards can be equally effective.
Most project team members are motivated by an opportunity to grow, accomplish, and apply their professional skills to meet new challenges. A good strategy for Project Managers is to reward the team and recognize them throughout the life cycle of the project rather than waiting until the project is concluded.

4.7 TUCKMAN LADDER – MODEL OF TEAM DEVELOPMENT

Each team goes through these stages. Some pass through them fast. Some take a little more time. It depends on the complexity, size, and culture of the team.

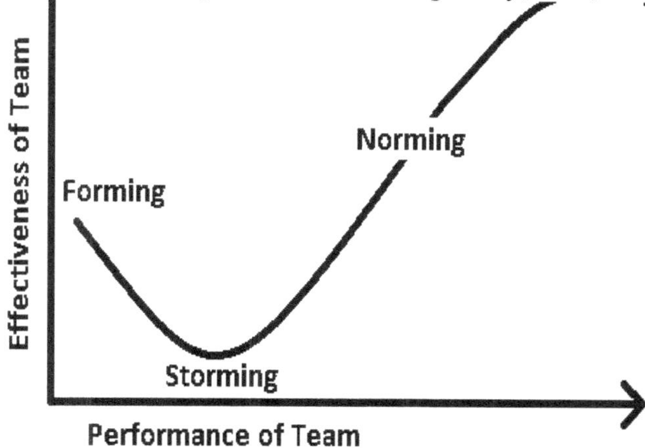

The first stage of team formation is:

FORMING
This phase is where the team meets and learns about the project and what their formal roles and responsibilities are. Team members tend to be independent and not as open in this phase.

STORMING
During this phase, the team begins to address the project work, technical decisions, and the project management approach. If team members are not collaborative and open to differing ideas and perspectives, the environment can become destructive.

NORMING
In the norming phase, team members begin to work together and adjust work habits and behaviors that support the team. The team begins to trust each other during this phase.

PERFORMING
Teams that reach the performing stage function as a well-organized unit. They are interdependent and work through issues smoothly and effectively.

ADJOURNING
In the adjourning phase, the team completes the work and moves on from the project. It's common for these stages to occur in order. However, a team may get stuck in a particular stage or slip back to an earlier stage based on the leadership and climate of the organization/team.

4.7.1 LET'S PLAY: TEAM STAGES

Identify and match the team stage in the given scenarios:

Scenario.	Team Stage
1. Kyle and Joanna are working together on the project POSH. They disagree on everything most of the time. They are at a point now where they are barely talking to each other.	Forming
2. Norman manages project APOLLO. Norman understands the team's aspirations, ensures that the team's enthusiasm is high, and allocates the right tasks to the right people. The team trusts Norman, and contributes with high enthusiasm. It seems like a great, happy group.	Storming
3. A new member, Amy, joined the task force; everyone seemed polite and offered assistance if she needed it. She is trying to understand her duties.	Norming
4. Now that the project is over, the team is analyzing the failures and is looking forward to meeting each other while packing their bags.	Performing
5. Sarah is torn by the behavior of her fellow colleague, Amy. She had differences of opinion, but now she has made up her mind to focus on her task, realizing that the points Amy made were not so bad after all and helped her arrive at a few good decisions.	Adjourning

4.8 CONFLICT MANAGEMENT

Now that your team is trained, working with each other, and producing project deliverables. They might run into some conflicts, as per usual inherent human nature. If the conflicts are small, you, as a Project Manager, do not need to get into them; they get solved on their own. But if conflicts are affecting project performance, or if they escalate, then as a PM, you need to take appropriate actions.

Conflict Happens

Some conflict is beneficial for the team, as it gets the team to think differently.

Sources of conflict include

- Scarce resources,
- Scheduling priorities, and
- Personal work styles.

Team ground rules, group norms, and solid project management practices, like communication planning and role definition, reduce the amount of conflict.

Good things to note about conflict

Successful conflict management results in greater productivity and positive working relationships.

- Differences of opinion can lead to increased creativity and better decision-making.
- If the differences become a negative factor, project team members are initially responsible for their resolution.
- If the conflict escalates, the Project Manager should help facilitate a satisfactory resolution.
- Conflict should be addressed early and usually in private, using a direct, collaborative approach.
- If the disruptive conflict continues, formal procedures may be used, including disciplinary actions.

Various Conflict Resolution Techniques:

FORCING

- Get your way.
- "I know what's right. Don't question my judgment or authority."
- It is better to take a risk causing a few hard feelings than to abandon a position you are committed to.
- You feel you have proved your point, but the other party feels defeated and possibly humiliated.

AVOIDING

- Avoid having to deal with conflict.
- "I'm neutral on that issue. Let me think about it."
- Disagreements are inherently bad because they create tension.
- Interpersonal problems don't get resolved, causing long-term frustration manifested in a variety of ways.

ACCOMMODATING

- Don't upset the other person.
- "How can I help you feel good about this encounter? My position isn't so important that it is worth risking bad feelings between us."

- Maintaining harmonious relationships should be our top priority.
- The other person is likely to take advantage of you.

COMPROMISING
- Reach an agreement quickly.
- "Let's search for a mutually agreeable solution."
- Prolonged conflicts distract people from their work and engender bitter feelings.
- Participants become conditioned to seek a convenient rather than an effective solution.

COLLABORATING
- Solve the problem together.
- "This is my position. What is yours? I'm committed to finding the best possible solution."
- The positions of both parties are equally important (though not necessarily equally valid). Equal emphasis should be placed on the quality of the outcome and the fairness of the decision-making.
- Participants find an effective solution.

As per the PMBOK, Collaboration/Problem-Solving is the BEST STRATEGY.

4.8.1 LET'S PLAY: CONFLICT MANAGEMENT

Appraisal discussions were taking place. Mark, the Project Manager, has a team of 35 people and had a lengthy task to discuss the results and the expectations to keep his team motivated. Here are a few scenarios of 1-1 discussions Mark had with his team members. **Find the conflict resolution technique selected by Mark:**

1. **Rita started crying when Mark handed over the appraisal results and told her that she was rated as an underperformer. Since it was difficult to converse, Mark said, "Why don't you go home today, sleep on it, and we will discuss your appraisal again tomorrow?"**

   A. Forcing

   B. Avoiding

   C. Accommodating

   D. Compromising

   E. Collaborating

2. **Mark to Rob: "Rob, I don't want to hear the same excuses again. The rest of the team is working harder and producing better results. I'm convinced that you should be rated an average of 5/10 as your final rating. If you have any complaints, speak to the Human Resource Department."**

   A. Forcing

   B. Avoiding

   C. Accommodating

   D. Compromising

   E. Collaborating

3. **Mark to Jason: "Jason, you can select either a promotion or a role change but not both. Let me know so that I can proceed."**

   A. Forcing

   B. Avoiding

   C. Accommodating

   D. Compromising

   E. Collaborating

4. **Mark, while addressing the team in the daily team meeting: Team, let's move beyond appraisal ratings. You are a dynamic group, and I'm sure this year we will rock."**

   A. Forcing

   B. Avoiding

   C. Accommodating

   D. Compromising

   E. Collaborating

5. **Noah, a member of the team, resigned. When Mark and Noah discussed the reasons, Noah mentioned that he needed to spend more time at home since his wife Carol was working. Mark knows that Noah is an asset to the team. He called a meeting with Noah and the human resource manager, Susan, to see if there could be a better option, such as allowing Noah to work from home.**

   A. Forcing

   B. Avoiding

   C. Accommodating

   D. Compromising

   E. Collaborating

4.9 DECISION-MAKING TECHNIQUES

We work in a group on projects, and there are times when we need to make a decision. It is easier if we have decided the ways to make the decision. For example, we will always go with the majority for any team outings. That makes one of the ground rules, and people would abide by it.
But there are times when the decision should be on merit or when everyone needs to say yes (very crucial decisions)

Decision-making criteria can be anything of the below techniques:

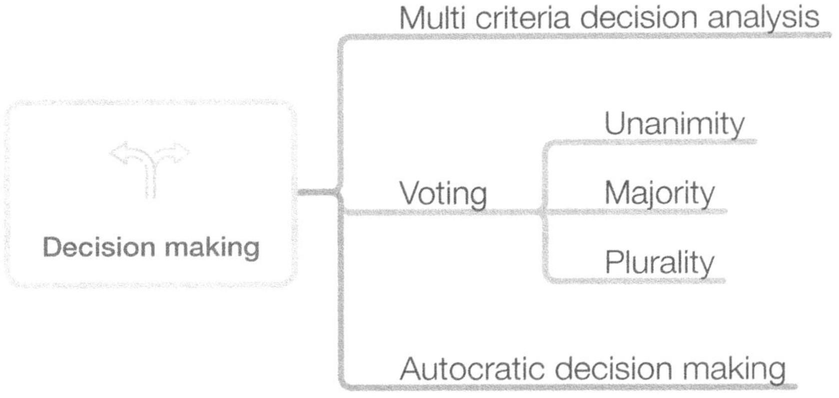

MULTI-CRITERIA DECISION MAKING

This is also called merit-based decisions. The table is called a decision table. You can have various parameters with ratings for each decision variable. The one which gets the most points is the decision to go with.
Let's take the example of the candidate selection process for a company:

Candidates	Presentation Level (Total 10)	Skills (Total 10)	Leadership (Total 10)	Culture Fitment (Total 10) Most Crucial	Overall $P+S+L+C*2$
Candidate 1	5	8	5	7	32
Candidate 2	7	7	7	8	37
Candidate 3	9	7	6	6	34

The candidate who gets the most marks is selected.

AUTOCRATIC DECISION-MAKING:

Autocratic is, as the name suggests is, made by one individual. The PM or senior management, or customer makes and announces a decision for you.
One individual makes the decision for the group.

VOTING

Voting is everyone vote for various options. Based on the voting decision criteria (majority/unanimous or plurality), the group makes a decision. Do understand that the decision-making criteria is announced and agreed upon before the group goes for voting. Various decision criteria for voting can be:

UNANIMITY (100% AGREEMENT)
Everyone has to agree to the proposed solution; else, the decision is not taken.

MAJORITY (50% OR ABOVE)
Support from more than 50% of the members of the group is required for the final agreement.

PLURALITY (MAXIMUM VOTES)
The largest set of people decides on the option. It can be less than 50%. This can be used when there are many choices to select from.

WHAT IS CONSENSUS-BASED DECISION-MAKING?

Consensus-based decision-making is based on a **deliberate process of consensus building,** whereby members of a group actively participate in finding a decision together that all members can feel comfortable with.

We can start by giving the options and get to know how people are feeling about it. This would give us the undercurrents of the decisions. We can use the following tools to understand the undercurrents:

FIRST TO FIVE
Fist to Five is quality voting. It has the elements of consensus built in and can prepare groups to transition into consensus if they wish. Most people are accustomed to the simplicity of "yes" and "no" voting rather than the complex and more community-oriented consensus method of decision-making. Fist to Five introduces the element of the quality of the "yes." A fist is a "no," and any number of fingers is a "yes," with an indication of how good a "yes" it is. This moves a group away from quantity voting to quality voting, which is considerably more informative. Fist to Five can also be used during consensus decision-making as a way to check the "sense of the group" or to check the quality of the consensus.

Fist to Five is accomplished by raising hands as in voting, with the number of fingers raised that indicates a level of agreement. The support for the issue/decision can be inferred as below:

Oppose				Favor	
0	**1**	**2**	**3**	**4**	**5**
FIST	1 finger	2 fingers	3 fingers	4 fingers	**Open Hand**
Block	Issues	Issues	Issues - Go	Go	Go
Strong Objection	Major Issues	Minor Issues	Minor Issues	OK as is	I love this
		Resolve Now	Resolve Later		Will actively champion

If this looks too complex, then one can use Roman voting. What is it?

ROMAN VOTING

Roman voting is showing support for the idea by using a thumbs up or Thumbs down if you do not support the idea. Sometimes a sideways thumb can be used, which means that you neither support the idea nor discourage the idea.

- A thumbs-up shows support.
- A thumbs down shows a block.
- A side thumb (if required) shows a neutral stand.

4.9.1 LET'S PLAY: DECISION-MAKING TECHNIQUES

Select the correct decision-making technique in the given scenarios:

1. Some changes were suggested, and a few of them were approved as all the members of the CCB agreed. Two changes were not approved, as Rob raised a question about them. There was a total of five board members in the CCB.

    A.   Plurality
    B.   Majority
    C.   Autocratic decision making
    D.   Unanimity

2. Jia, the Project Manager of Project NEXT, was having difficulty finding a suitable venue for the client meeting. She suggested a few locations, but they were rejected. It seemed as if the meeting were to be canceled. However, John, the client's supervisor, instructed everyone to meet at their headquarters.

    A.   Plurality
    B.   Majority
    C.   Autocratic decision making
    D.   Unanimity

3. A group of college students wanted to see the movie, Avengers. The movie is available in 3D, 4D, and IMAX 3D., 6 out of 10, opted for the 4D format. Hence, Ana booked the tickets accordingly.

    A.   Plurality
    B.   Majority
    C.   Autocratic decision making
    D.   Unanimity

4. Ria was in the process of selecting a book cover for her upcoming book. It was a matter of elimination rather than selection, as her choice was very specific. She asked for a general survey and selected the cover3. Cover3 was not liked by 52% of the people.

    A.   Plurality
    B.   Majority
    C.   Autocratic decision making
    D.   Unanimity

5. Noah is an interviewer for technical skills. A firm, SPAR, has a few open positions. There are three rounds of interviews, mainly technical, attitude, and management. Each interviewer assesses the candidates and provides the rating sheet to HR (Human Resource) Representative Monika. Monika will then compile

all the interviewer's scores to select the best candidate.

A.   Plurality

B.   Majority

C.   Autocratic decision making

D.   Unanimity

6.   **In the daily meeting, the PM asked everyone how is everyone feeling today. People responded by showing thumbs up and thumbs down. One girl showed a sideways thumb. Which technique was used by the PM?**

A.   Roman voting

B.   Thumbs voting

C.   Fist to Five

D.   Unanimity

7.   **Should we go live today? Most of the team members responded with open hand gestures. However, Ram showed a closed fist. What should the PM do next?**

A.   Go live

B.   Build consensus by asking Ram his apprehensions

C.   Ask team members to work with Ram to get him to say yes

D.   Don't go live, as Ram may have issues

8.   **Should we go live today? Most of the team members responded with open hand gestures. However, Ram showed a closed fist. Which technique is used here**

A.   Roman voting

B.   Thumbs voting

C.   Fist to Five

D.   Unanimity

4.10 LEADERSHIP STYLES

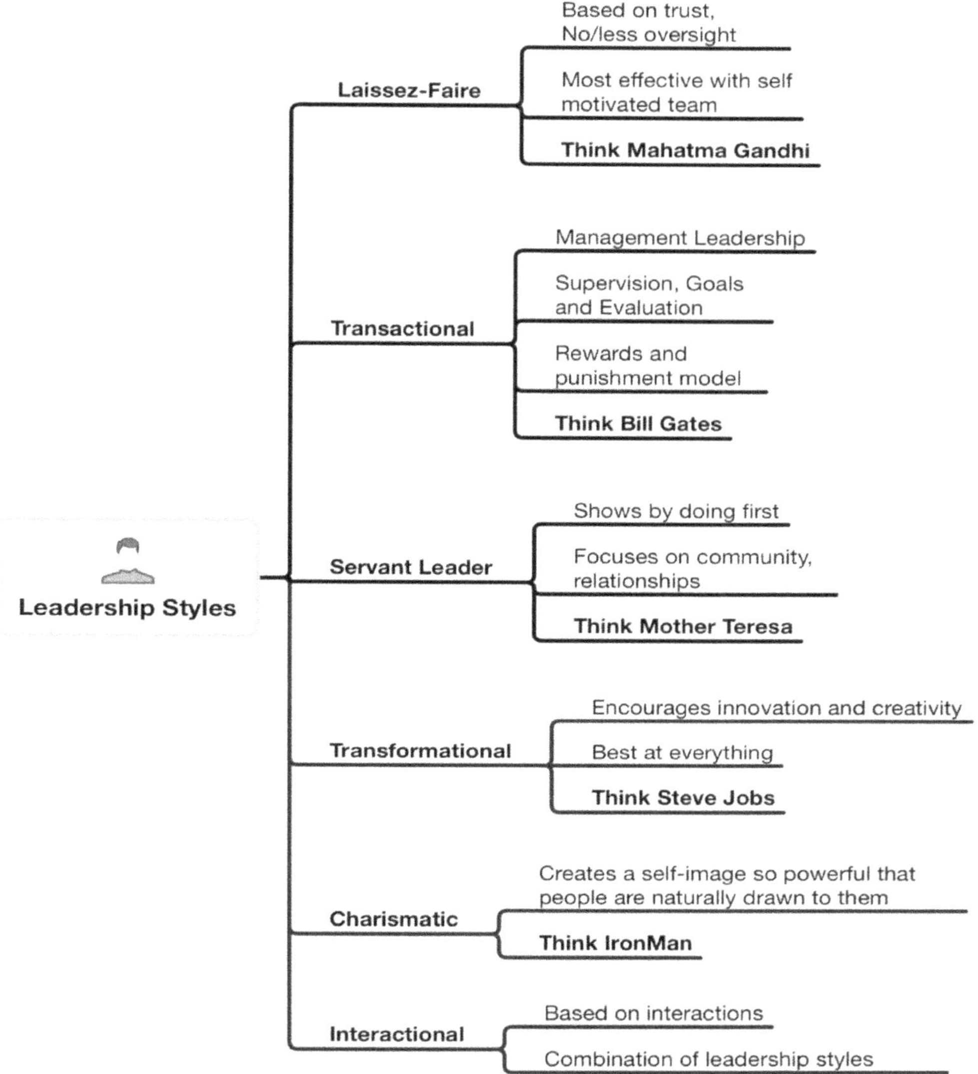

SERVANT LEADER?

→ Educate stakeholders

→ Support the team through mentoring and encouragement. Advocate for team members' training and career development. The quote "We lead teams by standing behind them."

→ Help the team with technical project management activities like quantitative risk analysis.

→ Celebrate team successes

→ Support and bridge-building activities with external groups

4.10.1 LET'S PLAY: LEADERSHIP STYLES

Match the leadership style displayed by the manager in the scenario:

Sno	Scenario	Answer
1.	Chris works in the organization BLUE. The team reports to him as he is the Functional manager. However, the team members are often busy with the project and usually are traveling. Chris does not bother anyone until and unless any escalation from fellow managers reaches him.	A. Charismatic
2.	Roy is an athlete and ensures that he gets his work done. Sometimes the logic works, and in some cases, the charm. He knows the audience, and he knows what will work with them.	B. Transactional
3.	Aron works with the team and ensures that he is always available for any need. If the team is working on weekends, Aron will make sure that he is present in the office just to talk to and motivate the team. He often laughs and says my job is to ensure you guys are fed and hydrated so that you can focus on work.	C. Laissez-faire
4.	Joy is busy setting the team goals for the coming year. The goal-setting exercise will help the team and her stay focused on the job at hand. It's a big task, and she wants to do justice to it.	D. Transformational
5.	When Liam speaks to the team, everyone listens. He is so clear in his thought processes and very good at painting the big picture. The new product which Liam is launching will take the market by storm. Everyone is excited to be part of this next big phenomenon.	E. Servant leader

4.11 EMOTIONAL INTELLIGENCE AND MBTI

Emotional intelligence/ quotient (EQ) is the ability to understand, use, and manage your own emotions. Mastering EQ will work positively to relieve stress, communicate effectively, empathize with others, overcome challenges, and defuse conflict.
EQ can help you build stronger relationships, succeed at school and work, and achieve your career and personal goals.
EQ helps you understand your feelings, turn intention into action, and make informed decisions about what matters most to you.
4 attributes commonly define emotional intelligence:

SELF-AWARENESS

Recognizing your own feelings and emotions and knowing how they change your thoughts and behavior. You are aware of your strengths and weaknesses and have self-confidence.

SELF-MANAGEMENT

Controlling impulsive feelings and behaviors, managing emotions in positive ways. Taking the initiative and adapting to changing circumstances.

SOCIAL AWARENESS

Having empathy. Understanding others' emotions, needs, and concerns. Observant to pick up on emotional cues and comfort others. You feel comfortable socially and recognize the power dynamics in a group or organization.

RELATIONSHIP MANAGEMENT

Developing and maintaining good relationships and communicating clearly. You inspire and influence others, work well in a team, and manage conflict.
You can start by knowing yourself and the reasons why you react the way you react. A few tools which can help with that are:
- DISK Analysis
- MBTI - Myer Brigg Type Indicator

Search for the assessment using the above tools, and you can get many links. One of the links which I liked is   https://www.16personalities.com.

4. MODULE END QUESTIONS

1. **You just received a communication from your client in which the client expressed her displeasure with the way the project is progressing so far. In your view, the project is progressing well. What is the best thing to do?**

    A. Reach out to your supervisor and ask her to call the client.

    B. Ignore her. The client does not have any facts.

    C. Send the progress report to the customer showcasing the fact that the project is on track.

    D. Arrange a meeting with the client to understand the issues and then plan accordingly

2. **Who is a Resistant stakeholder?**

    A. The stakeholder who talks badly about your personality

    B. The stakeholder who does not like you

    C. The stakeholder who has a negative mindset

    D. A stakeholder who does not want to change as per project change

3. **Michael categorizes the project stakeholders using the direction of influence. Kate is highly influential with senior management of the customer organization. Help Michael to place her in the appropriate category.**

    A. Upward influence

    B. Downward influence

    C. Outward influence

    D. Side-ward influence

4. **You are currently working as a Project Manager at SUPPL. You are given responsibility for moving the office infrastructure to the newly procured office. You are currently identifying project stakeholders and placing them in the appropriate power/interest quadrant. Which of the following stakeholder expectations should be closely managed?**

    A. High Power - Low Interest

    B. High Power - High Interest

    C. Low Power - Low Interest

    D. Low Power - High Interest

5. **What is the counterpart of the term Extraversion?**

    A.   Extroversion

    B.   Introversion

    C.   Sensing

    D.   Feeling

6. **Catherine is working towards introducing a new product in the firm. The stakeholders have asked her for certain information about the project. She is in the process of identifying the right communication method for information distribution to project stakeholders who are working at different locations. She decided to have the performance reports uploaded on the intranet where only specific stakeholders can access them. This information is available 100% of the time. Which sort of communication method has she opted for?**

    A.   Push

    B.   Interactive

    C.   Pull

    D.   Social

7. **A team wanted to go out for dinner on Friday. However, not everyone was on board for Friday, so the dinner was canceled and shifted to Monday, which was agreed on by everyone.**

    A.   Plurality

    B.   Majority

    C.   Autocratic decision making

    D.   Unanimity

8. **How would you recommend handling a senior stakeholder who has no interest in your project?**

    A.   Ignore him. He does not have any interest in my project

    B.   Identify areas of interest and try and meet often (virtually or physically)

    C.   Understand his information needs and work towards fulfilling them efficiently

    D.   Always copy him in the emails

9. **You started the project, and team members are getting on board. A few people joined the team last week, and a few more are joining now. Which stage is the team at?**

    A.   Forming

    B.   Storming

    C.   Norming

    D.   Performing

10. How does the Team Charter help the project?

A. It is an information radiator

B. It helps in meeting management

C. Team charter helps in planning better holidays

D. It helps to understand the expected behavior within the team and set clear guidelines, which in turn help the team to work better

11. In the daily status meeting, you asked your team how the morale is. They answered using Thumbs up or Thumbs down. You are using:

A. Roman voting to understand team morale

B. Fist of Thumb to understand team morale

C. Polling to understand team morale

D. Dot voting of thumb to understand team morale

12. The Project Manager told all the developers to work on weekends until a milestone is met, as there have been unexpected delays in the schedule.

A. Plurality

B. Majority

C. Autocratic decision making

D. Unanimity

13. Salience model describes classes of stakeholders based on their _________, _________, and _______. Fill in the blanks.

A. Influence, Impact, Power

B. Power, urgency, legitimacy

C. Influence, rights, legitimacy

D. Impact, rights, legitimacy

14. Ray is the project sponsor of the VANNA project. Ray diligently participated in the steering team meetings to ensure the smooth functioning of the project. He also reached out to Jia, the Project Manager, if she needed any help with resource mobilization for the project. How would you categorize Ray as a stakeholder?

A. Ray is a supportive stakeholder

B. Ray is a leading stakeholder.

C. Ray is a negative stakeholder.

D. Ray is a positive stakeholder.

15. A new team member, Jack, joined the team last month. For no reason, the team suddenly seems to be always at war with Jack. What is happening?

A. The team is in forming stage, and it will pass

B. The team is in the storming stage, and it will pass.

16. **The marketing team wanted to choose a perfect icon for the summer campaign. Everyone had their favorites, so the team decided to vote. The icon that was selected had the most votes. The selected icon was not liked by 55% of the people. What were the decision-making criteria?**

    A.   Plurality

    B.   Majority

    C.   Autocratic decision making

    D.   Unanimity

17. **The ability to understand and relate to others' emotions is _________, a core skill of emotional intelligence. Fill in the blank.**

    A.   Social skill

    B.   Empathy

    C.   Motivation

    D.   Engagement

18. **There are a lot of emails floating around. One of the emails which you got was marked as very urgent. So, you responded to all. One of the recipients wrote back to keep him out of these emails as he is not interested. What action would you take?**

    A.   Send him an email and apologize

    B.   Meet/call him to understand his information needs and update the communication plan accordingly

    C.   Do nothing - this is normal.

    D.   Acknowledge his email by responding to all.

19. **Gina is assigned a new project, RUGBY, as the Project Manager. She has 6 team members, 2 sponsors, and 1 client. She wants to inform all of them about the progress of her project. How many lines of communication are present in the project?**

    A.   45

    B.   36

    C.   3

    D.   50

20. **You and your senior manager have differences over which observation to be closed first. You set up a meeting with the senior management. He declined the meeting request. You called to confirm the availability, but he did not pick up the phone. Which conflict management technique did the senior manager use?**

    A.   Withdraw/Avoid.

    B.   Smooth/Accommodate

C.   Compromise/Reconcile

D.   Collaborate/Problem Solve.

21. **Select the correct order of team development stages:**

A.   Adjourning, Forming, Storming

B.   Storming, Norming, Adjourning

C.   Performing, Norming, Forming

D.   Forming, Adjourning, Storming

22. **Which of the following team development stages characterize the team stage where the team meets and learns about the project and its formal roles and responsibilities?**

A.   Forming

B.   Storming

C.   Norming

D.   Performing

23. **Ana is the Project Manager for project AXA. She has a few team members on board. Each team member came from a different background, and few of them lacked the necessary skills. People are still at a distance. They started working on some of the allocated work. Which team development stage is the team AXA?**

A.   Forming

B.   Storming

C.   Norming

D.   Performing

24. **You are the Project Manager working with KFCD. You are creating a communication plan for your project. A communication plan allows a Project Manager to document the approach for communicating most efficiently and effectively with stakeholders. You sent an information note to all the managers about the project's best practices. This communication would be classified as:**

A.   Horizontal communication

B.   Informal communication

C.   Upward communication

D.   Downward communication

25. **You work as part of a development team in an agile project. There are times when you are so angry that you do not want to talk to anyone on your team. This is leading to bad relationships and negative reviews. It has started affecting your mental well-being nowadays. Which EQ aspect should you start with to understand your emotions?**

A. Self-awareness

B. Self-management

C. Social awareness

D. Relationship management

26. Which of the following is NOT a valid Conflict Management Technique?

A. Force

B. Withdraw

C. Focus Groups

D. Avoid

27. Donald and Doris are currently in a conflict over the location of an upcoming store. Donald is emotional about the site, whereas Doris is more of a logical thinker. Both, after a lengthy discussion that involved storming out and tears, decided to go with their next store location, Boston. Both liked this option. Which conflict management strategy was used in the scenario?

A. Withdrawal

B. Problem Solve

C. Reconcile

D. Forcing

28. Today is the annual event in your company where everyone is asked to be in formal dress. One of your team members turns up in a casual dress. Your other team members raised their eyebrows and hands in a questioning way. What kind of communication is being used?

A. Paralingual

B. Nonverbal

C. Feedback

D. Active listening

29. In a communication model, the sender is responsible for, EXCEPT:

A. information is clear and complete

B. Encoding the information

C. Confirming the understanding

D. Confirming the agreement on the shared information

4. ALL ANSWERS

ANSWERS: 4.1.1 LET'S PLAY: STAKEHOLDER ANALYSIS

Power	Interest	Strategy
1. High	High	Manage Closely
2. High	Low	Keep Satisfied
3. Low	High	Keep Informed
4. Low	Low	No Extra Work-Monitor

ANSWERS: 4.2.1 LET'S PLAY: STAKEHOLDER ENGAGEMENT GRID

ENGAGEMENT LEVEL	DESCRIPTION
1. Unaware	Unaware of the project and potential impacts.
2. Resistant	Aware of the project and potential impacts and resistance to change.
3. Neutral	Aware of the project yet neither supportive nor resistant.
4. Supportive	Aware of the project and potential impacts and supportive of changes.
5. Leading	Aware of the project and potential impacts and actively engaged in ensuring the project is a success.

ANSWERS: 4.3.1 LET'S PLAY: COMMUNICATION DIMENSIONS

S.no.	Communication Characteristics	Category
1	Correct grammar, concise expression, clear purpose, coherent, logical flow, controlling the flow	5Cs of communication
2	Gestures	Nonverbal communication
3	Horizontal communication	With peers
4	Sending an internal note to the supervisor	Internal, upwards
5	Listening actively	Communication skills

ANSWERS: 4.5.1 LET'S PLAY: COMMUNICATION MODEL

Communication Element	Description
1. Sender	The entity that initiates the communication
2. Receiver	The entity for which the message is intended
3. Medium	Used for transmitting the message
4. Feedback	Response to message
5. Noise	This can change the message
6. Encoding	Done at the sender's end
7. Decoding	Done at receiving end
8. Acknowledgment	Confirming the receipt of the message

ANSWERS: 4.6.1 LET'S PLAY: COMMUNICATION TYPES

Question	Answer	WHY
1	Nonverbal	Dressed unprofessionally
2	Paralingual	Her tone of voice was sarcastic
3.	Feedback	Ron inquired, "Can you please repeat the question?"
4.	Communication competence	As he spoke, he made eye contact with them and made sure to confirm agreement with them.

ANSWERS: 4.7.1 LET'S PLAY: TEAM STAGE

Scenario	Team	Keywords
1. Kyle and Joanna are working together on the project POSH. They disagree on everything most of the time. They are at a point now where they are barely talking to each other.	Storming	"Barely talking to each other3
2. Norman manages project APOLLO. Norman understands the team's aspirations, ensures that the team's enthusiasm is high, and allocates the right tasks to the right people. The team trusts Norman, and contributes with high enthusiasm. It seems like a great, happy group.	Performing	"Enthusiasm is high and allocates the right tasks to the right people. The team trusts Norman, and contributes with high enthusiasm. It seems like a great, happy group."
3. A new member, Amy, joined the task force; everyone seemed polite and offered assistance if she needed it. She is trying to understand her duties.	Forming	"She is trying to understand her duties as of now."
4. Now that the project is over, the team is analyzing the failures and is looking forward to meeting each other while packing their bags.	Adjourning	"Looking forward to meeting each other while packing their bags."
5. Sarah is torn by the behavior of her fellow colleague, Amy. She had differences of opinion, but now she has made up her mind to focus on her task, realizing that the points Amy made were not so bad after all	Norming	"Focus on her task, realizing that the points Amy made were not so bad."

and helped her arrive at a few good
decisions.

ANSWERS: 4.8.1 LET'S PLAY: CONFLICT MANAGEMENT

Scenario	Conflict resolution technique
1. Rita started crying when Mark handed over the appraisal results and told her that she was rated as an underperformer. Since it was difficult to converse, Mark said, "Why don't you go home today, sleep on it, and we will discuss your appraisal again tomorrow?"	Avoid – The conflict stays at 100 percent.
2. Mark to Rob: "Rob, I don't want to hear the same excuses again. The rest of the team is working harder and producing better results. I'm convinced that you should rate it as the average for the final rating. If you have a complaint, speak to HR."	Forcing – One Point of View and decision is taken.
3. Mark to Jason: "Jason, you can select either a promotion or a role change but not both. Let me know so that I can proceed."	Compromising – Full resolution not implemented. One is not fully satisfied.
4. Mark, while addressing the team in the daily team meeting: Team, let's move beyond appraisal ratings. You are a dynamic group, and I'm sure this year we will rock."	Smoothing – Conflict is reduced by some percentage.
5. Noah, a member of the team, resigned. When Mark and Noah discussed the reasons, Noah mentioned that he needed to spend more time at home since his wife Carol was working. Mark knows that Noah is an asset to the team. He called a meeting with Noah and the human resource manager, Susan, to see if there could be a better outcome, such as allowing Noah to work from home.	Problem Solve – Group thinking to eliminate the problem to zero percent.

ANSWERS: 4.9.1 LET'S PLAY: DECISION-MAKING TECHNIQUES

Question	Correct Answer	Why?
1.	Unanimity	100% agreement
2.	Autocratic decision making	One person took the decision.
3.	Majority	The decision was liked by more than 50%
4.	Plurality	The decision was liked by less than 50%
5.	Multi-criteria decision analysis	A decision matrix is used. Check the keywords.
6.	Roman Voting	Thumbs up or down to show the response
7.	Build consensus by asking Ram about his apprehensions.	Once a person shows resistance, the next steps to understand and solve any resistance
8	Fist to Five	Usage of open palm or fist

ANSWERS: 4.10.1 LET'S PLAY: LEADERSHIP STYLES

Question	Answer	Why
1.	Laissez-faire	Minimum oversight
2.	Interactional	Combination of management styles
3.	Servant leader	Serving the team
4.	Transactional	Supervision, Goal setting, feedback
5.	Transformational	Vision, Inspiration

ANSWERS: 4. MODULE END QUESTIONS

1. D	In the case of any conflicts/perceptions, it's always good to reach out to the stakeholder and close it by providing facts. The first step in solving the issue is to understand and hear what the client says. It could be a matter of perception, and sending the status report may not help. The best thing to do is an interactive meeting (call/meetings). **_As a thumb rule, always select interactive meeting if the option is given._**
2. D	A resistive stakeholder is aware of the project and its potential impact and is resistant to change.
3. C	Clients, sellers, and any entity outside the project team are considered to be outside of the team. People having an influence on either of them are said to have outward influence.
4. B	Stakeholders with high power and high interest should be managed closely. Hence, B is the correct answer.
5. B	People can be divided into two dimensions on how one gains energy. Extraversion is by the outer self – meeting people, talking, and being with others. Introversion is when one gains energy by being alone, with nature, and gets inspiration through self. The terms introversion and extraversion were introduced into psychology by Carl Jung, although the popular understanding and current psychological usage vary. Extraversion tends to be manifested in outgoing, talkative,

	energetic behavior, whereas introversion is manifested in more reflective and reserved behavior
6. C	Information is available to the seeker when they need it is an example of pull communication.
7. D	Everyone will agree on the decision then only a decision is made – that's unanimous decision-making.
8. C	The stakeholder falls under High authority and Low interest. Don't copy them on emails. Work towards finding their information needs and provide to efficiently.
9. A	Forming. This phase is where the team meets and learns about the project and their formal roles and responsibilities.
10. D	The team charter sets clear expectations, and an early commitment to clear guidelines decreases misunderstandings and increases productivity.
11. A	Roman voting: Individuals vote with either a thumbs up (agreement) or thumbs down (disagreement).
12. C	A decision was made by one person to be followed. One person making a decision for all is Autocratic decision-making.
13. B	The salience model describes classes of stakeholders based on their power (ability to impose their will), urgency (need for immediate attention), and legitimacy (their involvement is appropriate).
14. B	Ray is participating in project activities and showing initiative to engage with other stakeholders. Ray is a supportive stakeholder. His active support of the project puts Ray in the leading stakeholder bracket.
15. B	The team is in the storming stage – this is when all confrontation comes out.
16. A	See the voting for the selected decision was liked/voted by less than 50% of the respondents. Still, a decision to select was made. This would mean that plurality (most votes) was the decision-making criterion.
17. B	The ability to understand and relate to others' emotions is empathy, a core skill of emotional intelligence.
18. B	Thumb rule – Whenever there are stakeholder issues/concerns/requests – always choose interaction. Choice B is interaction. Understanding the information needed and changing the communication plan is a continuous process.
19. A	The formula to calculate the lines of communication is $\{n*(n-1)\} / 2$. Here you have 9 people plus Project Manager. N is 10; hence Communication channel is $\{10*(10-1)\}/2 = 45$.
20. A	The manager used avoidance as the technique.
21. B	The right answer is Storming, Norming, and then Adjourning.
22. A	Forming is where the team meets and learns about the project and its formal roles and responsibilities. The team members tend to be independent and not as open in this phase.
23. A	- Forming is where the team meets and learns about the project and their formal roles and responsibilities. Team members tend to be independent and not as open in this phase.
24. A	Information sharing among peers is horizontal communication.

25. A	**SELF-AWARENESS** Recognizing your own feelings and emotions and knowing how they change your thoughts and behavior. You are aware of your strengths and weaknesses and have self-confidence.
26. C	Focus-Groups is not a valid Conflict Management Technique.
27. B	Both parties liked the decision. Problem solved. Incorporating multiple viewpoints and insights from differing perspectives requires a cooperative attitude and open dialogue that typically leads to consensus and commitment.
28. B	Nonverbal communication means your gestures, facial expressions, and physical appearance.
29. A	This is an EXCEPT question. Let's see who is responsible for what as per the communication model:

A. information is clear and complete - Sender

B. Encoding the information - Receiver

C. Confirming the understanding - Receiver

D. Confirming the agreement on the shared information – Receiver

A is the correct answer.

5. PREDICTIVE PROCESSES

This is a big section and hence is coved under a few chapters.

TOPICS WE COVER

1.1	Distinguish between issues, risks, assumptions, and constraints.
1.1	Review/critique project scope.
1.2	Demonstrate an understanding of project management planning.
1.2	Describe the purpose and importance of cost, quality, risk, schedule, etc.
1.2	Distinguish between the different deliverables of a project management plan versus a product management plan.
1.2	Distinguish differences between a milestone and a task duration.
1.2	Determine the number and type of resources in a project.
1.2	Use a risk register in a given situation.
1.2	Explain project closure and transitions.
1.4	Determine how to follow and execute planned strategies or frameworks (e.g., communication, risks, etc.).
1.4	Give examples of how it is appropriate to respond to a planned strategy or framework (e.g., communication, risk, etc.).
1.4	Explain project initiation and benefits planning.
1.5	Demonstrate an understanding of common problem-solving tools and techniques.
2.1	Determine the activities within each process.
2.1	Give examples of typical activities within each process.
2.1	Distinguish the differences between various project components.
2.2	Demonstrate an understanding of a project management plan schedule.
2.2	Apply critical path methods.
2.2	Calculate schedule variance.
2.2	Explain work breakdown structures (WBS).
2.2	Explain work packages.
2.2	Apply a quality management plan.
2.2	Apply an integration management plan.
2.3	Determine how to document project controls of predictive, plan-based projects.
2.3	Identify artifacts that are used in predictive, plan-based projects.
2.3	Calculate cost and schedule variances.
3.2	Determine inputs for scope.
3.5	Determine how to prepare and execute task management steps.

PLANNING

Since planning for predictive projects is elaborate – we plan for everything. This is a good time to refer to PMBOK6, as PMBOK6 has great details on predictive processes.

We plan for:
1. What is the acceptable level of work (Testing criteria)?
2. When would the project team deliver the product/work package?
3. How much will it cost?
4. How do we ensure the quality of the work?
5. Do we need to buy something from the outside? If yes, when?
6. Is there a possibility of things going wrong? How do we prevent/minimize that?
7. What about changes? How do we handle them?
8. How about access control and management of digital and physical goods?

All the above things are planned in detail, and the project execution will follow. The project plan contains many sections or sub-plans which answer the above questions.

Let's see the above questions again:

No	Question	Plan
1	What is the acceptable level of work (Testing criteria)	Scope management acceptance criteria
2	What is the schedule	Schedule management plan
3	How much will it cost?	Cost/budget
4	How do we ensure the quality of the work	Quality management plan
5	Do we need to buy something from the outside? If yes, when?	Procurement
6	Is there a possibility of things going wrong? How do we prevent/minimize that	Risk
7	What about changes? How do we handle them?	Change Management
8	How about access control and management of digital goods and physical goods?	Configuration Management

So the planning starts with scope, then schedule and other knowledge areas follow.

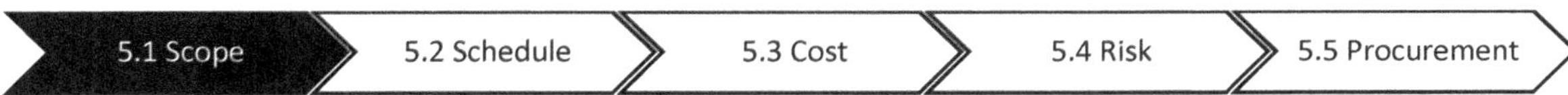

P.SCP - SCOPE

Let's understand a few projects and their requirements:
1. A company wants to launch an advertising campaign to accelerate growth.
2. There is a need to develop a residential complex for a senior citizen living space.
3. A website is to be developed to streamline the order management system. Currently, the orders are handled using manual processes, and it has become difficult to manage them seamlessly since the orders have grown extensively.

All the above scenarios show that some work should be completed to enable the business. A project starts with a need. It could be a need by your customer, senior management, or market demand.

It is of utmost importance that we understand what customers want, what is most valuable for them, and how the project delivers it.

PROCESS FLOW

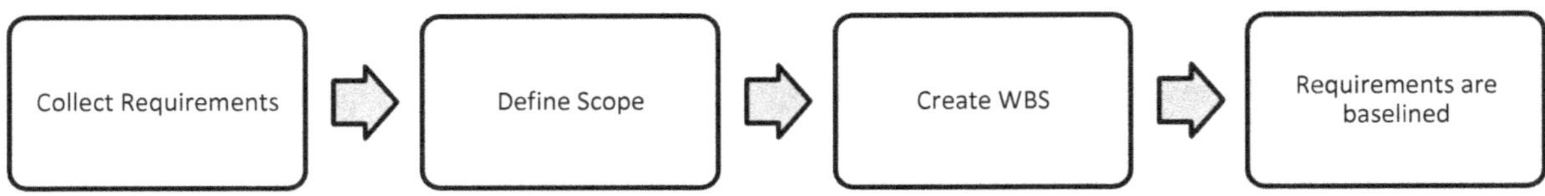

We discussed requirements and how to get and manage them in the business analysis chapter.

Before we move forward, let's understand the difference between the project and product scope. Both are project deliverables and should be considered while planning for the project deliverables.

P.SCP.1 PRODUCT SCOPE AND PROJECT SCOPE

Automobile manufacturing units decided to design a future
car. The features they wanted were:

- The car should run on water.
- The car should have a mileage of 100 miles per
  gallon.
- Third, the car should be sleek enough to park in
  crowded areas.
- The car will be launched in developing regions like
  Asia and Africa, so the cost should be less than $10,000.

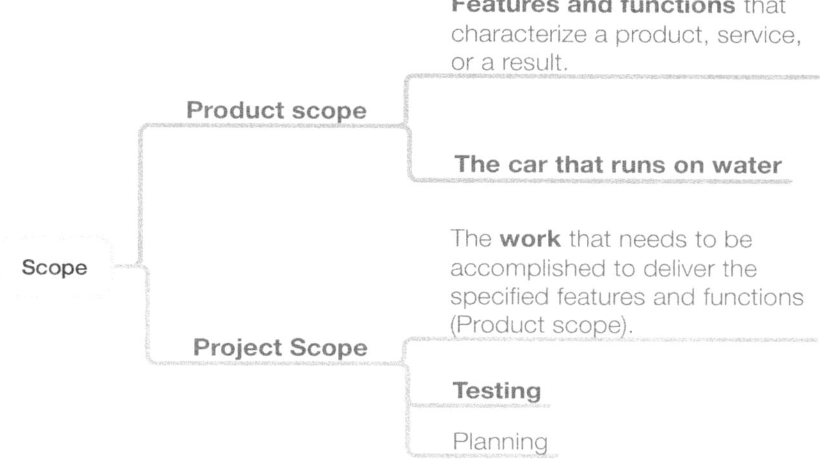

PRODUCT SCOPE

These are the features and functions that characterize a product, service, or result.
For future car projects, the **product scope is - the car that runs on water**. Everything
that the customer wants.
The customer owns the product scope and product specification.

PROJECT SCOPE

The **work** must be accomplished to deliver the specified features and functions (Product
scope).
The project scope for the future car will be - everything that needs to be done. This will
involve the following work (at a high level):

- Design of the car
- Cutting job to make the car body
- Painting
- Testing

P.SCP.1.1 LET'S PLAY: PRODUCT VS. PROJECT SCOPE

James is managing the project ACADEMY for an academic institute. The project is to develop collaboration software for teachers, students, and parents. To get the requirements, James conducted a focus group. The top requirements listed by the focus groups were:

1. Announcement board
2. Email and SMS notifications
3. Homework discussion forum
4. Events calendars
5. Online surveys

To get started on the project, the team needs to create a prototype and conduct a focus group to get an initial understanding from the user group. The project team must also identify the right solution platform to develop the required solution.

Select if the item in the description falls under product scope or project scope:

Description	Scope Type
1. Announcement board	A. Product Scope B. Project Scope
2. Conducting focus group	A. Product Scope B. Project Scope
3. Email notification	A. Product Scope B. Project Scope
4. Identifying the solution platform	A. Product Scope B. Project Scope
5. Planning for entire project activities	A. Product Scope B. Project Scope

P.SCP.2 DEFINE SCOPE – DEFINING BOUNDARIES

Once the project team gets the requirements, they sit with each other, brainstorm, and describe the IN-SCOPE and Out-of-SCOPE work. This will help the project team to set clear expectations for the team and customers.

THE PROJECT SCOPE STATEMENT CONTAINS THE FOLLOWING:

- → Product scope (Features required by customer)
- → Project scope (Work to be performed to achieve the desired features)
- → Major deliverables
- → Acceptance criteria of the product
- → Out-of-scope items/requirements
- → Assumptions
- → Constraints

PRODUCT ANALYSIS

This needs to be done to understand and develop the project features.

The first task in product analysis is to become familiar with the product! What does it do? How does it do it? What does it look like? All these questions and more need to be asked before a product can be analyzed. As well as considering the obvious mechanical, electrical, or other requirements, it is also important to consider the ergonomics, such as how the design was made user-friendly, and any other marketing issues. These all have an impact on the later design decisions.

Let's take an example of a bike to understand product analysis:

- → What is the function of a bike?
- → How does the function depend on the type of bike (e.g., racing, about-town, or child's bike)?
- → How is it made to be easily maintained?
- → How much should it cost?
- → What should it look like (colors, etc.)?
- → How has it been made to be comfortable to ride?
- → How do the mechanical bits work and interact?

ALTERNATIVES GENERATION

This technique is used to discover different methods or ways of achieving the same outcome. For example, if you do not have a particular type of resource, such as C++ developers, can you use Java developers, or are there any other self-made products that can be used to get the work done?

P.SCP.3 WORK BREAKDOWN STRUCTURE

Create Work Breakdown Structure (WBS) is the process of subdividing project work into smaller, more manageable units.

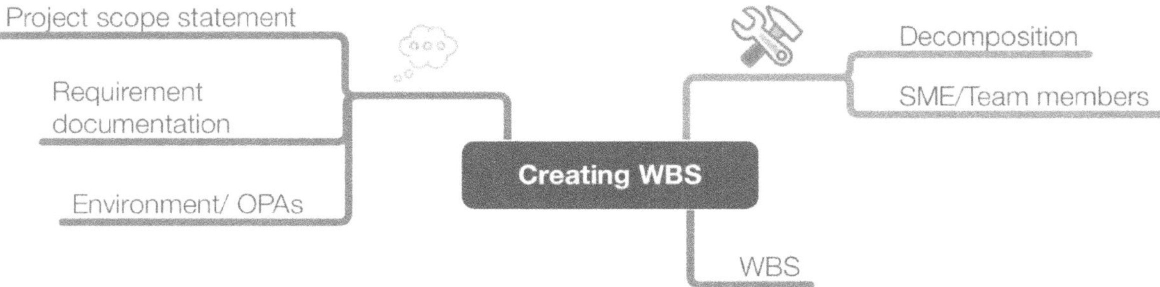

A project can never be completed by a single person. Hence, the overall work needs to be broken into smaller, manageable units to allocate to a team/vendor/department or a team member.

The main outcome expected from this process/activity is the work breakdown structure (WBS).

We start from IN-SCOPE items and decompose them into smaller work packages/deliverables to create a WBS.

The approved scope is called SCOPE BASELINE. A baseline can be changed only through formal change control procedures and is used as a basis for comparison with actual progress to manage the project.

DECOMPOSITION

Decomposition is a technique to divide and subdivide the project deliverables into smaller, manageable units called work packages.

Based on the complexity, project size, and urgency, you should decide on the ideal WBS size. Depending on the project, a work package can be one month long or as small as 6 hours. PMBOK does not specify the ideal WBS size.

In the case of agile projects, you would see the decomposition of 1-2 days of work because the overall phase (feature drop/Timebox) is 1 – 4 weeks long. So where do you see agile WBS?

WBS IN DETAIL

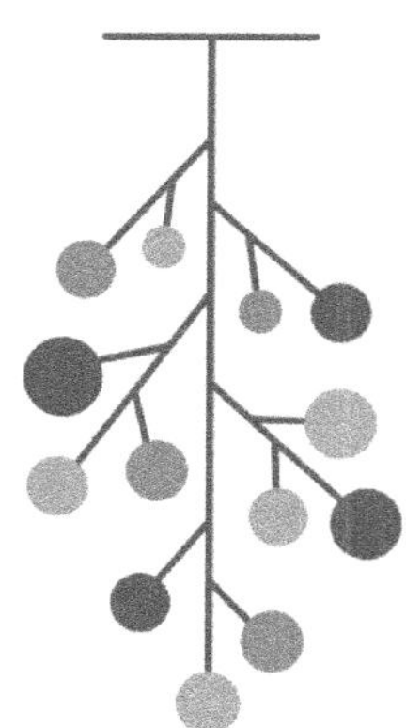

WBS is a deliverable-oriented hierarchical decomposition of the work to be executed by the project team to accomplish the project objectives.
It organizes and defines the total scope of the project.
Each descending level represents an increasingly detailed definition of the project work.
A Work Breakdown Structure is the foundation of project planning. It is a tool for breaking down a project into manageable parts and then detailing the

specific tasks and activities required to create each part (also called a work package). Can you think of an Agile artifact that can be compared to WBS?

Product Backlog.

A Product Backlog contains the overall scope of the work to be delivered in the upcoming iteration. Product Backlog grooming uses decomposition so the agile team can estimate and deliver the Iteration backlog. What are the decomposition criteria for PBIs? INVEST. You can also apply INVEST to WBS Items. Works perfectly.

Let's take an example of WBS so that we can understand the terms associated with WBS. The WBS can be represented in various ways, including graphical, textual, or tabular views. Regardless of the representation used, the WBS enables the project team to accurately predict and forecast costs, schedules, resource requirements, and allocations. A project WBS starts with the highest levels of work in the project. Each lower level breaks the work into smaller chunks. The breakdown continues to as many levels of detail as you need. There is no fixed number of levels for proper decomposition. Think of a tree. You invert it, so you get the trunk as the main parent, then branches and subbranches, and the last leaf can be equated as a **work package** or **deliverable**.

DELIVERABLE:

Any unique and verifiable product, result, or capability to perform a service that would be produced to complete a process, phase, or project.

DECOMPOSITION:

A planning technique that subdivides the project scope and project deliverables into smaller, more manageable components until the project work associated with accomplishing the project scope and providing the deliverables is defined in sufficient detail to support executing, monitoring, and controlling the work.

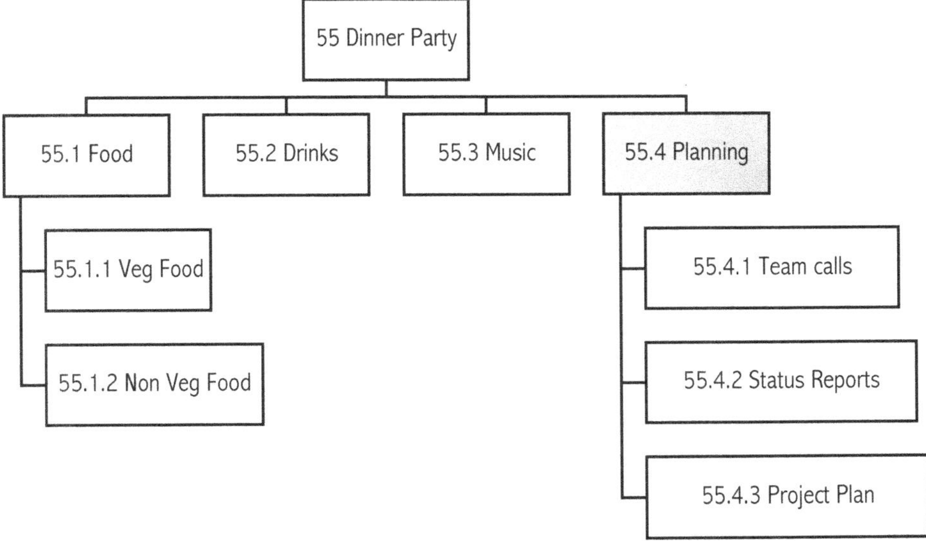

CODE OF ACCOUNT:

Each component in the WBS hierarchy, including work packages, is assigned a unique identifier called a code of account identifier. These identifiers can then be used in estimating costs, scheduling, and assigning resources to identify the component.
55.1 is a unique identifier that refers to food.

CONTROL ACCOUNT:

Think of a cost code. For example, when you travel, you fill out a reimbursement report and write the cost code to allocate your reimbursement to a particular project/department. Senior management can later analyze a cost code to understand the cost-benefit etc. A project is a cost code, also called a control account. If you or your senior management want to watch a particular WBS item spending, then that can also be mapped as a cost code. For example, 55.4 is mapped as a cost code so that management can see the efforts and spending on the planning activities. A management control point where scope, budget (resource plans), actual cost, and schedule are integrated and compared to earned value for performance measurement. Control accounts are placed at selected management points (specific components at selected levels) of the work breakdown structure. Each control account may include one or more work packages, but each may be associated with only one control account.

WORK PACKAGE:

A Work Package is a deliverable or project work component at the lowest level of each branch of the work breakdown structure.
55.4.3 is a deliverable – Project Plan.

THE 100% RULE:

The 100% rule is a core characteristic of the WBS. This rule states that the WBS includes 100% of the work defined by the project scope and captures ALL internal, external, and interim deliverables regarding work to be completed, including project management work. It makes sense as we started from the total IN scope and divided it to reach the WBS items.
The work outside the WBS is considered out of scope.
Think of Product backlog. Any feature required by the Product Owner, if not included in the Product Backlog, will never be developed.
Once the final scope is approved, the performing organization (an organization that does the work or where project execution occurs) is.
The CAPM exam assumes that you are one of the team lead/coordinators working in the performing organization.

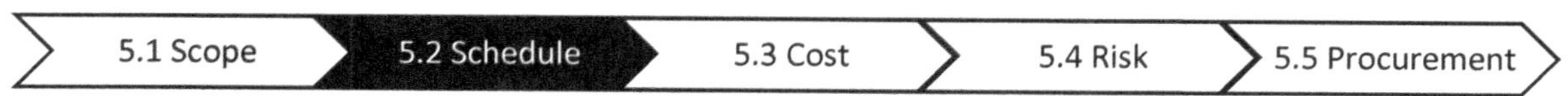

P.TME – SCHEDULE

For each WBS node, i.e., work package, we will break the task into activities so that they can be allocated and tracked.

The activities may have interdependence, so that we will establish that.

We will estimate for WHO will do the tasks and how long it will take.

We may arrive at a date-wise draft schedule based on who will do the tasks and how long the task will take.

More analysis by the team is also performed so that there is confidence that the schedule is achievable and in line with customer expectations. We also need to analyze the risks and see if the riskier items are planned to look at the risks.

The draft schedule is then sent to the stakeholders for their views, discussion, and alternations may arise, and finally, once everyone agrees, we achieve the schedule baseline.

SCHEDULE BASELINE:

The agreed and approved project deliverables schedule. The status report will consider the baselined schedule with the actual progress by the team to get the schedule status, i.e., behind schedule, on schedule, or ahead of schedule.

Let us see what goes in to arrive at the baseline schedule:

P.TME.1 - DEFINE ACTIVITIES

The goal of defining activities is to have the entire activity list and any additional information listed (i.e., activity attributes). Also, we list all the milestones.

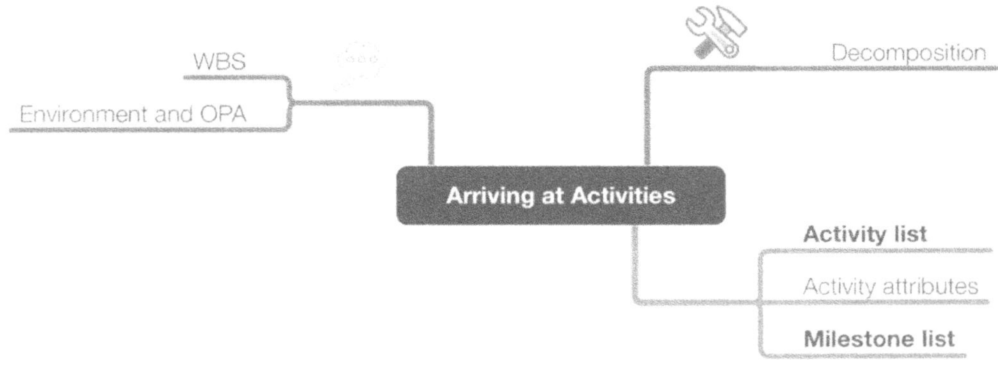

ACTIVITY LIST

We define the actions required for each WBS Item.

MILESTONE:

A milestone is a significant point or event in the project. When identifying all the activities, you want to identify **significant points** in the schedule, but why?
A milestone makes communication easier for all stakeholders. For example, instead of reporting 1000 tasks, you can mention a milestone completion status, and everyone will know. Often, a millstone may be attached with payments in case of a fixed-bid project.

DECOMPOSITION

Decomposition means subdividing. This technique can be used whenever we need to go modular, like creating WBS or Product Backlog Grooming.

ROLLING WAVE PLANNING

Rolling wave planning is an iterative planning technique where the work to be accomplished in the near term is planned in detail, while the work in the future is planned at a high level.
It is also called progressive elaboration.
The best example of rolling wave planning is that, in your plan, you would have detailed the overall work for the current phase along with the resource name, hours allocated along with all the leaves, and the work calendar. But, for the next phase, you might have broad-level activities that have no mention of resources because you don't know what type of resources you would get and when.

Let's take an example to understand what goes into elaborate WBS to a schedule.

DINNER PARTY

You are planning a party at home for the first time. A few of your friends are coming over (5 families with kids). There are demands:

→ Pizza for kids
→ Wine for women
→ Beer for a few folks
→ Cold drinks for few
→ Food should have vegetarian options along with non-vegetarian appetizers to go with drinks.
→ Special demand from kids for new-age music
A typical WBS for a dinner party is:

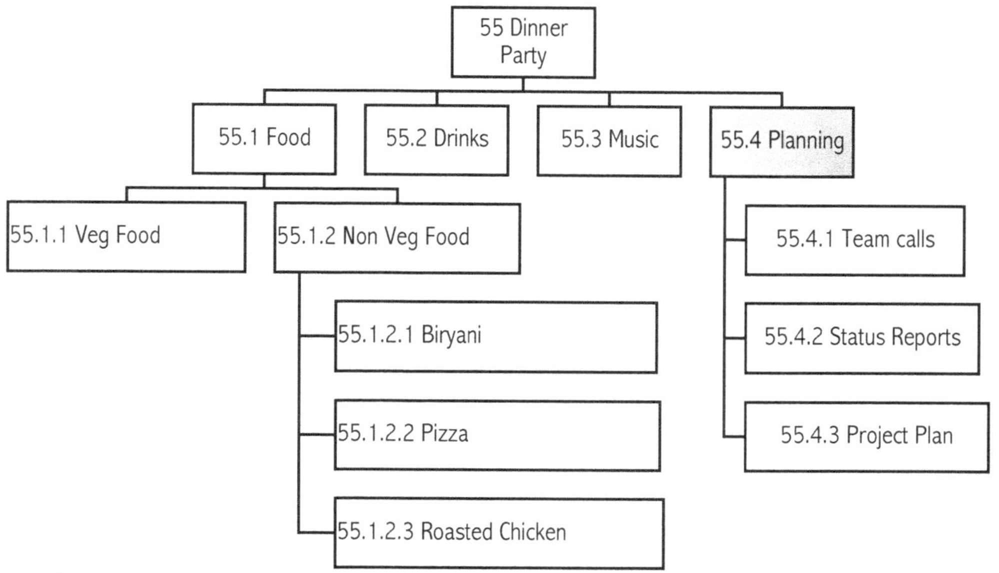

One of the WBS items 55.1.2.1 is biryani as the non-veg option as the main course. You planned to make the biryani at home.

The ACTIONS to produce biryani are:

1. Buy raw ingredients like chicken, masala, and rice
2. Wash and prepare ingredients
3. Cook
4. Serve.
5. Clean

Once we have identified the activities, we may want to see if any relationship exists between them. For example, I cannot cook biryani until the ingredients are not washed and prepared. There is a finish-to-start relationship(FS). Let's learn more about relationships: Before we start understanding dependencies, let's understand a few more terms:

P.TME.2 SEQUENCE ACTIVITIES

Identifying relationships amongst activities, if any.

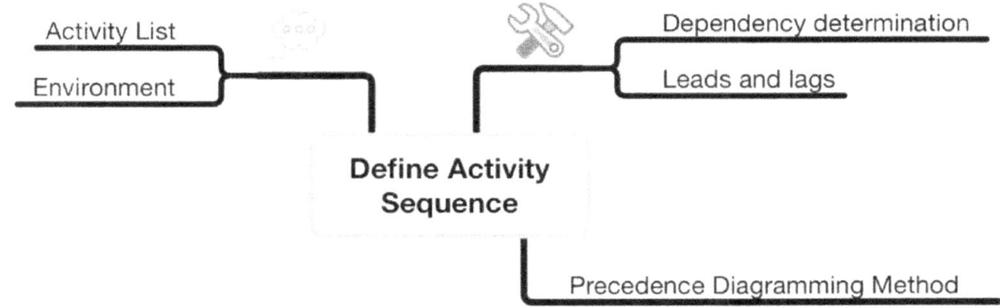

ACTIVITY DEPENDENCIES

Before we understand the different types of dependencies, let us understand the key terms:

PREDECESSOR

A predecessor activity is an activity that logically comes before a dependent activity on a schedule.

SUCCESSOR

A successor activity is a dependent activity that logically comes after another activity on a schedule.

In the given picture, A is the predecessor, and B is the successor. This means that Activity B will start only after Activity A finishes. Activity A lasts 4 days, and B lasts 3 days. This is an FS relationship.

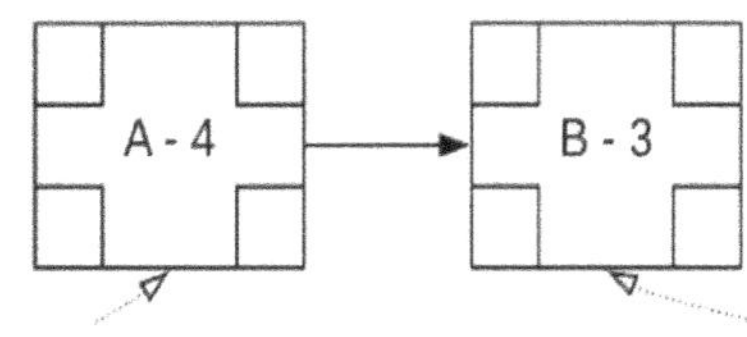

What are other types of relationships?

There are typically 4 types of activity dependencies:

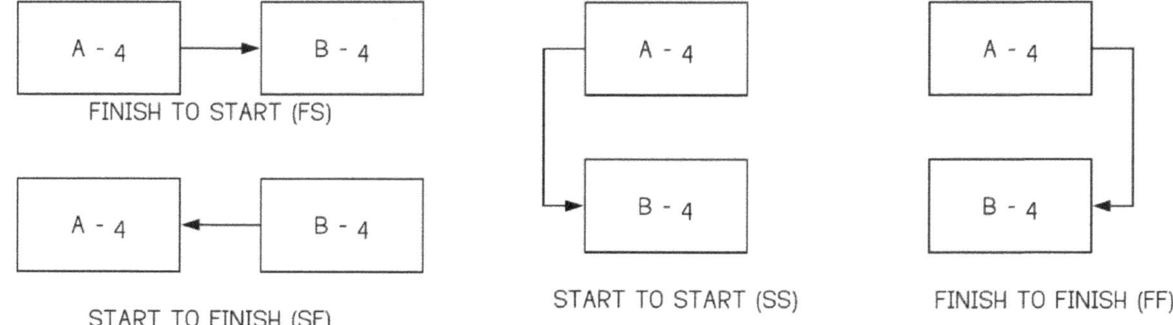

FINISH-TO-START (FS):

Successor activity cannot start until a predecessor activity has finished.

Example: The awards ceremony (successor) cannot start until the race (predecessor) has finished.

FINISH-TO-FINISH (FF):

Successor activity cannot finish until a predecessor activity has finished.

Example: Writing a document (predecessor) is required to finish before editing the document (successor) can finish.

START-TO-START (SS):

Successor activity cannot start until a predecessor activity has started.

Example: Level concrete (successor) cannot begin until pouring foundation (predecessor) begins.

START-TO-FINISH (SF):

The predecessor activity cannot finish until the successor activity has started.

Example: The first security guard shift (predecessor) cannot finish until the second shift (successor) starts.

There are other dimensions of action/node dependency:

MANDATORY DEPENDENCIES:

Mandatory Dependencies are contractual or physical limitations. They are also called Hard Logic dependencies. One has to wait for them. You cannot Fastrack (we will learn this soon) the dependent activity if need be.

Example: In a construction project, it is not possible to erect the superstructure until after the foundation has been built.

DISCRETIONARY DEPENDENCIES:

These are "Best practices" within a particular application area. They are also called preferred logic, preferential logic, or soft logic.

These are the type of activities that can be executed in parallel if you face a shortage of time in the schedule.

Example: In a software project, it is advisable that you do not start development work until and unless you get a sign-off from the architect. But, in case you, as the Project Manager, think that the developers are free and you want to optimize time, then you can optimize the schedule and can start the development tasks with the developers.

EXTERNAL DEPENDENCIES:

External Dependencies involve relationships between project activities and non-project activities. They can be regulatory dependencies.

Example: In the case of telecom roll-out projects, you cannot start deployment until the government grants you the licenses. The team cannot control them, and hence they have to plan accordingly.

INTERNAL DEPENDENCIES:

These are internal between the team and can be controlled. The plan can be changed/managed if there are internal dependencies.

Example: In your team, one of the modules is dependent on the other module's output.

LEADS AND LAGS

LEAD

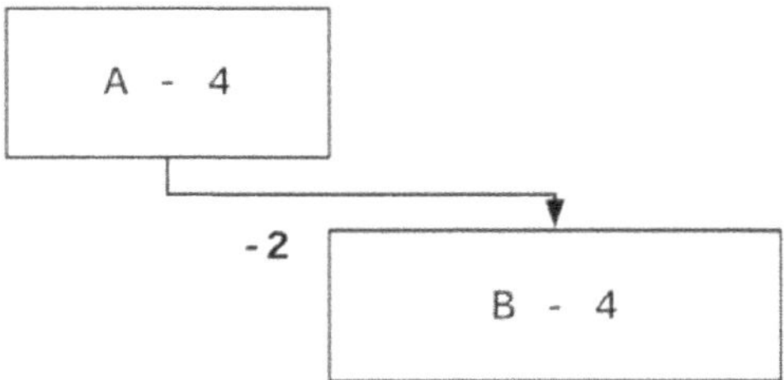

Lead is the amount of time whereby a successor activity can be advanced with respect to a predecessor activity. In the above picture above, Activity B has a LEAD or 2 Days.

LAG

Lag is the amount of time whereby a successor activity will be delayed with respect to a predecessor activity.

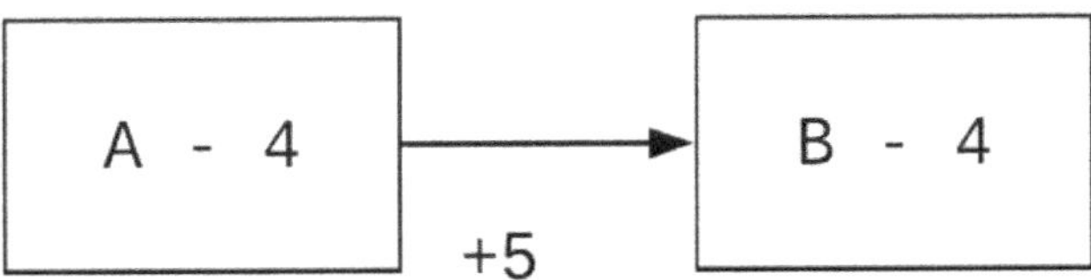

In this picture, Activity B has a LAG of 5 Days.
To avoid confusion, Map the Lead with the minus and the Lag with the plus.
Lead means that you would be doing the successor activity ahead of time, i.e., – X days.
Lag means that you would WAIT for X time, i.e., + X days.

PRECEDENCE DIAGRAMMING METHOD

The precedence diagramming method (PDM) is a technique used for constructing a schedule model where activities are represented by nodes and are graphically linked by one or more logical relationships to show the sequence in which the activities are to be performed.

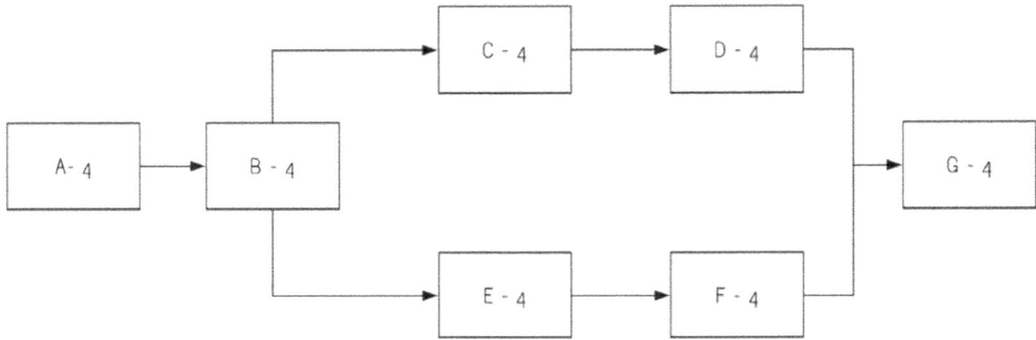

Activity-on-node (AON) is one method of representing a precedence diagram.

P.TME.3 ESTIMATIONS

We estimate resources, durations, costs, and many other things.
The estimations can be broadly categorized into the following buckets:

ANALOGOUS ESTIMATIONS

When you do not have time to do detailed analysis and estimations, we go with quick estimates. What are these? Based on historical information, we may roughly estimate the project as a whole (at the time of bidding when you don't have many details) or at the start of the project when there is not much clarity on the tasks.
Since the estimations are on a broad level, we understand the risk of unforeseen changes or things going wrong, and we may add some paddings to estimates. Still, the estimates are at a high level and may go wrong often.

This is called TOP-Down Estimates.
This method is most useful when you need more information about the current activity/project.

Keyword: Similar projects

BOTTOM-UP ESTIMATIONS

Opposite to top-down estimates, here we break down all possible details till WBS or till tasks to arrive at detailed estimations.

This process may take time but will yield the most accurate estimates.

Keyword: Detailed estimates (WBS/Task Level)

PARAMETRIC ESTIMATIONS

If 10 * 10 sq. feet takes 2 mins to paint, how much time would it take to paint 100* 100 sq. feet of the wall?

This is an example of parametric (calculations) estimation. Any estimate that is arrived at using calculation is a parametric estimate. The function point estimate is one of the examples in the software industry. The parametric estimate accuracy is as good as the underlying data on which the estimations are based.

Historical data is used to arrive at the calculation unit. If the historical calculations are flawed, then the outcome may be faulty. Hence to use parametric estimates, one needs to continually update the underlying calculations and estimations.

Keyword: Calculations

THREE-POINT ESTIMATIONS

What if your boss comes over to your desk and asks you, "How much time would you take to complete XYZ task?"

What do you do?

You calculate the task duration in your mind, add some buffer time, and then give him some hours or days. You did the right thing. However, if in case there were dependencies and you had an optimistic view, then you probably would not be able to give results on a required day.

Would it have been better if you had told him:

Boss, it will take ten days to complete if everything goes well (optimistic scenario). It will take 15 days if something goes wrong (a pessimistic scenario), and most likely, I should be able to deliver something by the 12th day (a most likely scenario).

Similar problems may arise in big turnkey projects – think the construction of a bridge – a lot many things may go wrong.

So for big projects, we rely on 3-point estimations, where the estimations are calculated based on best scenarios, worst scenarios, and most likely scenarios.

Now this will give us 3 different estimates, but our customers (they may be government bodies) want to hear one figure. So to arrive at the final estimates, we may calculate the Expected estimate on various distribution patterns of risks. Here you see:

TRIANGULAR DISTRIBUTION

The triangular distribution is also called the Average distribution. Here the overall final estimation is arrived at by giving equal weightage to all three estimations.

Final Estimate = (O + ML + P) / 3

BETA DISTRIBUTION

Beta distribution sees the world differently. The theory believes that the chances of most likely to happen are more than pessimistic scenarios or optimistic scenarios. Think Bell Curve.

To be precise, the chances of the most likely scenario to happen are 4 times that of pessimistic or optimistic scenarios. So the final calculation is done using the same principle in mind:

Final Estimate = (O + 4 * ML + P) / 6.

Where:

- O is the Optimistic estimate,
- ML is the Most Likely estimate and
- P is the Pessimistic estimate.

ESTIMATE ACTIVITY DURATIONS AND RESOURCES

Once the activities are identified, we estimate who will do them, the kind of skills needed for the job, and how many people will do it. How long will it take? All of this analysis is done keeping the schedule constraints in mind.

P.TME.3.1 LET'S PLAY: ESTIMATION TECHNIQUES

Identify the Estimation techniques.

1. **You started to work on the dinner menu. Keeping the last party in mind, you ordered the raw material for this one.**

   A.   Top-down Estimates

   B.   Bottom-up Estimates

   C.   Parametric Estimates

   D.   Three-Point Estimates

2. **You allocated 3 resources to a particular activity. The reason 3 resources were allocated is that you wanted to finish the activity within the next four days. It was assumed that 1 resource could complete the activity in 12 days.**

   A.   Top-down Estimates

   B.   Bottom-up Estimates

   C.   Parametric Estimates

   D.   Three-Point Estimates

3. **While estimating the project timelines, you estimated the most optimistic and the most pessimistic scenario along with the most likely conditions to arrive at the expected duration and then shared the time estimates with the senior management**

   A.   Top-down Estimates

   B.   Bottom-up Estimates

   C.   Parametric Estimates

   D.   Three-Point Estimates

4. **Sam detailed each activity with the project team. He discussed and finalized the activity-wise estimates and then combined all the days together to arrive at the final effort for the project.**

   A.   Top-down Estimates

   B.   Bottom-up Estimates

   C.   Parametric Estimates

   D.   Three-Point Estimates

DEVELOP SCHEDULE

The process of analyzing activity sequences, durations, resource requirements, and schedule constraints to create the Project Schedule Baseline.

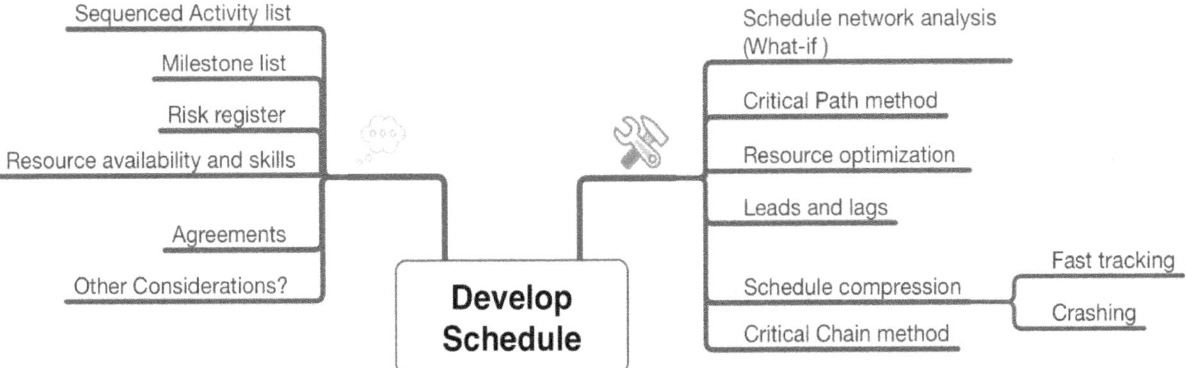

So far, we have decomposed the project to get the activities to achieve deliverables. We added dependencies, if any, and durations for each activity. However, we have not set the constraints until now.

→ There can be a time constraint. For example, the client may want to go live on X Date.

→ A resource constraint. For example, you cannot get more than five architects for a week.

→ Cost constraints or other constraints like quality etc.

All the constraints, especially time constraints, are applied at the time of arriving at the final schedule. Because a formal sign-off is taken in this process. A schedule baseline is the result of the process. The baseline schedule is established and circulated.

SCHEDULE NETWORK ANALYSIS

While applying the constraints, one would analyze the effects of each input on the entire project. It could be a simple analysis like:

→ What if I add another resource in activity C?

→ What if I do the activity in parallel

P.TME.4 Schedule Compression

Schedule compression techniques are used to shorten the schedule duration without reducing the project scope, to meet schedule constraints, imposed dates, or other schedule objectives.

CRASHING
A technique used to shorten the schedule duration for the least incremental cost by adding resources. Examples of crashing include approving overtime, bringing in additional resources, or paying to expedite the delivery of activities on the critical path. Crashing works only for activities on the critical path where additional resources will shorten the activity's duration. Crashing does not always produce a viable alternative and may result in increased risk and cost.

FAST-TRACKING
A schedule compression technique where activities or phases that are normally done in sequence are performed in parallel for at least a portion of their duration. An example is constructing the foundation of a building before completing all of the architectural drawings. Fast-tracking may result in rework and increased risk. Fast-tracking only works if activities can be overlapped to shorten the project duration.

Days	1 2 3 4 5 6 7 8 9 10 11 12 13 14 15 16 17 18 19 20 21 22
Normal	
Crashing	
Fast tracking	

P.TME.4.1- LET'S PLAY: SCHEDULE COMPRESSION TECHNIQUES

Identify the schedule compression technique used in the given scenarios:

1. **The Project Manager starts coding before the requirements are signed off by the customer.**

    A.   Fast Tracking

    B.   Crashing

2. **Ryan asked the project team to spend extra hours on weekends to complete the identified activity on time.**

    A.   Fast Tracking

    B.   Crashing

3. **The book publishing team started working on the format of the book while the academic team was in the last stage of editing the content.**

    A.   Fast Tracking

    B.   Crashing

4. **Due to a few issues, the project was behind schedule. To meet timelines, you asked the team to work overtime.**

    A.   Fast Tracking

    B.   Crashing

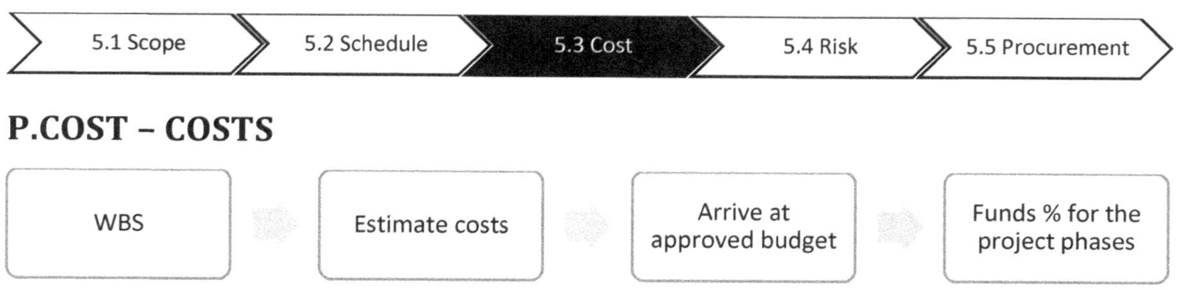

P.COST – COSTS

The costs for a project can be defined as:

- Currency (INR/USD)
- No of people working (in software, the cost is measured in person hours)
- Kilometers (cost can be derived as KMS in roadways project)
- Etc

The focus of the cost management plan is on how costs will be estimated and controlled. Many times, the project cost estimation may be in $, but sometimes it could be in person-hours. Many IT projects are given resources, and budgets are based on the person-hour formula. Similarly, many other industries can use their own method to measure costs.

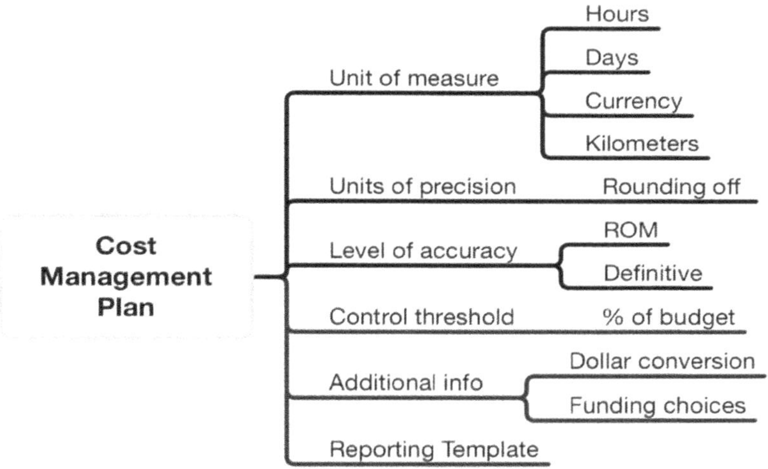

The Cost Management Plan describes how costs will be estimated and controlled. For a few industries, the cost can be person-hours, like IT. Roadways projects may calculate the cost in kilometers. What is the level of accuracy of estimates and other details?

The estimations on the project's costs can be derived using estimations techniques as we covered earlier.

P.COST.1 ESTIMATION RANGE

ROUGH ORDER OF MAGNITUDE (ROM)

The Rough Order of Magnitude or Order of Magnitude is a broad-level estimation. They can deviate by -25% to +75%.

DEFINITIVE ESTIMATE

The more you move in execution, the better you will be able to estimate. These estimates are called Definitive Estimates and can be as accurate as -5% to +10%

COST BASELINE AND FUNDING APPROVAL

Once the estimation for the project phase/project WBS items is done – we go to the management to get approval and allocation of the budget.
Please understand that it's the management that holds the budget.

The next step is to get the budget approved and funds allocated to the project. This is done along with senior management to arrive at the funding schedule and get the budget baseline (do you remember the definition of baseline??).

To understand the funding pattern and overall cost baseline, let's understand how a large project like a highway of 100 miles is constructed.
Are you given the funds for the entire construction? No - rather, you are allocated funds for the next 10 miles only (or one phase). This means that as per planned milestones, the project would be getting the agreed-upon funds. It is also agreed that the project will get a total of 1 million as funds. This is called Cost Baseline, or budget in other words.

P.COST.2 RESERVE ANALYSIS

Remember how, in the case study, I gave my daughter an extra budget than the cost estimates – why?
It was given to her to cover any risks that the project may encounter. Let's talk about risks and reserves.

CONTINGENCY RESERVES
To handle any risk in the project, the Project Manager sets aside some funds, also called contingency reserves.
The contingency reserves, once allocated, are part of the project budget, and the Project Manager controls them. Contingency reserves can be – additional money, extra time, extra resources, etc. You get the picture, right?

MANAGEMENT RESERVES
The senior management, which includes the program manager and portfolio manager, puts some funds aside to handle any risk that might arise in their portfolio or program.

The reserves which are kept in the project to work with any risk events

The Project Team plans for it and use it. You can identify them as - Schedule buffer, Resource Buffer, Cost buffer etc

The PM has full control on it.

The sponsor keeps some money aside for all the projects/operations/programs.

The Team does not own the funds and it is not considered as part of the budget

PM gets approval for this budget when the team asks from the sponsor (Think RED color Status Report)

These reserves are not in the project budget. The Project Manager has no control over these funds but may ask for them if and when any big, unforeseen risk emerges. The senior management may allocate a few funds from the management reserves to the Project Manager. Think of a dashboard that you prepare that shows a RED color status. The RED color signifies that you are asking for either more funds, more time, or more human resources. The senior management may then allocate more resources from the management funds.

P.COST.2.1 LET'S PLAY: RESERVE TYPES

Select the correct reserves.

1. **You are a Project Manager. You kept some reserve to address risks in your project while estimating costs. Project Cost Baseline consists of this reserve.**

   A.   Management Reserve

   B.   Contingency Reserve

2. **You have encountered a procurement risk that you did not plan for during planning. So, you do not have adequate funds to manage it. You approach your senior management for funds.**

   A.   Management Reserve

   B.   Contingency Reserve

3. **You, the Project Manager, manage and control this reserve.**

   A.   Management Reserve

   B.   Contingency Reserve

4. **You, the Project Manager, do not administer and control this reserve.**

   A.   Management Reserve

   B.   Contingency Reserve

P.QLTY - QUALITY

P.QLTY.1 COST OF QUALITY

While planning for costs, you need to calculate the overall cost of quality. Some examples of quality costs are testing costs, failure costs, etc. How many testers do we use? All the costs should be counted and estimated.

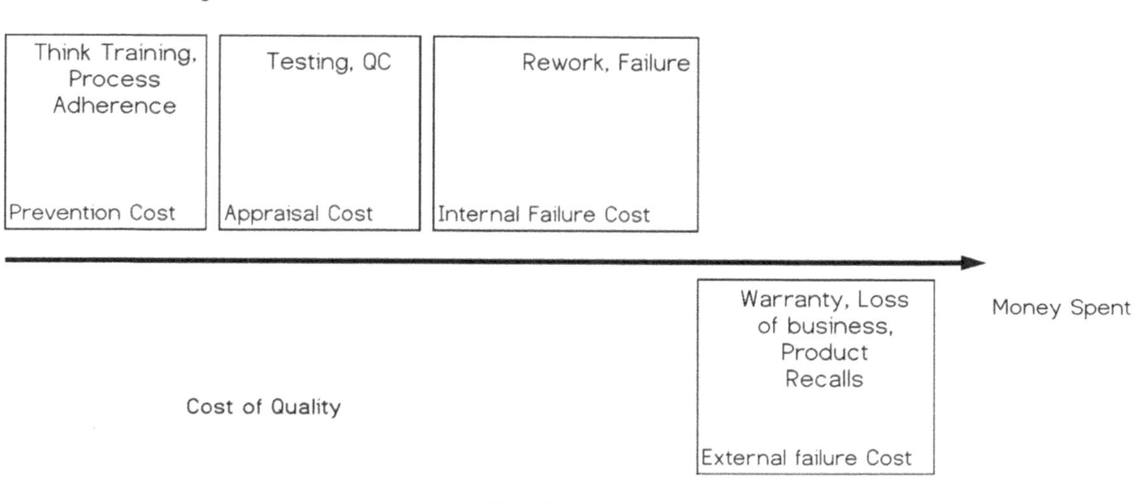

Cost of quality includes all costs incurred over the life of the product, which can be categorized as:

→ Investment in preventing non-conformance to requirements (Quality Assurance)

→ Appraising the product or service for conformance to requirements (Quality Control)

→ Failing to meet requirements (Rework)

→ Customer finding the problem is a huge cost and should be kept in mind while planning for quality management.

P.QLTY.2 - TEST, AUDIT, AND INSPECTION PLANNING:

As a project team, you will ensure the number of test cycles and testing methodologies so that the product which is handed over to the customer is usable and defect-free. A test plan is prepared. The audit schedule is prepared.

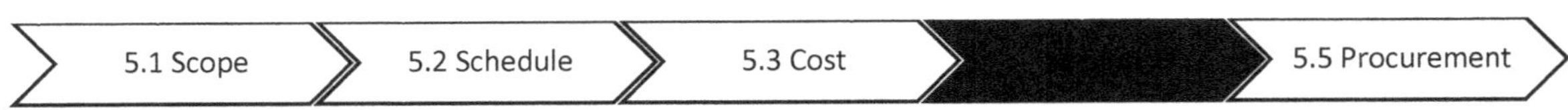

P.RISK - RISKS

The objective of identifying risks is to determine and list as many risks as possible. Participate in facilitation meetings with the customer. They can tell you the business risks. Ask an SME, and scan through all the earlier projects, historical data, and contracts; all of these can give you leads on what can possibly go wrong.

P.RISK.1 – IDENTIFY RISKS

We brainstorm and double-check assumptions and legal or contractual requirements to see if there are risks. We may also go through previous project's risks and see if we have planned for the project week links.

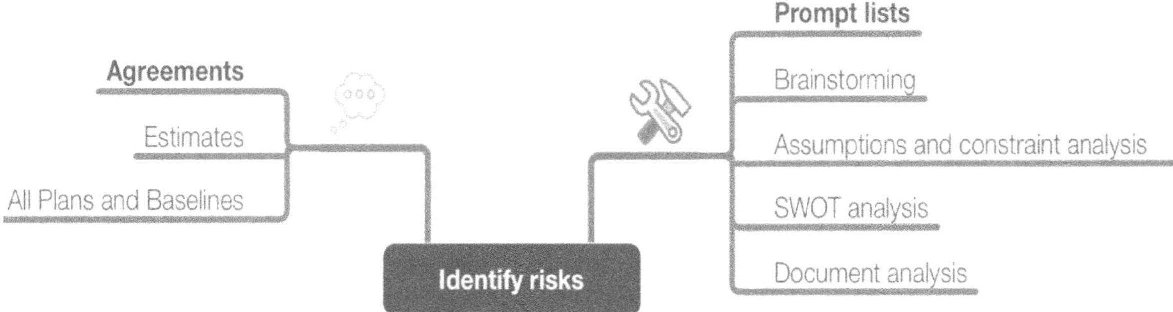

If you check all plans, baselines, and all the older projects, these can help us identify the project risks.

BRAINSTORMING

Brainstorming with project teams and customers can help you unearth many risks. Many mature organizations have risk checklists so that the team can simply find out the risk applicable to their project. Interviews with domain experts can help identify the risks with projects, especially complex domain-specific risks.

ASSUMPTION ANALYSIS

Assumptions can go wrong, and this may lead to risks. Check all of the assumptions from the documented requirements n and other plans. Check if they have any ambiguity or any chances of being untrue. Mark them as risks. Constraints, if not met, are a risk to project success. Identify and check all the constraints.

SWOT ANALYSIS

SWOT – Analysis

	Strengths	**Weaknesses**
Internal view	• What advantages do we offer? (USP) • What synergies can be created? • Which factors lead to success? • What makes us unique? • Which resources make us better?	• What disadvantages do we have? • What are we worse at than others? • What are our weaknesses? • What resources do we lack?
	Opportunities	**Threats**
External view	• What trends are there? • What opportunities are still untapped? • Are there positive societal changes? • Helpful legislative changes on the horizon? • Are there new technologies?	• What do competitors do? • Are there laws or regulations that can change? • Are there new technologies? • Other external factors that pose a risk? (Politics, economic situation, etc.)

This technique considers the project against each of the strengths, weaknesses, opportunities, threats (SWOT), and views to increase the extent of identified risks by including internal risks. The technique starts with the identification of the strengths and weaknesses of the organization, focusing on the project, team, or business area in general. SWOT analysis also is used to identify opportunities for the project that can arise from organizational strengths and any threats resulting from organizational weaknesses.

DOCUMENTATION ANALYSIS

You should always review all available documents for risk. It could be SLAs in contracts, milestones, or a baselined scope. All of these could have risk elements in them.

PROMPT LISTS

A prompt list is a predefined category of risks. An organization can develop its own prompt list for projects, or some of the domains also have a predefined prompt list. A few of the standard examples of prompt lists are:

PESTLE:
Political, Economic, Social, Technological, Legal, Environmental

TECOP:
Technical, Environmental, Commercial, Operational, Political

VUCA:
Volatility, Uncertainty, Complexity, Ambiguity
Using a prompt list ensures that the team checks the risks against each factor and identifies the risks in a structured manner. This ensures risk identification across all types

of risks, unlike brainstorming, which is quick and responsive but may be skewed toward some specific risks.

Using a category to define the risk in a structured way to identify the risk.

You might want to use an RBS (Risk Breakdown Structure) to ensure that you are not ignoring a certain type of risk and are adequately covered on all risks.

A mature organization might give you a risk template with the risk categories pre-populated – based on historical data. If your organization does not have one, then you might want to create a template and send it to them.

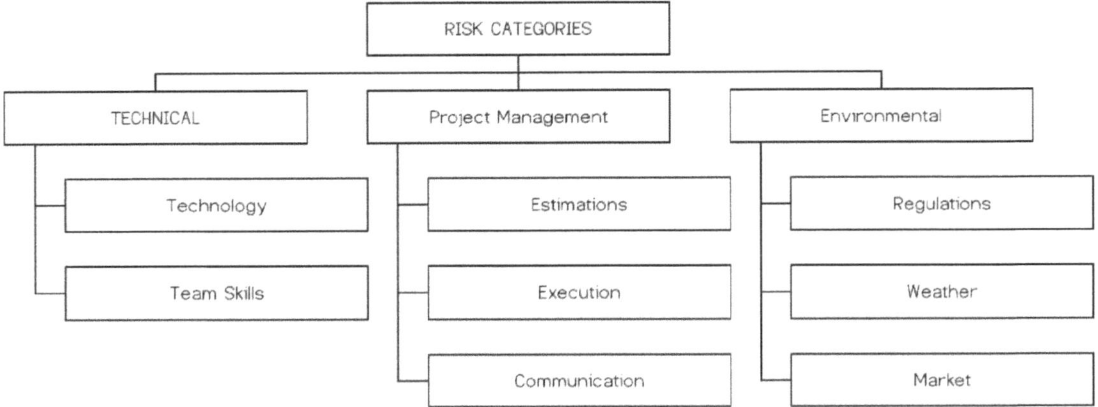

Once done, we arrive at the Risk plan,

P.RISK.1.1 LET'S PLAY: RISKS IDENTIFICATION TECHNIQUES

Match the following

Risk Scenario	Technique Used
1. You wanted to identify as many of the risks as possible in your project, so you called a joint meeting with the customer, PMO, your senior management, and the architect.	Interviews
2. You've sent a questionnaire to all the functional heads to find any risks to the success of the project. You did not want any biases, so these inputs were sought anonymously.	Documentation Reviews
3. You looked at the assumption log to ensure that the project success criterion may not get hampered by anything unexpected.	Brainstorming
4. You use the Fish Bone diagram technique to gain insight into the behavior of a risk.	Delphi
5. You meet personally with many different stakeholders: the sponsor, customer, team members, and experts. You seek answers to questions about what they think could go wrong on the project.	Assumption Analysis
6. You look through all the project documents, including contracts, to see any risk possibilities.	Root Cause Analysis

P.RISK.2 PERFORM QUALITATIVE RISK ANALYSIS

The goal of the qualitative analysis is to prioritize risks by assessing and combining their probability of occurrence and impact.

Once the risks are listed, then the next logical step is to find the risk priority. Some of us do it by instinct, but the most efficient method is to define and allocate probability and assess the impact of the risks and then arrive at the risk rating. In some projects, you can add the dimension of urgency to get overall risk ratings of the risks.

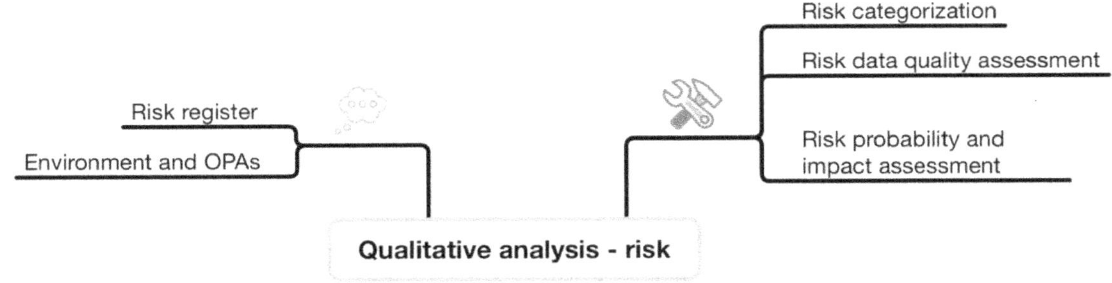

A risk register will be updated for risk priority and risk impact after this process.

RISK PROBABILITY AND IMPACT ASSESSMENT

While planning for risks, you should have agreed with your team on an impact and probability scale. Why?

In your mind, the impact could be high, or the probability of the event happening is high, but for others, it might not be. It is a good idea to discuss and decide on the definition of

PROBABILITY AND IMPACT MATRIX

A probability and impact matrix is a framework for mapping the likelihood of each risk event and its impact on project objectives if that risk occurs. Risks are prioritized as per the grid.

The probability and impact matrix shows how risk should be treated. For example, if the risk probability is low and the impact is also low, then accept the risk.

PROBABILITY ─────────────────────────── >>>>>			
PROBABILITY & IMPACT MATRIX	LOW	MEDIUM	HIGH
LOW	ACCEPT	MAY ACCEPT	MUST MANAGE
MEDIUM	MAY ACCEPT	MUST MANAGE	MUST MANAGE
HIGH	MUST MANAGE	MUST MANAGE	EXTENSIVE MANAGEMENT

If the risk probability is high and the impact is high, then put extensive management to control the risk.

BUBBLE CHART

Data is plotted and shown in many aspects. A bubble chart shows data on 3 aspects as given:

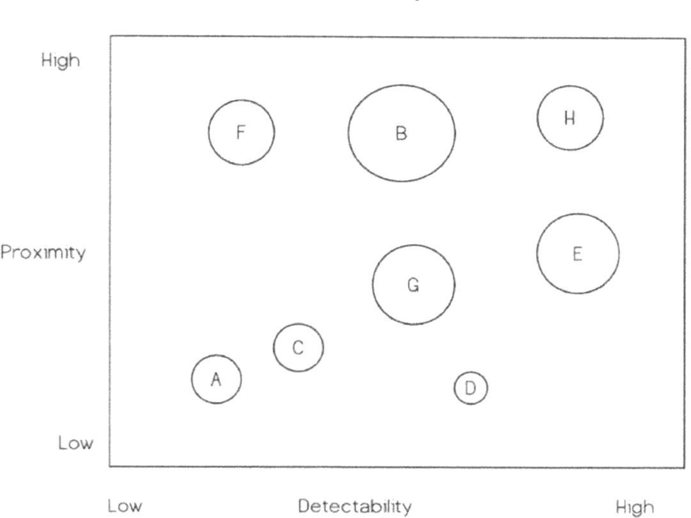

P.RISK.3- PLAN RISK RESPONSES

The process of developing options and actions to enhance opportunities and reduce threats to project objectives.

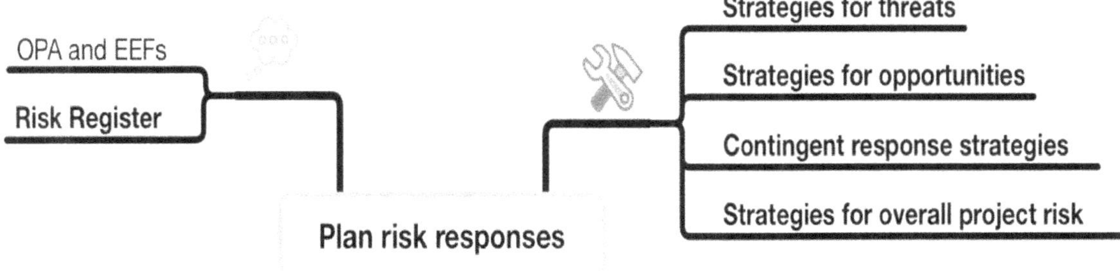

Once all the risks are identified and ranking is done, then you need to plan the responses for all the risks on the project. Now, some people use a term called mitigate, that's a popular expression but does not justify the overall response planning for risks.
You might have a few risks, but if planned/respond to with the right strategy, you can save money on the project.
    → A risk can result in more costs, also called THREAT.
    → Risk can lead to gaining money or saving money, also called OPPORTUNITY.

You know, threats – schedule slippage due to attrition, and so on.

But what is an opportunity – e.g., Airtel outsourcing all OSS work to IBM to save on costs as well as focusing on their customer because they had the risk of workforce attrition and technical competency. Did outsourcing save money for Airtel – yes, you bet!

So, in the Plan Risk Responses, we plan for all the threats as well as opportunities.

STRATEGIES FOR NEGATIVE RISKS OR THREATS

ESCALATE
- The risks which are out of the control of the project team are escalated
- The escalation level can be the program/portfolio level
- Senior management decides on the risk response

AVOID
- This involves actually changing the project plan so that a particular risk can't happen.
- Changing the project plan may inadvertently introduce new risks, called "Secondary risks."
- Risk probability becomes ZERO.

MITIGATE
- Steps are taken to reduce the likelihood and/or the impact of an identified risk.
- The risk which remains is called "Residual Risk."
- For example: keeping a buffer
- Risk probability or impact reduces but does NOT reach ZERO

TRANSFER
- Transfer to 3rd party.
- The risk probability and impact DOES NOT change
- Only the ownership changes
- For example - outsourcing

ACCEPT
Do Nothing

Let's summarize the risk response technique for threats:

Threat Strategy	Description	Changes in Probability	Changes in Impact	Extra Information
AVOID	Change the current course of action	Reduced to ZERO	No impact. Probability is zero	The alternate path/steps may introduce risks, also called secondary risks. They should also be assessed while planning for risk responses.
MITIGATE	Steps are taken to reduce the expected loss if a risky event happens	Reduced to an acceptable level	Reduced to an acceptable level	The overall risk does not become zero. Risk is reduced to an acceptable level. The remaining risk is called residual risk and is monitored

Strategy	Description	Changes in Probability	Changes in Impact	Any Extra Information
				and controlled throughout the project life cycle.
TRANSFER	Risk is transferred to the third party	No Change	The impact is transferred to another entity.	The overall risk management ownership is given to another entity. Examples can be outsourcing, insurance, and Annual maintenance (AMC).
ACCEPT	Do nothing	No Change	No Change	There may be some contingency reserves that are kept. No steps are taken to reduce the risk impact or probability.
ESCALATE	Escalate to senior management	No Change	No Change	Ownership changes

STRATEGIES FOR POSITIVE RISKS OR OPPORTUNITIES

ESCALATE
- The risks, which are out of the control of the project team, are escalated
- The escalation level can be the program/portfolio level
- Senior management decides on the risk response

EXPLOIT
- Increasing the probability to 100%
- Opposite of AVOID
- Assigning an organization's most talented resources to the project to reduce the time to completion or to provide lower costs than originally planned.

SHARE
- Sharing the ownership
- Opposite of TRANSFER
- Forming risk-sharing partnerships, teams, special-purpose companies, or joint ventures

ENHANCE
- Increase the probability and/or the impacts
- Opposite of MITIGATE
- Adding more resources to an activity to finish early.

ACCEPT
- Do nothing

Let's summarize the risk response technique for opportunities:

Strategy	Description	Changes in Probability	Changes in Impact	Any Extra Information

EXPLOIT	Change the current course of action to realize the opportunity	Increased to 100%		Steps are taken for the opportunity to be realized, and benefits are reaped.
ENHANCE	Steps are taken to increase the expected gains and/or increase the probability.	Increased	Increased	
SHARE	The benefits are shared with the third party	Shared	Shared	Joint Ventures (JV) are assigned to handle the risks together and gain benefits together.
ACCEPT	Do nothing	No Change	No Change	This is a common response to handling a threat and opportunity.
ESCALATE	Escalate to senior management	No Change	No Change	Ownership changes

The parallel between threat and opportunity responses:

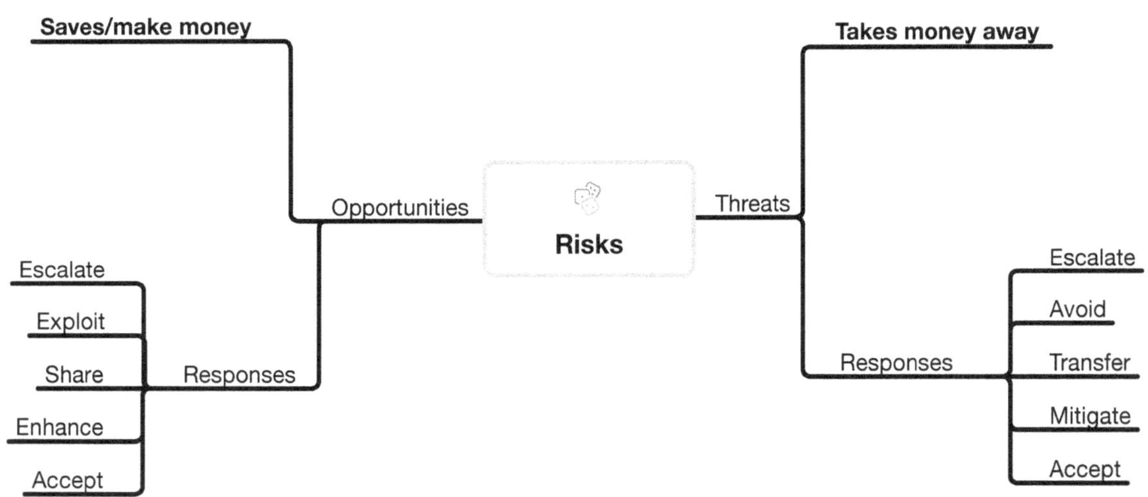

P.RISK.3.1- LET'S PLAY: RISK RESPONSES

You planned to go out for an outing with your friends for a few days. To ensure that everything is nice and smooth, you anticipated a few risks and implemented a strategy to handle them. Identify the strategy/response selected for each scenario:

1. **A chance of heavy rain could lead to car skids. You purchased new tires to avoid an accident due to rain.**

   A. Avoid
   B. Mitigate
   C. Transfer
   D. Accept

2. **You canceled the rappelling activity as the weather forecast was not favorable.**

   A. Avoid
   B. Mitigate
   C. Transfer
   D. Accept

3. **The weather forecast has a 99% probability of rain, but the team decided to go on a river rafting activity. Everyone said, "We will stop if the weather conditions turn bad."**

   A. Avoid
   B. Mitigate
   C. Transfer
   D. Accept

4. **Driving a car in rainy weather can lead to accidents, but at the same time, it's a beautiful view. So, you hired a cab to take you out for mountain scenery. You had to pay for the cab, but it was worth the money.**

   A. Avoid
   B. Mitigate
   C. Transfer
   D. Accept

5. **Before traveling, you noticed that the main route had a traffic jam, so you took a longer route to avoid the jam. The new route has a toll and goes through a national park. This was the best time spent watching the scenery.**

   A. Avoid
   B. Mitigate
   C. Transfer
   D. Accept

P.RISK.3.2 CONTINGENT RESPONSE STRATEGIES

These are predefined responses to certain events which have known triggers and can induce a big impact. Think disaster recovery drill, file, and data backups, etc.
Some responses are designed for use only if specified events occur. For some risks, it is appropriate for the project team to make a response plan that will only be executed under certain predefined conditions if it is believed that there will be sufficient warning to implement the plan. Events that trigger the contingency response, such as missing intermediate milestones or gaining higher priority with a supplier, should be defined and tracked. Risk responses identified using this technique are also called contingency plans or fallback plans and include unique triggering events that set the plans in effect.

STRATEGIES FOR OVERALL PROJECT RISKS

Risks are applicable to a project as a whole. Think dynamic technology or working in a non-friendly climate. The overall project risks can be handled by the techniques shown in the mind map.

Strategy	Description
Avoid	Reducing the probability to zero.
Exploit	Increasing the probability to 100%
Transfer/share	Work with sellers to share the benefits or losses.
Mitigate /enhance	Depending on the risk/opportunity, take steps to increase or decrease the probability or the impact or both.
Accept	Do nothing,

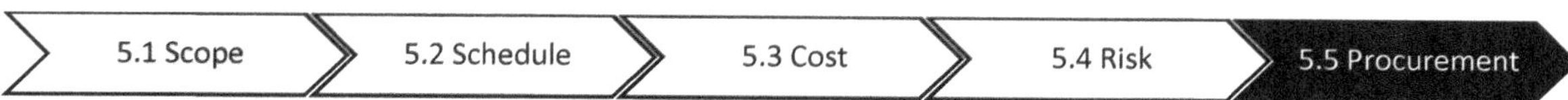

P.PROC – PROCUREMENTS

P.PROC.1 – PLANNING PROCUREMENTS

Plan procurements document what, how, and when a buying for the project will take place.

Plan Procurement Management is part of the planning process group and results in documenting the analysis of make or buy, along with:

- What to buy (statement of work)
- When to buy
- What would be the contract terms?
- How to select the seller
- Do we need independent consultants?
- How to check for the quality of the deliverables
- When to release payments

MARKET RESEARCH

You, or the procurement team, do market research to see if the product or services are available in the market. If it is, then you will also research the price range and probable sellers.

MAKE-OR-BUY ANALYSIS

A make-or-buy analysis is a general management technique used to determine whether a particular work can best be accomplished by the project team or should be purchased from outside sources.

Various factors can influence the make or buy, such as:

- Is it cheaper to buy from outside?
- Is the workforce adequate within the current organization?
- Do we have enough ramp-up time?
- Is it too risky to be executed (Remember transfer as risk response)?

P.PROC.2 - TYPES OF CONTRACTS

SCENARIO 1:

I want to get a custom-made dinner table and chair set. The dinner table's design is documented in detail and taken from one of the home furnishing magazines.

I called the carpenter and showed him the design. He had a few questions, and I had all the answers at that time, not requiring any research. After all the detailing on design, wood type, and color, I asked him the primary question:

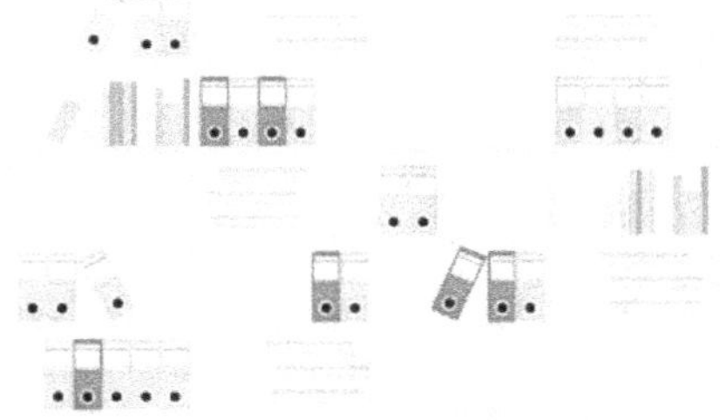

"What is the price, and how much time for this?"
He responds that $500 is the amount with a 30-day turnaround.
I agreed.
The carpenter has the final price after considering all the raw materials and service costs.
What if the wood price changes tomorrow?
Do I (the buyer) pay him more than the contract (USD500)?
No. Why? Simply because of the contract which we signed. We signed on a fixed price for the whole unit. As a buyer, I'm safeguarded by this type of contract.

SCENARIO 2:

After a few days, I realize that I need a good set of Almira cupboards covering one of the walls of my bedroom. I had no clue about the design or the type of wood, but I knew that I needed an Almira. So, I called my carpenter again.

He gave me the following options:

- → Option 1: Wood-type teak, USD 30.00 per square foot
- → Option 2: Wood-type Hardwood - USD 25.00 per square foot. I said OK for option 1, and he started work.

Whenever we use words such as; PER PERSON, PER HOUR, or RATE, these contacts are Time and material contracts.

SCENARIO 3:

After a few days, my Society Residence Association (RWA) called me and asked me to get a memento for the prize distribution event.

I asked them about what design, material, or any other specifications. They said, "We trust you, get whatever you like."

So, I called my carpenter again.

I had no answers to any of his questions. I told him that I didn't know what I wanted, but let's try and create something beautiful for RWA.
He mentioned that since the specifications are not clear, he would not be able to quote any amount. To which I said, "Don't worry about that part. I would

reimburse you for all legitimate costs and your service fee." The guy went back home happy.

If the wood price changes tomorrow, who will bear the increased cost? I do, as the buyer. This type of contract is called the COST PLUS contract.

FIXED-PRICE CONTRACTS

Buyers must precisely specify the product or services being procured.

FIRM FIXED-PRICE CONTRACTS (FFP)
→ The cost for goods is set at the outset and does not increase unless the scope of work changes.
→ Any price rise due to an unfavourable environment is the responsibility of the seller, who is obligated to complete the effort.

FIXED-PRICE INCENTIVE FEE CONTRACTS (FPIF)
→ Business incentives are tied to achieving agreed metrics.

FIXED PRICE WITH ECONOMIC PRICE ADJUSTMENT CONTRACTS (FP-EPA)
→ The administration period spans a considerable period of years, as is desired with many long-term relationships.
→ E.g., inflation changes or cost increases

COST PLUS CONTRACTS

When the extent of work cannot be accurately defined at the start and needs to be adjusted, or when high risks may exist in the effort.
Seller is compensated - all actual costs, plus a fee.

COST-PLUS FIXED-FEE CONTRACTS (CPFF)
→ The fee is paid only for concluded work and does not change due to seller performance.

COST-PLUS INCENTIVE FEE CONTRACTS (CPIF)
→ Predetermined incentive fee based upon attaining certain performance
→ Both the buyer and seller share costs based upon a pre-negotiated cost-sharing formula, e.g., an 80/20

COST PLUS AWARD FEE CONTRACTS (CPAF)
→ A Predefined FIXED AWARD is set based on SLAs

TIME AND MATERIAL CONTRACTS

Hybrid Type Of Contractual Arrangement, Aspects of BOTH Cost-reimbursable And Fixed-price Contracts. The full value of the transaction and the specific quantity of items to be delivered may not be specified by the buyer at the time of the contract award. Conversely, T&M contracts also resemble fixed unit price arrangements when certain parameters are specified in the contract.
T&M contracts are often used for:
→ Staff Augmentation

  → Acquisition of Experts
  → Any outside support

Buyer pays a rate for resources/services/products.

The Keywords to identify this type of contract is:

→ Per Hour
→ Per Unit

RELATIONSHIP BETWEEN CONTRACT AND RISKS

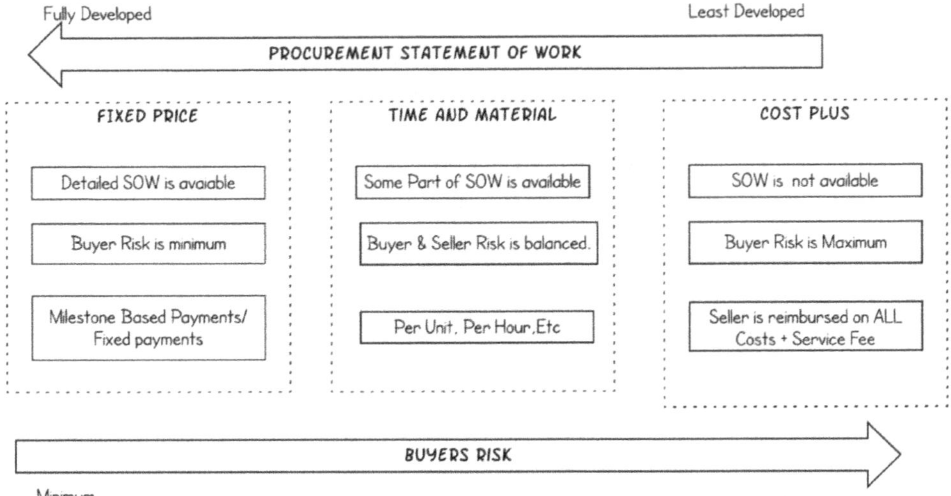

P.PROC.2.1 LET'S PLAY: CONTRACT TYPES

Map the right contract with the definition:

Description	Contract Type Used
1. A contract having special provisions allowing for predefined final adjustments to the contract price due to changed conditions, such as inflation or cost increases (or decreases) for specific commodities. Otherwise, the cost does not change	Cost Plus Incentive Fee
2. The seller is reimbursed for all allowable costs for performing the contract work and receives a percentage based upon achieving certain performance objectives as set forth in the contract. The seller also shares losses as per the contract agreement.	Fixed Price with EPA
3. Contracts that specify rates per hour or categories of materials at specified rates per unit.	Fixed Price
4. In this contract, the buyer should precisely specify the product or services to be procured. Any changes to the procurement specification can increase the costs to the buyer.	Time and Material

EXECUTION

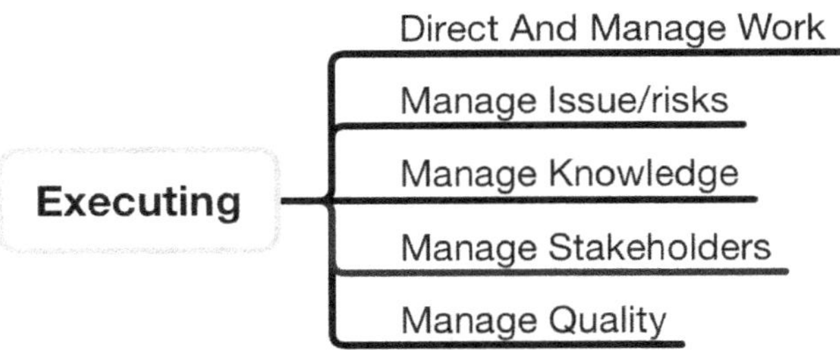

E.INT.1 - DIRECT AND MANAGE PROJECT WORK

Direct and Manage Project Work is doing the work as per the plan and implementing the approved changes.

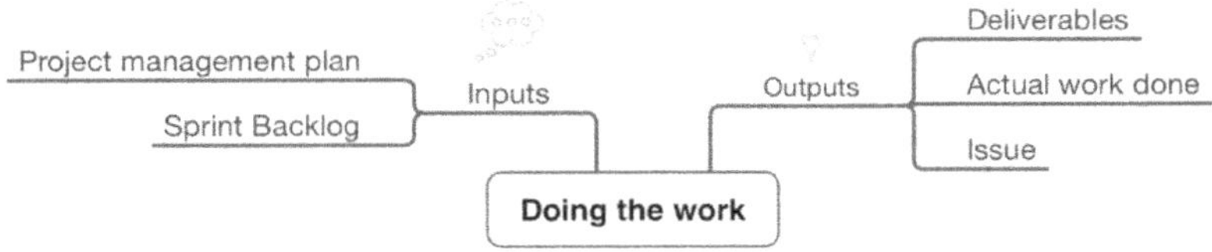

What happens here?

My team started working on the assigned work as per the plan and work assignments. In many projects, I have successfully used whiteboards for daily meetings. My team would meet (daily stand-up meetings) and discuss topics like:

- What did I complete yesterday?
- What is my plan for today?
- Discuss issues
- Discuss and allocate any interdependency

ACTUAL WORK DONE/ WORK PERFORMANCE DATA/ ACTUAL STATUS

Actual work completed by the team is noted and compiled. Software or whiteboard information radiators (Charts) can be used. The team gives information on the following:

→ Actual hours spent,
→ Actual money spent,
→ Actual work completed
→ % of tasks completed
→ % of money spent
→ Work start status

DELIVERABLE

Tangible or intangible results produced at the end of a process, phase, or project are referred to as a deliverable. A deliverable is to be tested first before customer acceptance.

E.INT.2 MANAGE PROJECT KNOWLEDGE

While underway, a project creates much knowledge that can be preserved to help other projects, and thus the organization, tremendously.

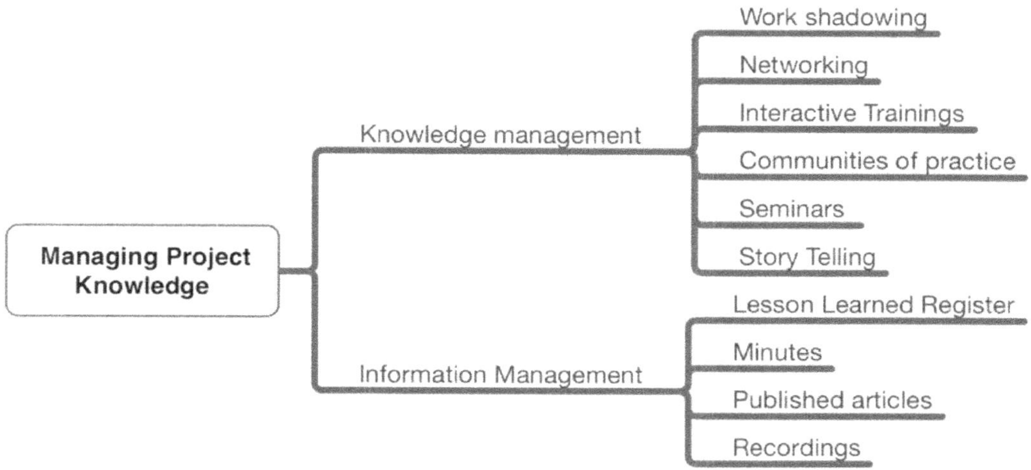

The knowledge categories:

TACIT KNOWLEDGE

The knowledge is personal, i.e., a belief system, know-how, insight, or experience. It's not documented. You learn while you are working with the team. For example, if you check any office manual or instruction manual, you will not know where the cafeteria is. But when you join the office, you find out. This is an example of tacit information.

EXPLICIT KNOWLEDGE

This is the documented knowledge. For example – what is the employee vacation policy, etc.
In a project, it's easy to get and document explicit knowledge, but ensuring the tacit information is also documented for future projects or the success of an ongoing project is a great challenge.
There are various tools suggested to help manage knowledge:
- Networking
- Informal discussions
- Communities of practice
- Shadow and reverse shadow
- Knowledge fairs
- Interactive training etc.

Tools to document knowledge are information management tools:
- Lessons learned

- Recording training sessions
- Discussion of records (Minutes)
- Creating new processes using the knowledge of experienced personnel

E.INT.2.1 LET'S PLAY: TYPE OF KNOWLEDGE

1. **The knowledge that can be easily documented**

   A.   Tacit Knowledge

   B.   Explicit Knowledge

2. **Usual mechanism to share this knowledge is forums, informal interactions, and observations**

   A.   Tacit Knowledge

   B.   Explicit Knowledge

3. **This type of knowledge can be found in the OPAs**

   A.   Tacit Knowledge

   B.   Explicit Knowledge

4. **Belief systems, Know-how is a type of:**

   A.   Tacit Knowledge

   B.   Explicit Knowledge

E.INT.3 ISSUES AND RISKS

ISSUE:

A current condition or situation that may have an impact on the project objectives. In other words, it is an action item that the project team must address. An Issue is:
- → A present event
- → Has happened on the project
- → You have to work on it NOW
- → The response is adhoc to an issue and is called WORKAROUND
- → They are documented in the Issue log till the closure

RISK:

A future event that may happen or not, and if that event does happen, will impact the product objectives. A risk is:
- → A future event
- → Have some probability (it may happen)
- → You can respond to the risk (even elimination can be on the response)
- → They are documented in the Risk Register for further assessment and planning.

E.INT.3.1 - LET'S PLAY: IDENTIFY A RISK OR ISSUE

The Visconti Country project is nearing completion (your new home), and you should take possession of the new home in about a month. You have been working to manage and control the schedule and cost as per the initial estimates. However, the project came with particular challenges. Select if these are issues or risks.

1. **You received a letter from the bank stating that the mortgage rate has increased by 1%. This will increase the project spending by at least 10%**

   A. Risk

   B. Issue

2. **Heavy rains are forecasted in the next week. This could delay the project's completion by a few days.**

   A. Risk

   B. Issue

3. **Few of the workers went on strike.**

   A. Risk

   B. Issue

4. **Some of the windows you bought were the wrong size and should now be returned. This is a lot of rework.**

   A. Risk

   B. Issue

5. **A new shopping mall is planned near your house. If that comes up in the next two years, it will significantly increase property valuation.**

   A. Risk

   B. Issue

MONITOR AND CONTROL

The work which we do is following to manage and control the project:

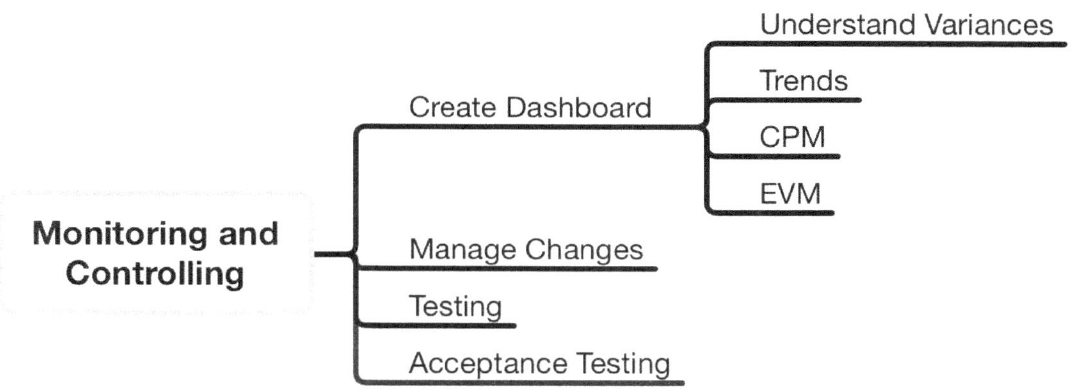

MC.1 - MONITOR AND CONTROL PROJECT WORK

The process of reviewing the project by creating Project Progress Reports that compare the current progress with the baseline.

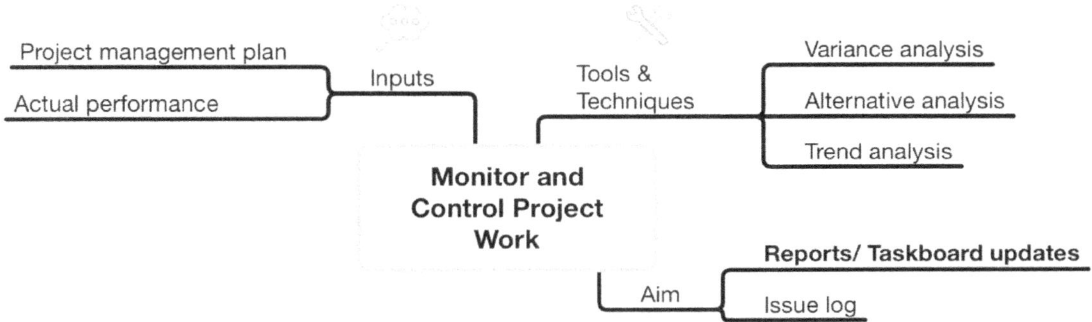

A report Is called a WORK PERFORMANCE REPORT and can be referred to as a status report or dashboard in normal project discussions.
Data analysis techniques, like variance analysis, 'What-if Analysis,' Earned Value Analysis, and Trend Analysis, are used to control the project.

In the case of Agile teams, the daily meeting is the place where the burndown charts are plotted to see the variations. Then, instead of creating a report, an agile team updates the progress charts/task boards so that information can be available to all stakeholders.

MC.2 CHANGE MANAGEMENT

While executing the project, a change may be requested by a stakeholder. For example, a team member might want a change to the timeline. The client may need to add a few new items to the scope, or the PM may want to change a milestone date.

THE CHANGE MANAGEMENT PLAN ADDRESSES QUESTIONS LIKE:
→ What would be classified as a change?
→ Where would it be documented?
→ Which Impact Analysis template be used?
→ Are there any change management tools available?
→ Who decides if the change Is implemented or rejected?
→ Who is on the Change Control Board (CCB)?
→ How will approved changes be implemented?

A CCB/ authorized person decides to approve or reject each change request. This results in an Approved Change Request.

CHANGE MANAGEMENT PROCESS

Change Control Board (CCB) Meetings are required to understand the nature of the change and its impact. The CCB can decide to look at the plan, schedule, and overall business outcome. Then, the CCB can decide to approve or reject the change. They can also request more information or that changes be implemented later. These meetings should be pre-planned as laid out in the change management plan. The CCB should be identified at the time of planning and informed of their roles as well.

All the changes should be documented so that the origin of the change and what happened to the change can be understood along with the impact analysis. In addition, the change control tool should have the ability to log the changes and trace them.

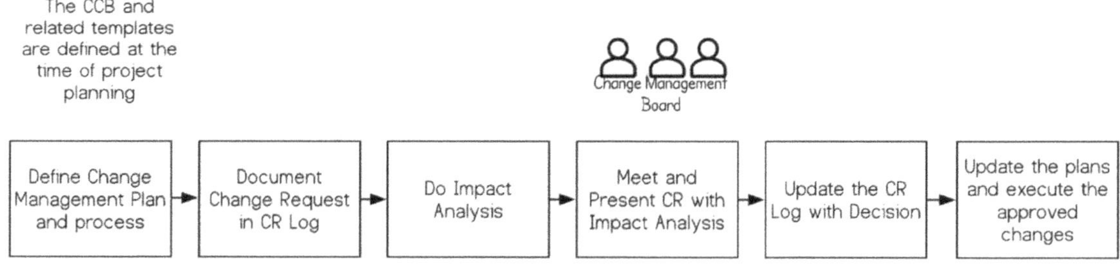

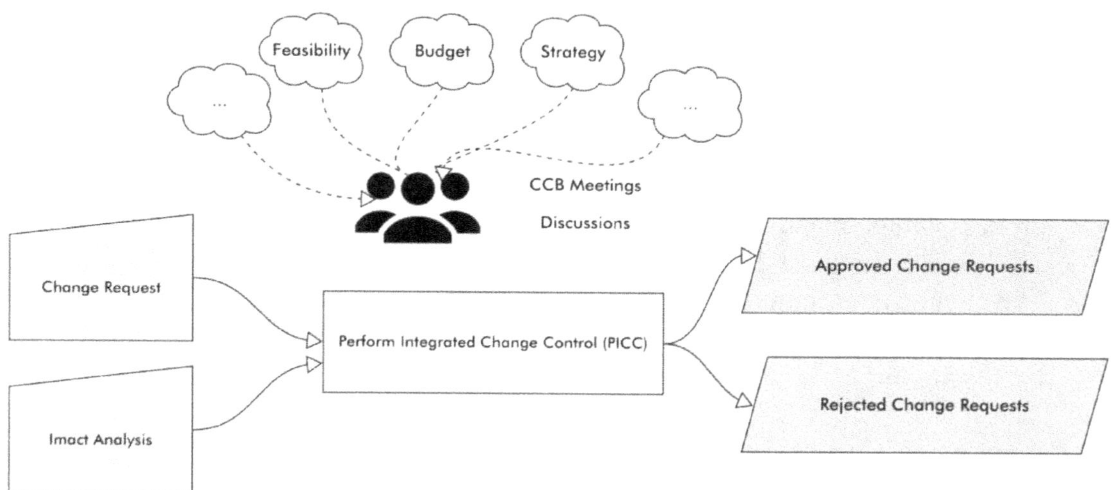

Approved changes will undergo planning and execution again. As a result, the project baselines will generally change when the approved changes are incorporated into the plan, resulting in changes in baselines.

A TYPICAL CHANGE MANAGEMENT PROCESS:

Perform Integrated Change Control is one of the processes under the monitoring & controlling process group and is part of the Integration Management Knowledge Area. Therefore, you can expect many questions on change management in the CAPM exam.

A FEW SCENARIOS:

- A team member comes to you and proposes changes to a high-level design for security module interfaces. He feels confident that introducing those changes will lead to less effort and more secure and decoupled interfaces.
- You (Project Manager) and a few senior team leads are meeting with the customer to get the prototype signed off. The customer feels the screen is too bland and needs a better UI (User Interface).
- Your senior manager informs you that the interrelated BPO project has a few process changes, so the current project (under you) needs to change to match the updated workflow.

What do you think of the given situations? Are these change requests? Would you implement them?

According to PMBOK, the above scenarios can induce changes to the project plan and, therefore, should be considered change requests. These changes may impact the project's schedule/quality/scope/risk and should follow the Integrated Change Control process.

REAL-LIFE

Real life may not perfectly align with PMBOK theory, but a change request is never implemented immediately until and unless you are using agile methodology.

Typically, the process, as advised by PMBOK, is as follows:

1. Document the CR in the Change Request Register.
2. Assign the CR to an SME (Subject Matter Expert) for an Impact Analysis
3. Present the cumulative Impact Analysis forms to CCB (Change Control Board)
4. CCB meetings need to be periodic and interactive.
5. The CCB accepts or rejects the CRs
6. The approved CRs go back for planning.

7.   The PM revises plans and gets approvals. A new baseline is in place now.

KEY TAKEAWAYS
- → There is always a CCB.
- → There is always a Change Management Plan.
- → Any change, even a reduction of scope, must go through the Change Management process, which means:
- → The Change Request documentation is added to the Change Request Register.
- → The change is executed according to agreed-upon plans.
- → Never implement unapproved changes, however small they seem. (Remember this for the exam.)

AGILE PROJECTS AND CHANGE REQUESTS

Agile is change based project life cycle. Iterations are time-boxed and are of a small time frame (Typically 1-4 weeks). The Product Owner keeps evaluating the requirements and keeps changing the priority using the Product Backlog Grooming. This would ensure that the high-value specifications are discussed and implemented in the upcoming iterations. **In case a change is advised to a developer while they are working on the Sprint/Iteration, The developer should redirect the request to the Product Owner.** The product owner has the ultimate authority to make any changes in the Product backlog. In an urgent case, if a change is required in the ongoing iteration due to some ad-hoc regulations or business requirements, the Product Owner can request the development team to stop working on the PBI item. The team and the Product Owner can then take a call to replace the PBI with another user story or terminate the ongoing iterations (only an exception scenario).

CHANGE REQUESTS

A change request is a formal proposal to modify a process, deliverable, or baseline. Most people think of a change request as a change in scope sought by the client, but that's an incomplete view.
A change request is any deviation from the plan.

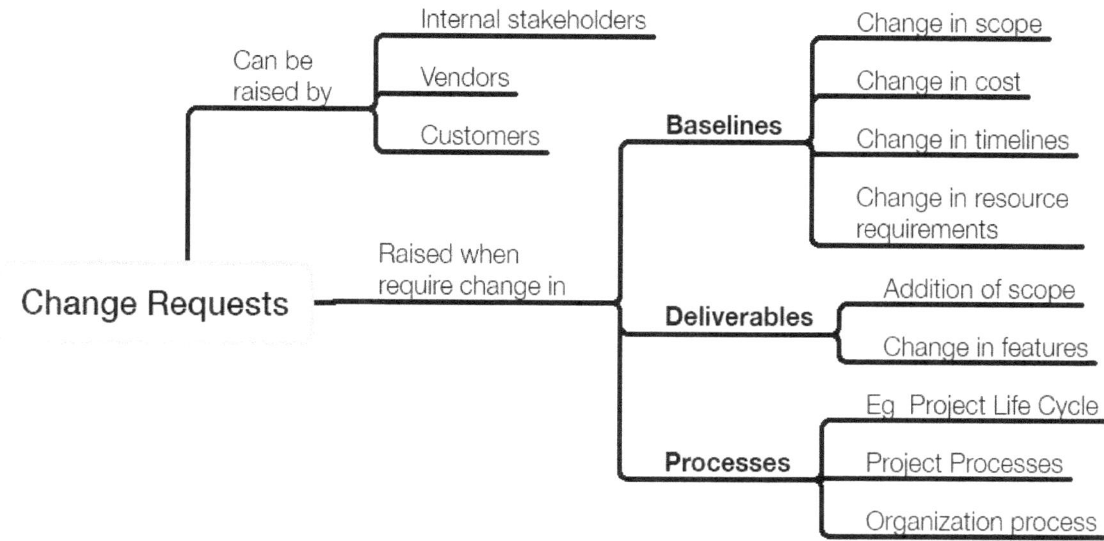

WHO CAN RAISE A CHANGE REQUEST?

Who can ask for it? A customer, a team member, or maybe senior management when they are preparing to take away your resource.

Most of you are not even aware that when you use a RED status in the status report, you are actually asking for a change. This change request could be changed in the baselines. Significance of colors:

- Green – In control
- Yellow – A warning sign
- Red color – Out of control (Issue – needs management intervention)

The red color in a status report is a change request in the project. For example, a red status shows that your project is delayed or overspent and hence may need more time or resources, or money. That's a deviation from the plan and hence is a change request which was raised by you.

MC.2.1 LET'S PLAY: IDENTIFY THE CORRECT CATEGORY

Mia is remodelling her friend Emma's villa. Emma lives with her son S and daughter D. This is a tricky task, as the requirements are unclear. Emma wants a breezy look with wooden furniture. However, when Mia started decorating the study, the teenage daughter, D, requested the slim copper furniture that is very popular right now. The painting was completed in two days. Mia has spent ten days, as of now, on the task. According to how the work has been going, Mia may have to spend the next 60 days on the remodelling project. The kitchen and two other bedrooms are not started yet. The objective is to redo all the bedrooms, the kitchen, and the study.

1. **Emma wants a breezy look with wooden furniture.**

    A.   Deliverable

    B.   Actual Work Status

    C.   Change Request

2. **The teenage daughter, D, has requested slimmer copper furniture that is very popular.**

    A.   Deliverable

    B.   Actual Work Status

    C.   Change Request

3. **The wall color was completed in two days.**

    A.   Deliverable

    B.   Actual Work Status

    C.   Change Request

4. **Mia has spent ten days as of now on the tasks.**

    A.   Deliverable

    B.   Actual Work Status

    C.   Change Request

5. **The kitchen and two bedrooms are yet to be started.**

    A.   Deliverable

    B.   Actual Work Status

    C.   Change Request

MC.3 CONTROL QUALITY AND MANAGE QUALITY

After the deliverables are made by the team, what happens next? Do you hand it over to the customer for acceptance testing? No, you don't. Your team tests the finished deliverables for any defect.

Manage quality is preventive. Before my team starts working on the tasks, I will enable them. Providing training and creating a checklist so the team produces fewer or no defects is the target for Manage quality.

Manage Quality/Quality Assurance	Control Quality/ QC
• QA aims to **prevent** defects with a focus on the process used to make the product. • **PREVENTIVE** process. • Also referred to as QA	• QC aims to identify defects in the finished product. Focus on Finding **DEFECTS**. • INSPECTION • Also referred to as QC

Sampling

sampling involves choosing **part of a population** of interest for inspection.
An example can be: Selecting ten engineering drawings at random from a list of seventy-five. Why should you use sampling? **Sampling reduces time and costs**.

Attribute Sampling

- Result either conforms or not (Boolean)
- Eg – Pass or Fail

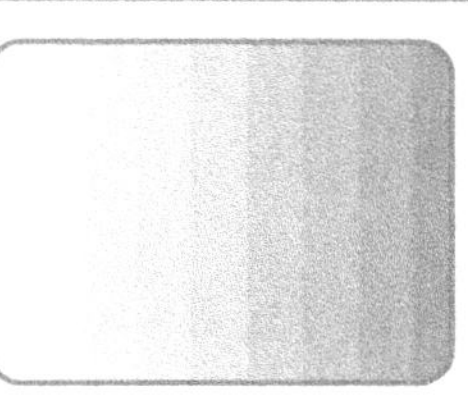

Variable Sampling

- Data is in the "**variable**" form, and the result is rated on a continuous scale. that measures the degree of conformity
- Eg – 80% of people know configuration management

ATTRIBUTE SAMPLING (BOOLEAN)
The result either conforms or does not conform. Results in a Yes or NO. It can be captured using a checklist.

VARIABLE SAMPLING
Data is in the "variable" form, and the result is rated on a continuous scale that measures the degree of conformity.
E.g., 80% of people know configuration management.

INSPECTION

Referred to as reviews, peer reviews, audits, or walkthroughs. Examining the deliverable and checking whether it conforms to the specification or not.

TESTING/PRODUCT EVALUATIONS

Organized and structured investigations to find defects in the produced deliverables. Different domains may need specific testing. For example, a software application may need unit, integration, and system testing.

MC.3.1 LET'S PLAY: QA VS. QC

Scenarios depict some actions. These actions are taken to ensure the quality of the product. Select the process where the actions are taken:

1. **The applications developed by your team had many errors, and it was reoccurring—things like using a variable without context, etc. To control, you defined coding standards.**

   A.　Manage Quality (QA)

   B.　Control Quality (QC)

2. **You work in a cheese factory as a cheese taster. Some of the cheese you tasted was rejected because it did not conform to the quality standard.**

   A.　Manage Quality (QA)

   B.　Control Quality (QC)

3. **You work as a magazine editor for a leading fashion brand. You have created a Quality Task Force that is responsible for proofreading and reviewing the content before anything is published.**

   A.　Manage Quality (QA)

   B.　Control Quality (QC)

4. **Your team is working on a website development project for one of your clients. Before starting the project, you organized training to share the best practices of website development with your team. You also shared with them the lessons learned from previous similar projects.**

   A.　Manage Quality (QA)

   B.　Control Quality (QC)

5. **You work as a marketing manager. You have bought a subscription for an application that checks your marketing collateral for errors and formatting before it is released.**

   A.　Manage Quality (QA)

   B.　Control Quality (QC)

MC.4 QUALITY TOOLS

CAUSE AND EFFECT DIAGRAM

Also known as fishbone diagrams or as Ishikawa diagrams. The problem is the Head of the Fish, and all the probable causes are listed. The fishbone diagram could be industry-specific or could be standardized, showcasing primary and secondary causes.

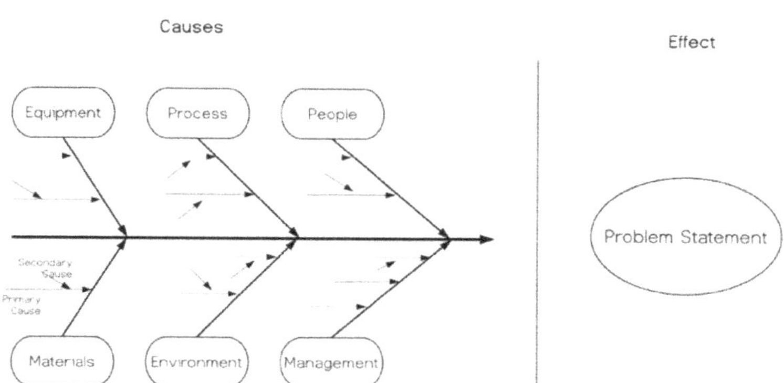

HISTOGRAM

You have a problem in real life or in operations that is reoccurring. What would you do? Hmm, you would do Root Cause Analysis (RCA). But what after RCA??
You should visually compare all the root causes to eliminate the top few. You do it by plotting a histogram.

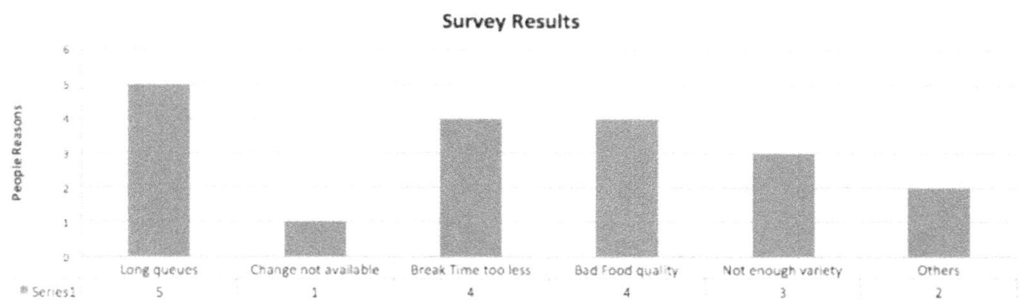

MATRIX DIAGRAM

Data is represented using various representations. For example, the relationship can be represented using matrix charts. Various representations are available using L, T, Y, C, X, and roof-shaped matrix.
You can learn more about matrix charts here:
http://asq.org/learn-about-quality/new-management-planning-tools/overview/matrix-diagram.html

MIND MAPPING

Visual representation of related ideas.

FLOWCHARTS

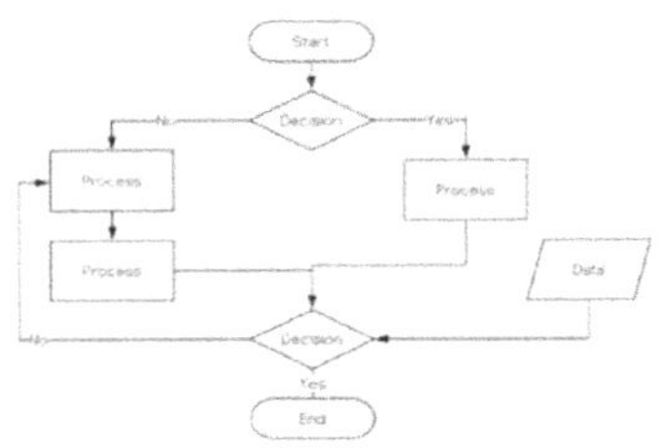

Flowcharts are used to analyze the process to find out unnecessary waiting time or non-usable process components and hence are also referred to as process maps.

TREND CHARTS

Single variable plotted over a period of time.

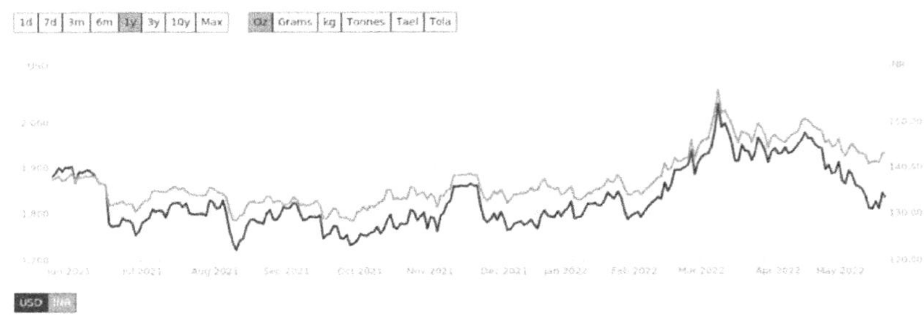

SCATTER DIAGRAMS

Scatter diagrams are also called **correlation charts**. This is because it shows a **relationship** between 2 variables.

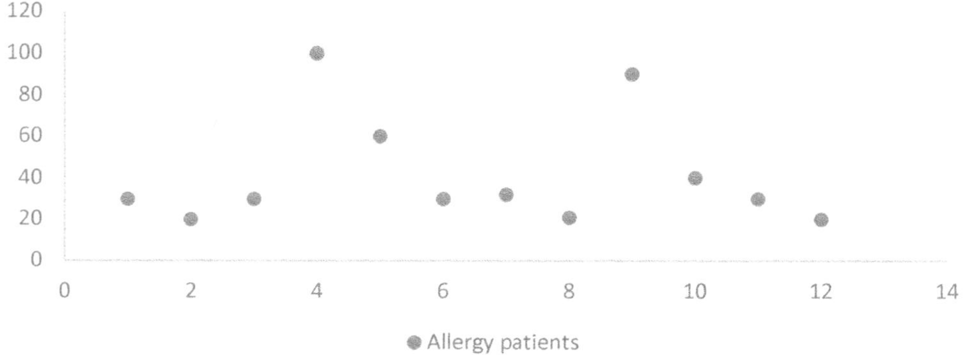

CHECKLISTS

A checklist is an easy way to implement a standard. The corresponding standard requirements are listed in a usable manner, and the concerned user will conform to the listed items. Items with a space to put check boxes.

1. A checklist is a tool used to ensure that a set of tasks or items are completed or reviewed systematically and accurately. It is a list of items or tasks that need to be accomplished, often in a specific order, and is used to track progress and ensure that nothing is overlooked or forgotten.

2. Checklists can be used in a variety of contexts, such as for quality assurance, safety inspections, project management, event planning, or daily tasks. In addition, they are often used in professions where accuracy and attention to detail are critical, such as aviation, healthcare, and manufacturing.

3. Checklists can be created in various formats, such as on paper, in digital form, or as a series of prompts or questions. As a result, they are highly customizable and can be adapted to fit specific needs or requirements.

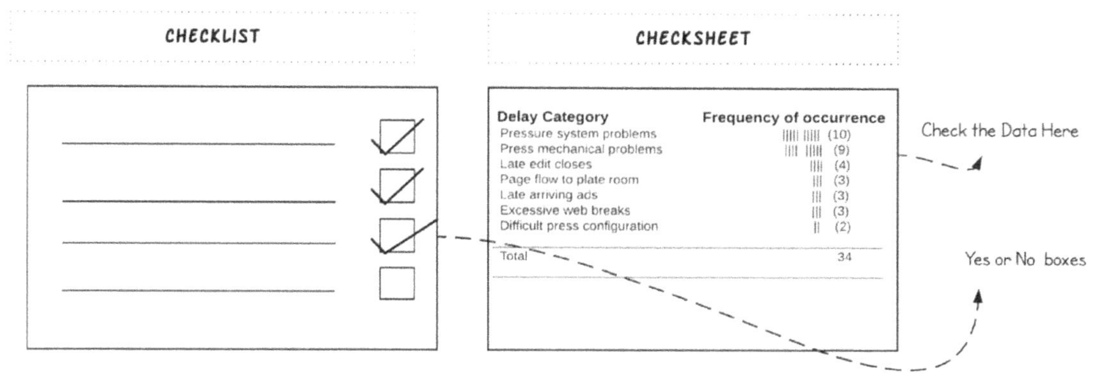

Checklist Vs Checksheet

CHECK-SHEETS

Also known as tally sheets.

A check sheet, also known as a tally sheet, is a simple data collection tool used to record the frequency or occurrence of specific events or items. It is a way of organizing and collecting data in a systematic manner for analysis.

A check sheet typically consists of a table with categories or items listed on the left-hand side and a series of tally marks or other symbols on the right-hand side. When an event or item is observed or encountered, a tally mark or symbol is added to the corresponding category or item. This allows for easy tracking and counting of occurrences over time.

Please do not confuse them with the checklist. Checklists are data points/checking points with Yes and No tick marks. The check sheets have columns for data.

MC.4.1 LET'S PLAY: QUALITY TOOLS

Match the quality tools used in the scenarios:

Scenario	Quality Tool
1. Costs incurred over the life of the product by investment in preventing nonconformance to requirements, appraising the product or service for conformance to requirements, and failing to meet requirements	Flow Charts
2. Also referred to as process maps because they display the sequence of steps and the branching possibilities that exist for a process that transforms one or more inputs into one or more outputs.	Cost of Quality (COQ)
3. The problem statement placed at the head of the fishbone is used as a starting point to trace the problem's source back to its actionable root cause	Histogram
4. Vertical bar chart is used to identify the vital few sources that are responsible for causing most of a problem's effects.	Control Charts
5. ______ are used to determine whether or not a process is stable or has predictable performance. Upper and lower specification limits are based on the requirements of the agreement.	Fish Bone Diagram

MC.5 Problem-Solving

Problem-solving is required in various project stages and is vital for managing project issues. Listed are typical steps to solve a problem:

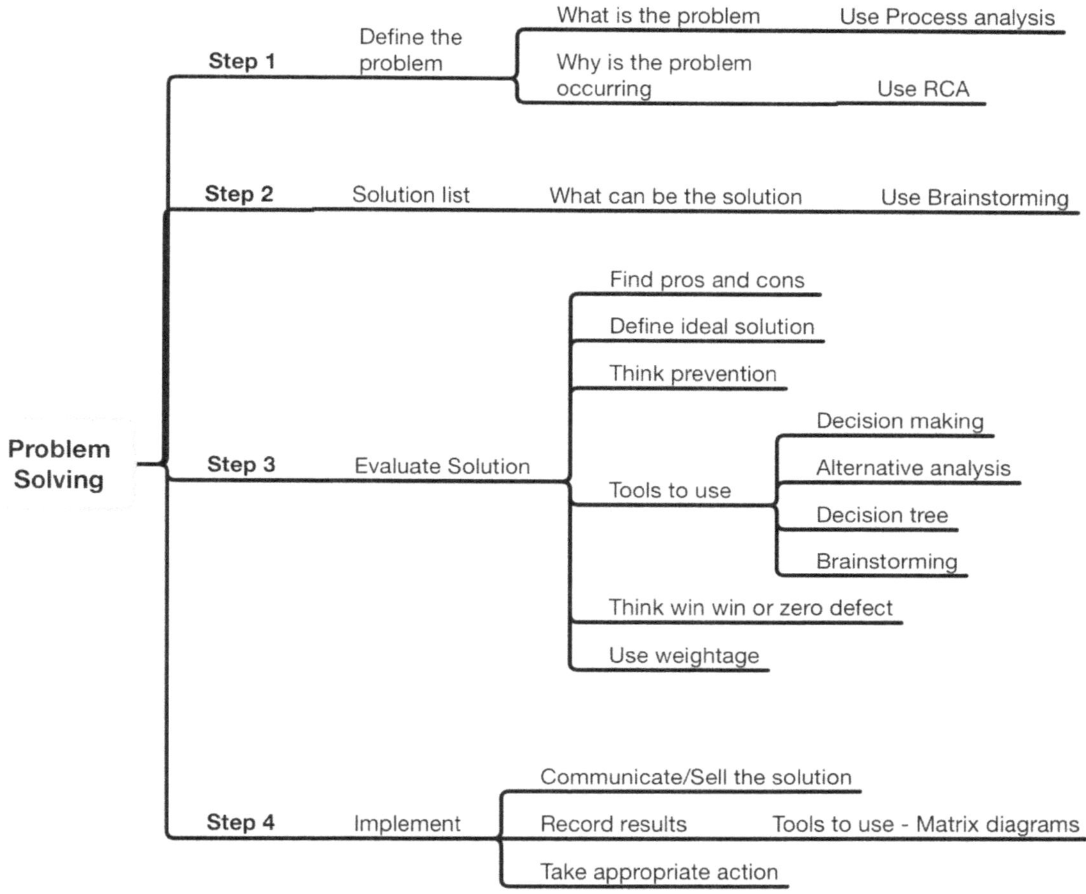

MC.6 THE DELIVERABLE JOURNEY

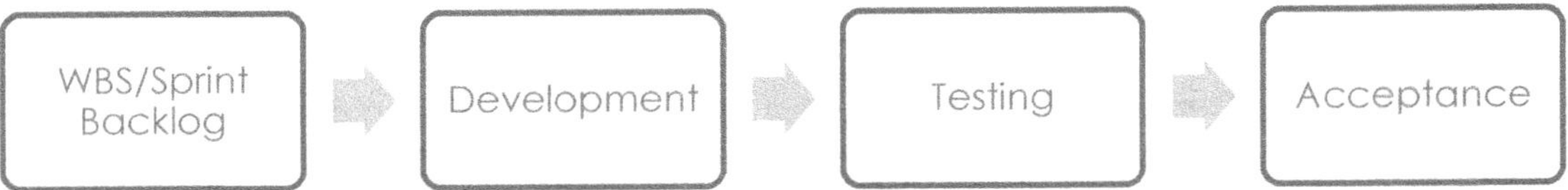

A deliverable is planned at the time of planning from the IN SCOPE items. The team works on it and develops it. Before we show this deliverable to the customer, It should be reviewed for errors (Who does it? QA/Testers)
In the case of predictive teams, you can have another set of testers in agile. The development team typically tests the work themselves and ensures that the deliverable meets the DOD. What is DOD? Refer Agile section if you do not know the full form of DOD.

VALIDATE SCOPE/ACCEPTENCE

Validate scope is the process of formalizing acceptance of the completed project deliverables. You can map it with ACCEPTANCE TESTING.
The goal of Validate Scope is to drive acceptance from the client and get sign-off on accepted deliverables.

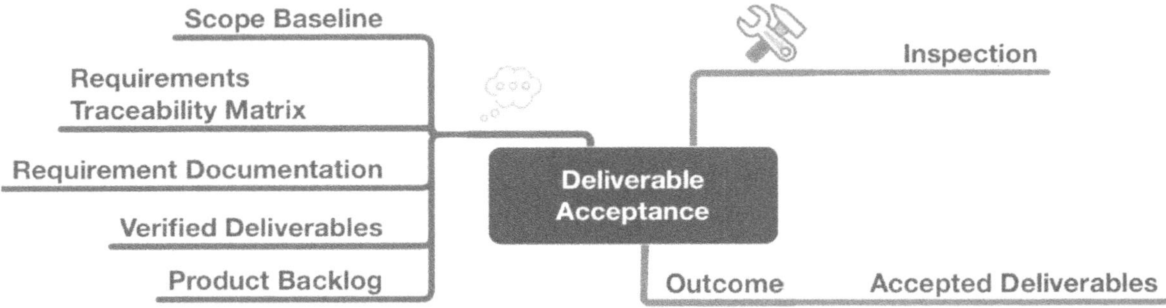

Upon completion of the Validate Scope process, if everything goes well, the client accepts the deliverables and provides a sign-off on the deliverables. In case the client does not accept the deliverables, changes have to be made. This results in Change Requests.
Validate Scope process is performed by the customer/Sponsor.
Which meeting in agile is equivalent to validate scope process? Who accepts the deliverables?

INSPECTION

The client/sponsor/Product Owner will run acceptance test cases that are either written by their team or provided by you to them. As a best practice, it's always good to have the Acceptance Test Criteria defined right at the time of getting requirements and put them as part of the deliverable testing criteria.

CLOSING

C.1 CLOSE PROJECT OR PHASE

Administrative closure occurs when a project or phase is complete. After the customer accepts all the due deliverables, a formal process to close the project starts.
This process is NOT about acceptance testing. The deliverables, as per the agreements, have been created, tested, and accepted. The process is kicked off when all of that is achieved or when the customer request to terminate the agreement. Yes – The process is also followed for pre-mature project closures.

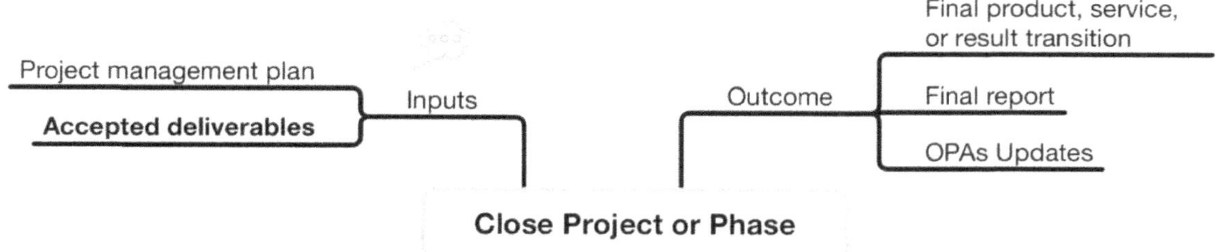

It is critical to achieve two things in this process:

→ One: Hand over the deliverable to the customer or the operations team

→ Two: Create a project final report to document the project's performance.

In addition, you will get all the updated documents from the project team (manuals, help files, etc.), And conduct a retrospective meeting to ensure you capture the lessons learned in the completed project/phase. Why is this necessary? So that other Project Managers can take precautions to avoid certain pitfalls or do things better.
Activities involved in administrative closure are:

- Verify agreement details with the customer

- Get FINAL formal acceptance by the customer

- Create and circulate the final project performance report

- Close the procurements

- Communicate the project's final status to the required stakeholders

- Conduct a retrospective meeting to gain insights from the team

- Update lessons register

- Update and archive all project documents

- HANDOVER

- Release project resources (possibly conduct formal feedback sessions)

- Celebrate a job well done.

5. MODULE END QUESTIONS

1. ______is an analytical technique used to determine the basic underlying reason that causes a variance, defect, or risk. (Fill in the blanks)
Select one:

    a. process analysis

    b. Alternative analysis

    c. Root cause analysis

    d. Document analysis

2. Project success is measured by the perception of the project, which includes the team and the Project Manager, their actions, and their communication styles. Effective managers spend most of their time in:
Select one:

    a. Creating Work Performance Reports

    b. Communicating

    c. Working on scheduled activities

    d. Managing risks

3. You are using the hybrid project. The design phase uses an adaptive methodology to get design feedback and provide value to the customer. Later the design is moved into development in a predefined manufacturing process. The project uses the design phase and development phase, and testing phase. What should be the ideal relationship between the design and development phases?

Select one:

    a. Start to finish

    b. Finish to Start

    c. Start to start

    d. Finish to Finish

4. You are preparing the estimates for the project SPARTA. You discuss the data with a fellow Project Manager and get relevant information from the Project Management Office. Once you have the base data, you work out the estimate using function point analysis (A function point is a unit of measurement to express the amount of business functionality an information system, as a product, provides to a user. This is typically a calculation-based analysis where the cost, in dollars or hours, of a single unit is calculated from past projects/standards). Which estimation technique did you use?
Select one:

    a. Bottom-up

    b. Analogous

    c. Three Point

    d. Parametric

5. The following are examples of deliverables EXCEPT:
Select one:

    a. The planning team submitting the Project Management Plan

    b. The software development team developing the application software

    c. Team member Zena updating the activity-Z start date in the project management
        information system

    d. Portfolio Manager creating the Project Charter

6. You are invited to a steering team meeting where you need to present the project's status to the audience. You are also asked to forecast the total estimated cost for the current cost performance in view. Which of the following EVM terms would be helpful to describe the information sought?
Select one:

    a. Budget at Completion

    b. Actual Costs

    c. Estimate at Completion

    d. Estimate to Complete

7. You realize that you cannot start one of the activities without getting the requisite approval from a government regulatory body. What type of dependency is described in the scenario?
Select one:

    a. Mandatory - Internal dependency

    b. Mandatory - External dependency

    c. Discretionary - Internal dependency

    d. Discretionary - External dependency

8. The project NEIL has a CPI of .98 and SPI of .7. How is the project doing?
Select one:

    a. The project is ahead of schedule and is overspent

    b. The project is ahead of schedule and is under budget

    c. The project is behind schedule and is under budget

    d. The project is behind schedule and is overspent

9. Due to similar defects in many deliverables, the team checked for the root cause and implemented an additional step in the process. Adding an additional check decreased the defects by a significant percentage. Changing the process to include the additional step is:
Select one:

    a. A preventive action

b. A corrective action

c. Defect repair

d. Process audit

10. You are engaged in a book publishing project. Your team is checking the book contents for grammatical mistakes (proofreading). This is achieved by using automated software. Which quality activity is performed by using the automated software?
Select one:

a. Using automated software reduces grammar mistakes by identifying the defects and hence should be classified as a corrective action.

b. Using automated software reduces grammar mistakes by identifying the defects and hence should be classified as inspection.

11. Many deliverables were found with defects. The testing team sent the deliverables back to the developers so that they could correct the deliverable, and then the fixed deliverable could be resubmitted for the next testing cycle. What is done here?
Select one:

a. Testing

b. Preventive Action

c. Control Quality

d. Corrective Action

12. One of the activities is delayed beyond recovery days. If the project goes with the same plan, it will get delayed by at least a few weeks. Your management has told you that no delay is acceptable and that arranging new resources for the project will take substantial time and is not a valid option. Also, the organization's policy is no overtime and no work on weekends. No employee can be asked to do more than 40 hours of work. What is the best option you are left with?
Select one:

a. Do work in parallel

b. Put more resources into the project

c. Analyze the schedule to see if a few activities can be shortened or can be overlapped

d. Reduce the scope

13. Knowledge can be split into two types. Tacit and explicit. Tacit knowledge can be managed and used in projects by using the following:
Select one:

a. Communities of practice, networking, and storytelling

b. Formal training and documentation

c. User manuals and instructions update

d. Lesson learned register and retrospective meetings

14. Correlation charts are also called:
Select one:

a. Control Charts

b. Histograms

c. Scatter diagrams

d. Pareto diagrams

15. Crashing is preferred over fast-tracking when:
Select one:

a. Project SPI < 1

b. Project CPI is <1

c. Project CPI is >1

d. Project SPI >1

16. ABC Expressway is a 6-lane, 165 km long, controlled-access expressway. It connects City A with City B. You are managing the project to set up the toll booths. Setting up the toll booths with toll charges requires getting approvals from the government before you proceed towards setting up the cabin. The contract, which was sanctioned, approves you to set up the booths. However, the final discussions about toll charges are yet to happen. Can you fast-track the activity of setting up the booths?
Select one:

a. Yes. This project is entitled to set up the booths along with tool tickets. We will do it as per the plan.

b. No. Government approval is always mandatory

c. Yes. After checking the contract, work can start on setting up the booth while the toll charges approval takes place

d. No. Paperwork is a MUST before we carry out any activity

17. Please help Ana invest in preventive cost spent to reduce the overall cost of quality in her project. What would these costs be considered?
Select one:

a. training costs

b. Inspections cost

c. Reviews cost

d. Warranty period costs

18. A change control board is:
Select one:

a. A formally chartered group to support the project by establishing change management protocols

b. A formally chartered group responsible for reviewing, evaluating, approving or rejecting changes to the project

19. The client asked for a business-critical change at the last minute. The change seems to be minor at the outset. You are convinced that your team should be able to accommodate the change within the given timelines. What is the BEST thing to do?
Select one:

a. Compress the schedule to accommodate the request

b. Accept the change and start implementing

c. Consult the sponsor before taking any action

d. Ask the subject matter expert to analyze the impact of change

20. Project activity A has a duration of 2 weeks with a 20% probability of exceeding the timelines. What does it translate to?
Select one:

a. It is definite that activity A will be finished in 2 weeks.

b. It is only 20 % possible that activity A can finish within 2 weeks

c. It is 80% probable that activity A will finish within 2 weeks

d. Activity A will finish within 2 weeks with a plus or minus of 20%

21. Rough Order of Magnitude Estimation has tolerances of:
Select one:

a. -50% to +50%

b. -25% to +75%

c. -15% to + 25%,

d. -5% to +10%

22. You work in aerospace, designing the aviation control panel. The emphasis is to simplify the control panel so that it is easier for the pilots to understand the indicators. What should the team use to ensure that the Pilot finds it easier to use the control panel?
Select one:

a. Design for X

b. User interface design

c. Histograms

d. Pie charts

23. What does a negative Cost Variance indicate for any ongoing project?
Select one:

a. The Earned Value currently exceeds the Planned Value.

b. The Planned Value currently exceeds the Earned Value.

c. The Earned Value currently exceeds the Actual Cost.

d. The Actual Cost currently exceeds the Earned Value.

24. Which tool will help you to arrive at the root cause of any issue?
Select one:

a. Trend Analysis

b. Scatter diagrams

c. Design of Experiments

d. Ishikawa diagrams

25. Which diagramming technique can show the relationship between two variables?
Select one:

a. Matrix diagrams

b. Histogram

c. Flowcharts

d. Scatter diagram

26. Definitive Estimate tolerance is?
Select one:

a. -50% to +50%

b. -25% to +75%

c. -15% to + 25%

d. -5% to +10%

27. You allocated three more resources to a critical activity to overcome a critical delay. Which technique did you use?
Select one:

a. Fast Tracking

b. Crashing

c. Analyzing Schedule

d. Control Schedule

28. A project is considered complete only when:
Select one:

a. The acceptance testing is signed off

b. Quality Control is achieved

c. The customer has taken the handover of deliverables

d. The handover is completed, and a final report is circulated

29. A project shows CPI as 0.9 and SPI as 0.8. What does this information convey?
Select one:

a. The project is delayed

b. The project is ahead of schedule

c. The project work is per plan

d. Not adequate information was provided

30. What is a milestone?
Select one:

a. Milestones are marked for payments.

b. Milestones are similar to regular schedule activities, with the same structure and attributes.

c. Milestones depict a significant point or event in a project.

d. The schedule should always have milestones.

5. ALL ANSWERS

ANSWERS: P.SCP.1.1 LET'S PLAY: PRODUCT VS. PROJECT SCOPE

Description	Scope Type	Why?
1. Announcement board	Product Scope	Part of the customer's requirements
2. Conducting focus group	Project Scope	Project activity
3. Email notification	Product Scope	Part of the customer's requirements
4. Identifying the solution platform	Project Scope	Project activity
5. Planning for entire project activities	Project Scope	Project activity

ANSWERS: P.TME.3.1 LET'S PLAY: ESTIMATION TECHNIQUES

1. You started to work on the dinner menu. Keeping the last party in mind, you ordered the raw material.	Analogues estimate	Keyword: Similar
2. You put 3 resources into a particular activity. The reason 3 resources were allocated is that you wanted to finish the activity in the next Four days. It was assumed that 1 resource could have completed the activity in 12 days.	Parametric estimate	Keyword: Calculation
3. While estimating for roll-out date for your project, you estimated the most optimistic scenario and most pessimistic along with the most likely conditions and then gave your estimates to senior management	3-point estimates.	Keywords: Optimistic, Pessimistic, and Most Likely
4. Sam detailed each activity with the project team. He discussed and finalized the activity-wise estimates and then combined all the days together to arrive at the final effort for the project.	Bottom-up estimates	Keyword: Detailed out

ANSWERS: P.TME.4.1- LET'S PLAY: SCHEDULE COMPRESSION TECHNIQUES

1. The Project Manager starts coding before getting the requirement sign-off from the customer.	Fast-tracking	(Work in Parallel)
2. Bond got his team to put in extra hours to complete an activity on time.	Crashing	(Extra Hours/team within an activity/activities)
3. The book publishing team started working on the format in parallel while the academic team was reviewing the content.	Fast-tracking	(Work in Parallel)

4. Due to a few issues, the project was behind schedule. To meet timelines, you asked the team to work extra hours.	Crashing	(Extra Hours/team within an activity/activities)

ANSWERS: P.COST.2.1 LET'S PLAY: RESERVE TYPES

1. You are a Project Manager. You kept some reserve to address risks in your project while estimating costs. Project Cost Baseline consists of this reserve.	Contingency Reserve
2. You have encountered a procurement risk that you did not plan for during Planning. So, you do not have adequate funds to manage it. You approach your senior management for funds.	Management Reserve
3. You, the Project Manager, manage and control this reserve.	Contingency Reserve
4. You, the Project Manager, do not administer and control this reserve.	Management Reserve

ANSWERS: P.RISK.1.1 LET'S PLAY: RISKS IDENTIFICATION TECHNIQUES

Risk Scenario	Technique Used
1. You wanted to identify as many of the risks as possible in your project, so you called a joint meeting with the customer, PMO, your senior management, and the architect.	Brainstorming
2. You've sent a questionnaire to all the functional heads to find any risks to the success of the project. You did not want any biases, so these inputs were sought anonymously.	Delphi
3. You looked at the assumption log to ensure that the project success criterion may not get hampered by anything unexpected.	Assumption Analysis
4. You use the Fish Bone diagram technique to gain insight into the behavior of a risk.	Root cause analysis
5. You meet personally with many different stakeholders: the sponsor, customer, team members, and experts. You seek answers to questions about what they think could go wrong on the project.	Interviews
6. You look through all the project documents, including contracts, to see any risk possibilities.	Documentation Reviews

ANSWERS: P.RISK.3.1 LET'S PLAY: RISK RESPONSES

Scenario	Response Strategy	Why?
1	Mitigate	Probability is reduced to some extent.

2	Avoid	The risk probability is reduced to zero.
3	Accept	Do nothing.
4	Share	You gained (not money), and you shared with a
5	Exploit	Opportunity increased to 100%.

ANSWERS: P.PROC.2.1 LET'S PLAY: CONTRACT TYPES

Description	Contract Type Used
1. A contract having special provisions allowing for predefined final adjustments to the contract price due to changed conditions, such as inflation or cost increases (or decreases) for specific commodities.	Fixed Price with Economic Price Adjustment Contracts
2. The seller is reimbursed for all allowable costs for performing the contract work and receives a predetermined incentive fee based upon achieving certain performance objectives as set forth in the contract.	Cost Plus Incentive Fee Contracts
3. Contracts that specify rates per hour or categories of materials at specified rates per unit.	Time and Material Contracts
4. In this contract, the buyer should precisely specify the product or services to be procured, and any changes to the procurement specification can increase the costs to the buyer.	Firm Fixed Price Contracts

ANSWERS: E.INT.2.1 LET'S PLAY: TYPE OF KNOWLEDGE

Question	Answer
1. The knowledge that can be easily documented	Explicit Knowledge
2. Usual mechanism to share this knowledge is forums, informal interactions, observations	Tacit Knowledge
3. This type of knowledge can be found in OPAs	Explicit Knowledge
4. Belief systems, Know-how is a type of:	Tacit Knowledge

ANSWERS: E.INT.3.1 - LET'S PLAY: IDENTIFY A RISK OR ISSUE

Sno.	Question	Answer	Reason
1.	You received a letter from the bank stating that the **mortgage rate has increased by 1%.** This will increase the project spending by at least 10%	Issue	Probability = 100% Has happened. The impact is 1%
2.	Heavy rains are **forecasted** in the next week. This has the **potential** to delay the project's completion by a few days.	Risk	Future event It may happen or not.
3.	Few of the workers went on strike.	Issue	Already happened. Present.

4.	Some of the windows you bought were of the wrong size and should now be returned. This is a lot of rework.	Issue	Already happened. To be sorted now
5.	A new shopping mall is planned near your house. **If that comes up** in the next two years, it will **significantly increase** property valuation.	Risk	Future event. Have some probability and impact. It can be treated as an opportunity.

ANSWERS: MC.2.1 LET'S PLAY: IDENTIFY THE CORRECT CATEGORY

1.	**Emma wants a breezy outlook with wooden furniture:**	Deliverable	A breezy outlook with wooden furniture is the project scope. The scope is further divided into smaller deliverables.
2.	**The request from the teenage daughter, D, was to get slim copper furniture that is popular**	Change Request	Deviation from the original request.
3.	**The wall color took two days to complete**	Actual work status	Took 2 days to complete is information about the task. This is schedule data
4.	**As of now, Mia has spent ten days on the task**	Actual work status	Ten days. Work reported and the time spent on that is actual data on the task
5.	**The kitchen and two other bedrooms are yet to be started.**	Work Status	Report on work completion status

ANSWERS: MC.3.1 LET'S PLAY: QA VS. QC

Scenario	Answer	Why
1. The applications developed by your team had many errors, and it was reoccurring. Things like using a variable without context etc. To control, you defined coding standards.	Manage Quality	Defining coding standards will prevent errors from happening. Preventive actions are performed in Manage Quality processes.
2. You work in a cheese factory as a cheese taster. Some of the cheese you tasted was rejected because it did not conform to the quality standard.	Control Quality	Cheese is the end product if you test the product for faults that comes under Quality Control. The activity results in finding defects. You find defects in Control Quality Process.

3. You work as a magazine editor for a leading fashion brand. You have created a Quality Task Force that is responsible for proofreading and reviewing the content before anything is published.	Control Quality	Don't get fooled here by the word "Quality Task Force." Check what the work of the quality task force is. They are proofreading and reviewing the end deliverables. The activity results in finding defects. You find defects in Control Quality Process. The activity results in finding defects. You find defects in Control Quality Process.
4. Your team is working on a website development project for one of your clients. Before starting the project, you organized training to share the best practices of website development with your team. You also shared with them the lessons learned from previous similar projects.	Manage Quality	Training will eliminate the source of the defects and hence would be classified as preventive action. Preventive actions are part of the Manage Quality process.
5. You work as a marketing manager. You have bought a subscription for an application that checks your marketing collateral for errors and formatting before it is released.	Control Quality	Checking the deliverable can be automated, but this is again performed on the finished product to check for errors. QC, my friends. The activity results in finding defects. You find defects in Control Quality Process.

ANSWERS: MC.4.1 LET'S PLAY: QUALITY TOOLS

Scenario	Quality Tool
1. Costs incurred over the life of the product by investment in preventing nonconformance to requirements, appraising the product or service for conformance to requirements, and failing to meet requirements	Cost of Quality (COQ)
2. Also referred to as process maps because they display the sequence of steps and the branching possibilities that exist for a process that transforms one or more inputs into one or more outputs.	Flow Charts
3. The problem statement placed at the head of the fishbone is used as a starting point to trace the problem's source back to its actionable root cause	Fish Bone Diagram

4. Vertical bar chart is used to identify the vital few sources that are responsible for causing most of a problem's effects.	Histogram

5. _________ are used to determine whether or not a process is stable or has predictable performance. Upper and lower specification limits are based on the requirements of the agreement.	Control Charts

ANSWERS: 5. MODULE END QUESTIONS

Sno.	Correct Answer	Reason
1.	The correct answer is Root cause analysis.	Root cause analysis (RCA). Root cause analysis is an analytical technique used to determine the basic underlying reason that causes a variance, defect, or risk. A root cause may underlie more than one variance, defect, or risk. It may also be used as a technique for identifying the root causes of a problem and solving them. When all root causes for a problem are removed, the problem does not recur.
2.	The correct answer is: Communicating.	A successful project manager should be good at managing stakeholders, and they spend 80% of their time managing them - how do you manage a stakeholder by interacting and communicating with them.
3.	The correct answer is: Finish to Start.	The design should be complete before the development phase. Finish to start relationship.
4.	The correct answer is: Parametric.	Parametric estimating is an estimating technique in which an algorithm is used to calculate cost or duration based on historical data and project parameters.
5.	The correct answer is: Team member Zena updating the activity-Z start date in the project management information system.	Just check if someone is spending time performing the task which produces a WBS work package allocated to them.
6.	The correct answer is: Estimate at Completion .	The total cost at the end of the project is referred to as Estimate at Completion. ETC is how much more money is required to complete.
7.	The correct answer is: Mandatory - External dependency	Mandatory dependencies are those that are legally or contractually required or inherent like the work. External dependencies involve a relationship between project activities and non-project activities. These dependencies are usually outside the project team's control.
8.	The correct answer is: The project is behind schedule and is overspent	Your project is behind schedule, and the budget is overspent. PMBOK does not use the words "under budget or over budget."

9.	The correct answer is: A preventive action	Reducing future defects by changing the process is a preventive action
10.	The correct answer is: Using automated software reduces grammar mistakes by identifying the defects and hence should be classified as inspection.	Using automated software reduces grammar mistakes by identifying the defects and hence should be classified as inspection.: TRUE.
11.	The correct answer is: Corrective Action.	Update the deliverable so that the defects are corrected is Corrective Action.
12.	The correct answer is: Analyze the schedule to see if a few activities can be shortened or can be overlapped.	Let's see all the options. Choice A needs people to work overtime which is denied. So, option A is not feasible. Option B – Put more resources into the project is also denied. Choice C - We need to analyze the schedule to see what can be possible and achievable, and then changing the plan accordingly seems the only valid choice. Choice D – Reduce the scope and be one valid choice, but the decision cannot be taken until the reduction in scope is discussed with the customer. Out of all the choices given, Choice C is the most correct option at this time.
13.	The correct answer is: Communities of practice, networking, and storytelling.	Tacit knowledge can be managed and used in projects by using Communities of practice, networking, and storytelling.
14.	The correct answer is: Scatter diagrams.	Correlation charts are also called scatter diagrams.
15.	The correct answer is: Project CPI is >1	This is a good question :) Crashing requires money. You can crash only when the CPI is > 1, i.e., and when the project has financial reserves.
16.	The correct answer is: Yes. After checking the contract, work can start on setting up the booth while the toll charges approval takes place.	Understand that two activities are in discussion - Setting up the booth and toll charge. The toll charge is external mandatory, but setting up the booth is internal (part of the contract). Read this line: The contract, which was sanctioned, approves you to set up the booths. So you can set up the booth and let the toll charge decision happen in parallel.
17.	The correct answer is: Training costs.	Out of all the activities, the only preventive activity is training. Ana should spend more on training so that the team delivers a better, error-free product. Thus, reducing the overall cost of quality.
18.	The correct answer is: A formally chartered group responsible for reviewing, evaluating, approving or	A CCB is a formally chartered group responsible for reviewing, evaluating, approving or rejecting changes to the project as per the PMBOK.

	rejecting changes to the project.	
19.	The correct answer is: Ask the subject matter expert to analyze the impact of change.	Even if you think that changes have minimum impact, you need to know the impact... A good practice is to understand the impact of the change. Follow the change management process.
20.	The correct answer is: It is 80% probable that activity A will finish within 2 weeks.	Project activity A has a duration of 2 weeks with a 20% probability of exceeding the timelines means that it is 80% probable that activity A will finish within 2 weeks.
21.	The correct answer is: -25% to +75%	Rough Order of Magnitude Estimation has a range of -25% to + 75%
22.	The correct answer is: Design for X	Design for X, also referred to as DfX, means designing the products with some focus. Designing for usability would be the focus while designing the aviation control panel.
23.	The correct answer is: The Actual Cost currently exceeds the Earned Value.	The formula for cost variance is: EV- AC. That means that the actual cost spent on the project is more than the earned value of the project.
24.	The correct answer is: Ishikawa diagrams.	The best tool to perform RCA is the Fish Bone diagram, also called the Ishikawa diagram.
25.	The correct answer is: Scatter diagram.	The Scatter diagram shows a relationship between the 2 variables.
26.	The correct answer is: -5% to +10%	As more information is known, Definitive Estimates could narrow the range of accuracy to -5% to +10%.
27.	The correct answer is: Crashing.	Adding resources to shorten an activity is crashing.
28.	The correct answer is: The handover is completed, and the final report is circulated.	The project is considered complete and closed only after completion of the process close project/ phase. Two main tasks in the project closure are handover and the creation of the final report, along with OPA updates.
29.	The correct answer is: The project is delayed	The project is behind schedule as SPI <1
30.	The correct answer is: Milestones depict a significant point or event in a project.	"A milestone is a significant point or event in a project.

6. NEXT STEPS

THE 21 DAYS TEST PREP PLAN

Phase	Day	What Needs to be done	Reference Material	Hours Commitment
Week 1-2 Revise	1	Business Environment	PMBOK 6 - Chap 1- 3	2 hours
	2	Business Environment - Int	PMBOK 6 - Chap 4	2 hours
	3	Business Analysis - Scope	PMBOK 6 - Chap 5	2 hours
	4	Agile Question	Agile Standard	2 hours
	5	People - Team Management	PMBOK 6 - Chapter 9	2 hours
	6	People - Stakeholder	PMBOK 6 - Chapter 13	2 hours
	7	People - Communications	PMBOK 6 - Chapter 10	2 hours
	8	Project Schedule Management	PMBOK 6 - Chapter 6	2 hours
	9	Project Cost Management	PMBOK 6 - Chapter 7	2 hours
	10	Project Quality Management	PMBOK 6 – Chapter 8	2 hours
	11	Project Risk Management	PMBOK 6 – Chapter 11	2 hours
	12	Project Procurement Management	PMBOK 6 – Chapter 12	NA
	13	Buffer - If you missed any day		NA
Week 3 Simulate	14	Full-Length Test	Search and gain more information using the wiki	3 Hours
	15	Full-Length Test		3 Hours
	16	Full-Length Test		3 Hours
	17	Full-Length Test		3 Hours
	18	Full-Length Test		3 Hours
	19	Buffer - If you missed any day		NA
	20	Buffer - If you missed any day		NA
Go/No Go	21	80% in the last 2 full-length tests - Schedule the Exam		NA

*You can refer following documents for optional studies.
  1. Agile Practice Guide available at PMI.org
  2. PMBOK 6th Edition available at PMI.org

7. FULL-LENGTH TEST

3 hours to test your knowledge. All the best.

Since the test questions need to be updated, you can attempt the full-length test at Lms.kavitasharma.net.

Just register at the learning site. It's a free test, and you can find the associated study capsules on the website.

Here is the full URL for your reference.

https://lms.kavitasharma.net/course/view.php?id=106

8. ABOUT KAVITA SHARMA

Kavita Sharma
Significant Contributor
PMBOK- Sixth Edition

Kavita Sharma has two decades of project management experience in IT, Project Management, Program Management, Account Management, and Project and Leadership Coaching.
She worked with Microsoft, Tech Mahindra, Sapient, and Satyam in her career. While working as an end-to-end program manager, she managed multi-skilled virtual teams ranging from 30 - 90 members having widespread skill sets.
In the last few years (approx. 10), she has evolved as a great mentor to the CAPM aspirants and conducts project management workshops. She authored many books, including the best Seller:
Pass CAPM in 21 Days - Study Guide.
You can see her name in the PMBOK as a significant contributor and CAPM (eLearning by PMI) reviewer.
Her focus is now shifting to mindfulness. We hope to see something new from her pretty soon.
YouTube: https://www.youtube.com/channel/UCLjfEAI-EmgzsDQnXiTth9g
LinkedIn: https://www.linkedin.com/in/kavitasharmaCAPM
Official Website: https://KavitaSharma.net

THANK YOU

Hi, this is Kavita Sharma. Thanks for buying the book and staying with it till the end. I assume that you have gone through the book and stayed with it. And that is the reason you are reading this page.
A lot of effort has gone into producing this book.
I keep receiving feedback from people like you and ensure that the feedback is acted upon. That's the reason you see book updates.
The credit goes to all of you.
I hope that you found the book helpful. If there is any feedback do write to me. I will look forward to hearing from you.
You can reach me at kavita.sh@gmail.com.
Thanks, and wishing you success.
Kavita Sharma
Author, Coach, and Thinker

DISCLAIMER

With this book, I have put in my best effort to bring you the right tools to pass the CAPM examination. However, this should not be interpreted as a promise or guarantee of your success. Any positive or negative outcome is ultimately dependent on your competency, commitment, and the overall effort put into the CAPM exam preparation.
You have the right tools with you. Use them and pass the CAPM exam.